JOYCE'S MESSIANISM

JOYCE'S MESSIANISM

Dante, Negative Existence,
and the Messianic Self

GIAN BALSAMO

University of South Carolina Press

Published in Columbia, South Carolina,
by the University of South Carolina Press

Manufactured in the United States of America

08 07 06 05 04   5 4 3 2 1

Library of Congress Cataloging-in-Publication Data

Balsamo, Gian, 1949–
    Joyce's messianism : Dante, negative existence, and the messianic self / Gian Balsamo.
        p. cm.
    Includes bibliographical references and index.
    ISBN 1-57003-552-0 (alk. paper)
    1. Joyce, James, 1882–1941—Criticism and interpretation. 2. Dante Alighieri, 1265–1321—
Appreciation—Ireland. 3. Joyce, James, 1882–1941—Knowledge—Literature. 4. Dante Alighieri, 1265–1321—Influence. 5. Negativity (Philosophy) in literature. 6. English fiction—
Italian influences. 7. Negation (Logic) in literature. 8. Messianism in literature. 9. Self in literature. I. Title.
    PR6019.O9Z52566 2004
    823'.912—dc22

                                                                                                    2004013880

To and for A.B.

CONTENTS

Abbreviations   x

Prologue: Sepulchral Intimations   1

Part One
Coordinated Influences: Augustine, Dante, and Vico

1   **Negative Self**   9
    Dante's Negative Poetics   9
    The Logic of Negative Representation   11
    Joyce's Negative Hero   15

2   **Negative Existence**   20
    Negative Interpretation   20
    Vico's Vestigial Theory of Language   23
    Vestigial Interpretation in *Finnegans Wake*   26
    Vestiges of Negative Cult   27

3   **Messianic Self**   29
    Augustine's Journey unto Death   29
    Negative Biography   33
    The Crisis of Irony   36
    Logorrhea of Messianism   38

Part Two
Joyce's Negative Protagonists

4   **Gabriel Conroy's Necropolitan Journey**   45
    Necropolitan Matrix   45
    Sepulchral Adumbrations   49
    Negative Biography   52
    Epiphany of Negative Self   54

5   **Stephen Dedalus's Silence in Progress**   60
    Christic Poet   62
    Poet of Maternal Absence   64
    Augustinian Poet   68

Dantesque Poet   71
Abortive Poet   73

6   **Stephen Dedalus's Poetry of the Afterlife**   76
The Sepulchral Muse   76
Literary Influences   78
Death and the Maiden   82
The Muse from the Crypt   86
The Extirpation of Poetry   90

7   **Leopold Bloom's Burial Meal**   93
Incorporation by Death   93
Purgation by Death   99

8   **Shem's Scripture**   108
Sacramental Immolation   108
Revision of the Christ Type   113
Corpus of Scriptural Poetics   115
Word and Flesh   118
Organic Bio-Graphy   120

Epilogue: Necropolitude   122

Acknowledgments   129
Notes   131
Bibliography   157
Index   169

JOYCE'S MESSIANISM

ABBREVIATIONS

FW James Joyce. *Finnegans Wake*. New York: Penguin, 1976.
P   James Joyce. *A Portrait of the Artist as a Young Man*. New York: Penguin, 1976.
U   James Joyce. *Ulysses*. Edited by Hans W. Gabler with Wolfhard Steppe and Claus Melchior. New York: Vintage, 1986.

PROLOGUE

SEPULCHRAL INTIMATIONS

"One of these days I'll be out back, swinging my scythe / Or holding my hourglass up to the moon, and Strand will appear / In a jacket and tie." The topic of Mark Strand's poem "2002" is the author's own death—Stephen Dedalus's premier concern as a poet. Rubbing his hands impatiently, Death foretastes his encounter with Strand:

> [. . .] and together under the boulevards'
> Leafless trees we'll stroll into the city of souls. And when
> We get to the Great Piazza with its marble mansions, the crowd
> That had been waiting there will welcome us with delirious cries[1]

Stephen would never write of his own terminal fate in such elegiac terms. The image of a delirious crowd waiting for the poet's arrival at the exotic burial place—a "Great Piazza" more suitable for a mob lynching than an entombment—exemplifies a degree of teasing self-enamorment[2] that Stephen would never condone. Stephen is a believer in "waking to the consciousness of [oneself] in darkness and secrecy and loneliness."

The reasons why Stephen Dedalus is a laconic and ultimately abortive poet are intricate, but they have as their essence the dictate of secrecy that binds him to the death of his mother. One must not confuse laconism with sterility. As a young expatriate, Stephen mastered an astounding wealth of poetic argument; his Parisian exile, prematurely interrupted by his mother's death, was meant to open the floodgates of his artistic self-expression. As a prodigal son returned home to his mother's funeral, Stephen is as eloquent as ever, a jester, a chatterbox—and yet one knows, obscurely, that his integrity will keep him from writing poetry for years to come.

Poetry is the daughter of memory, and Stephen's memories are undergoing a terrifying metamorphosis. His recollections of his mother are fading away, gradually substituted by the hallucinatory remembrance of a jealous specter. It is as though in dying his mother had robbed him of part of himself. Twenty-two years ago she had experienced—on his behalf—his own inception to the realm of phenomenal experience; she will have now preceded him in the unexperienceable obliteration of this very realm. Her memory is the repository of these two experiences that, impossible to him as they are beyond the influence of his poetic will, frame the entirety of his own existence. But he is losing her memory. And with it he is losing his previous sense of identity. It is the first stage of his own death, the dress rehearsal of the performance he will never intentionally deliver. Memories fall from him "like gangrened limbs."[3]

Since his return to Dublin Stephen has been facing a dilemma that exceeds rational comprehension. His younger siblings have been left in dire straits by their mother's death. Stephen's financial obligation toward his own family is a matter of simple computation, his teaching position at Mr. Deasy's school its expeditious solution. But we see him squander his earnings in pubs and brothels. This absurd compulsiveness frames the all-pervasive dilemma that on June 16, 1904, Stephen chooses to stare straight in the face. His new sense of responsibility is buried in the crypt of his mother's sacrifice for him. His new sense of self derives from his incorporation of her perennial remembrance. The deliberative space of his new interiority is framed by an uninterrupted state of mourning. The ineluctable yet impossible experience of his own death throws him into a constant, postmortem repetition of the vigil at his mother's bedside.

Stephen's presumed responsibility toward his next of kin, trivial indeed to assess since it is sanctioned by habit and communal custom, is rooted in the legacy of his mother's sacrifice for him. He feels yet a deeper existential obligation, meant to integrate the loss of his own source of life. This obligation is encrypted in a cathartic, purifying secret that "retains something of the thaumaturgical tradition": the secret, called Messianic in the present study, that is "tied to . . . the experience of the sacrificial gift."[4] The individual biography of ordinary obligations, orbiting the transacting logic of reciprocity, survival, exchange, care, gratitude, duty, retribution, is merely parasitic of the Messianic secret whereby the crypt of his mother's mourning nurtures the cradle of Stephen's future poetic creation.

To Stephen poetry is becoming another name for the wake as permanent existential condition. The truth of his poetry will not have been uttered in the language of ordinary experience—nor will have been the truth of his existential condition. Before writing honest and sincerely felt verses, exorbitant of convention, prevalent tradition, and artistic mannerism, Stephen needs to invent a vocabulary capable of expressing the irresistible, repulsive fecundity of his own mortality—which he sees encrypted, as a sort of vivifying power, in the putrefaction of his mother's corpse. He needs to reinvent his own self and his own biography, to bestow upon himself a personal biography entirely comprised of the impossible transaction of one death, his mother's, in return for his own. As we know, Stephen goes as far in this undertaking as envisioning himself as a vampire sucking blood from the maternal menses. But he goes no farther, not on the day of June 16, 1904. Having imaginatively incorporated his mother's ovum at the precise instant of its sterile decomposition, he lacks the words to fertilize it.

The sacramental tradition of the sacrificial gift depends on rites of incorporation, and what turns an ordinary act of incorporation into a manducatory sacrament is the liturgical repetition of a previous, vital event. In his mother's rejected ovum Stephen incorporates at once the virtual host of his two defining yet impossible experiences, that is to say, those of his own birth and his own death. However grotesque, no less repulsive and bloody than a crucifixion, this symbiotic kiss of the menses echoes the amorous sacrament of reciprocal incorporation celebrated on Howth Head by Leopold and Molly Bloom in 1888. Leopold's existential stance on June 16, 1904, vacillating between hope in the integrity of his family and despair in the future of his marriage, is entirely informed by the remembrance of this closed-loop embrace. He remembers Molly and himself enact a semblance or a fantasy of androgynous self-sufficiency by trading all at once seminal and nutritional secretions. This memory goes back to Leopold's youthful courtship of Molly on Howth Head, on September 10, 1888. Leopold and Molly were engaged in heavy petting among the rhododendrons. Molly was chewing a seed cake, which she forced into Leopold's mouth when they kissed. This mouth-to-mouth, semifluid nutrition flowing from her to him was almost immediately followed by the seminal counterflow that impregnated Molly with their daughter Milly (born nine months later, on June 15, 1889) (*U,* 17:2275–77, 17:865).

In time this autarkic emblem of Leopold and Molly's love for each other has come to incorporate to itself the death of their short-lived son, Rudy, whose demise pervades their relationship with long-term, cathartic effects, as devastating as they turn out to be ultimately cohesive. Blazes Boylan could even colonize Leopold's matrimonial bed permanently, but never extinguish Molly's existential attunement with this shared ideal.

The reader who misses the sacramental core of Stephen's and Leopold's existential paralysis in *Ulysses* will find it hard to assign any special relevance to their respective, opposite attitudes toward nutrition; Stephen fasts all day long after his breakfast in the company of Buck Mulligan and Haines, while Leopold keeps eating as though there were no tomorrow (for him and Molly), taking all of his many and complex culinary decisions under the aegis of the burial meal.

Stephen lacks the words, literally, to fertilize his own creative life. He has no faith in the power of words to vivify his permanent dialogue with his mother's memory. Determined not to succumb to the hypocrisy of an existence wasted on the reciprocity of transaction, he cannot conceive of that *negative existence,* pervaded by sacramental rather than ordinary experience, that would exonerate him from his stultifying obligations. After all, his material indebtedness toward his next of kin should only be as great as he makes their symmetrical obligations toward him.

Stephen's poetic inspiration sways between the self-enamorment that, as remarked above, he is unwilling to condone, and the maternal model of self-sacrifice that, however subversive of petty reciprocity, is ultimately imbued, in its Catholic configuration, with the patriarchal conformism that engendered the Marian legend. He is dissatisfied with both sources of inspiration. Self-centered frivolity belongs, in the same dimension of deterministic consequence and reciprocal obligation, with the "nightmare of history" that he is trying to evade; the sacrificial legend of Marian altruism pertains to the metaphysical indoctrination that he repudiated at the eve of his French exile. *Tertium datur,* a third option is indeed available in the realm of Joycean aesthetics, but not to Stephen. He is incapable of the existential revolution envisioned by his creator in *Finnegans Wake.*

Only in his last book does Joyce show us how the alternative biography of one's existence, informed by the tradition of the vigil for the dead, is exuberant of both the mundane experience of reciprocal obligation and of the otherworldly escapism of metaphysical justification. The present study identifies such an alternative with the negative existence of a Messianic self engaged in open and polemical confrontation with the dictates of common experience.

Stephen Dedalus is not alone in the defeat suffered by his abortive poetry. Having vanquished the lure and vanity of ordinary experience, his three great precursors —Augustine, Dante, and Mallarmé—also lose the power of poetic utterance at the threshold of the ultimate human experience, which they all confuse with metaphysical transcendence. Augustine, Dante, and Mallarmé's respective faculty of poetic speech exhales its last breath to make room for the Word that keeps Death at bay. On reaching the crossroads where the annihilation of physical decomposition encounters the idealization of death as "the impossibility to die,"[5] they renounce writing. The three of them belong, together with Stephen, in the illustrious tradition of San Juan de la Cruz's *noche oscura*: silence signals their supreme poetic performance, the homecoming, the intimacy with the Divine, reached at the conclusion of strenuous poetic labors, at the climax of their relentless struggle against the norms of ordinary experience. Beyond ordinary experience, Augustine, Dante, Mallarmé, and Stephen Dedalus meet the extraordinary experience that silences them all. Why does Joyce keep talking, then?

The pièce de résistance of the present study, several of whose arguments challenge the current debate about mystical and (negative) apophatic experience, attempts to provide this question with a nonmetaphysical answer. This "pièce" consists of the vestigial theory of language that, derived to Giambattista Vico from the Augustinian tradition, pervades the textual tapestry of *Finnegans Wake.* Augustine and Vico share a common view of linguistic performance in this, that they both hypostasize the presence in the human mind of a linguistic endowment that precedes the experience of language apprehension.[6] Augustine speaks of his own memory, the place where he meets God's Word, as a place of "hidden crevices" (*in cavis abditioribus*) wherein the "things themselves" of language (*res vero ipsas*) resided even before he learned them.[7] Vico speaks of a "mental vocabulary" (*dizionario di voci mentali*),[8] a sort of genetically transmitted neural endowment containing a priori all classical and vernacular languages. Given the linguistic patrimony inherent in either the "hidden crevices" of Augustine's memory or in Vico's "mental vocabulary," the scenario is not improbable that vestiges from archaic belief systems would percolate inside the information embedded within our innate (i.e., genetically wired) faculty of linguistic expression.

Such a scenario may be derived for instance from certain recent considerations of Noam Chomsky on a priori beliefs and our ignorance of how these beliefs might turn out to be fixed within semantic and phonetic structures.[9] It is a scenario consistent with Émile Durkheim's hypothesis that the contractual nature and legalistic implications of modern forms of religious cult, identifiable with the rise of individual responsibility and deliberative interiority, are the logical consequence in the evolution of the cult of archaic, forgotten religions: prayers, chants, sortileges, and canonic formulae would be the linguistic attractors, in this case, of inherited belief.[10] Our deep-seated drive to communal altruism may be the offspring of nature and nurture, of the interplay between evolutionary adaptation and historical evolution, in other words, without any need for transcendental, supernatural, otherworldly guidance. So may be our inescapable indebtedness to the principle of sacrificial catharsis.

Once the linguistic space of deliberative interiority is posited as genetically embedded and susceptible of evolutionary articulation, the dictate of secrecy that binds Stephen Dedalus to the death of his mother comes to coincide with that "phylo- and ontogenetic history" Derrida identifies with the history itself of God's name.[11] Stephen's paralyzing predicament consists of a dilemma between history (the symmetrical obligations of his domestic circumstances) and poetic vocation (the asymmetrical obligations of his poetic gift). Nourished by his uninterrupted conversation with the specter of his mother, his sense of responsibility, his sense of selfhood, and his interiority rebel against the prospect of devoting his existence to the mortifying tasks of the breadwinner. He refuses to submit in sum to the contingencies of history, either personal or communal. On the other hand, his mother's specter, which signifies his partial memory of the natural *and* the nurtural transmission of his poetic gift, stands for the metaphysical tradition of a faith that seems to call him to this very senseless, fatalistic sacrifice on behalf of his siblings. Hence, Stephen cannot write either in the mode of ordinary (historical) or in the mode of extraordinary (metaphysical) experience. Admirably enough, he embraces silence as a supreme gesture of defiance.

Shem in *Finnegans Wake* represents Joyce's solution to Stephen's paralysis. No less pregnant with poetic argument than Stephen after his vampirish ingestion of the expelled ovum of maternal fecundity, Shem dies to ordinary and common experience in order to conceive and then give new birth to himself as the anonymous Messiah of mortal eloquence. He inscribes the inviolable secret of his interiority upon every square inch of his own body, using his skin as parchment, for all to see. And yet, not every bystander can read his body, just as no more than a few eager readers can read *Finnegans Wake* or rare experts can decipher the sortileges inscribed on an Egyptian mummy. The liturgical text tattooed on Shem's skin is primarily vestigial; it belongs in the crypt; innate to some mourners' instinctive recognition, it is opaque to the linguistic skills of most. Shem inscribes this parchment using the waste matter of his own excrement as ink, turning thereby the inevitable putrefaction of his own corpse into the corpus of the Augustinian Word that never dies, making thereby his own body contemporary with the unfolding of the secret history of God's name.[12]

No wailing crowd will have been solicited at Shem's wake—only a fistful of fellow human beings, devotees of the written word, for whose assembly no "Great Piazza" is needed but only one small mound, the anonymous altar that Shem's remains will have made an inch taller. Within the dimension of negative existence, within the coordinates of an open and polemical confrontation with the dictates of common experience, Shem's gesture is not more eccentric than Christ's Crucifixion, or Stephen's kiss of the menses, or Leopold and Molly's closed-loop exchange of food and semen. It universalizes their catharsis. In the tradition of the medieval cycle drama, Christ too "stretched" his body on the cross like a "parchment" and then rubricated it like a medieval manuscript, with the inscription of the "bloody letters" from Holy Writ.[13] Shem's novelty is almost imperceptible, entirely contained in his stubborn enactment of the putrefaction that awaits all organic life, even that of sacrificial blood. Shem's Messianic biography is a biography of the mortal body. It is neither factual and deterministic nor metaphysical and transcendental. It is sacramental though—not because Shem is an inimitable Messiah transubstantiated into holy nourishment, but rather because he chooses to exist in uninterrupted communion with all the mortals who share his irremediable fate in extinguishment and decomposition. Shem will have turned his own body into a manifesto of human solidarity in front of death. The difference from Crucifixion is slight, as I said, the advancement vis-à-vis Stephen and Leopold's existential catharsis is minimal, but of this minimal slightness is made the evangel, the good news of *Finnegans Wake*.

PART ONE

Coordinated Influences
Augustine, Dante, and Vico

NEGATIVE SELF

Dante's Negative Poetics

According to John Freccero, Dante's *Paradiso* is made possible by maculae, the shadows of appearances that are not really there but allow one to see, by contrast, that which would remain invisible were it not for the chiaroscuro provoked and permitted by these shadows. The poetry of the *Paradiso* acknowledges its own limitations, as medium, via-à-vis its own subject; yet, it recurs to these shadowy limitations to suggest the limitless invisibility, impervious to the senses, of a place without extension or duration, called paradise, which does not reflect light against darkness but *is* light itself in its own relentless, boundless, unconditional giving—unreflecting, unreflective, neither transparent nor opaque medium, the condition of possibility of all media that are deployed in time and space. To Freccero the *Paradiso* displays a negative poetics of nonreferentiality.[1]

According to Eric Auerbach, the pilgrim of the *Inferno* undertakes a necropolitan journey that transcends his conscious experience of time and space, yet affords him a complete notion of the permanence of his own historical condition. The afterlife experienced by the pilgrim is "eternal and yet . . . full of history." Just as the souls in the afterlife are engaged in an eternal repetition of their decisive actions in life, so is Dante's pilgrim revealed that his decisive actions on earth will have been played out over and over again after his death "in tremendously concentrated form." The pilgrim's trespassing of natural boundaries and, first of all, of the unexperienceable threshold of physical death, affords him a negative contact with the "indestructible" givenness of his own existence. To Auerbach the *Inferno* displays an existential poetics of negative historicity.[2]

Immersed in the negative poetry of nonreferentiality, the pilgrim experiences divine light in its unconditional giving. Immersed in the existential poetry of negative historicity, he experiences human finitude in its indestructible givenness. His experience of the afterlife is at once mystical and phenomenal.

Contemporary discussions of apophatic experience have been dominated by two equivalent experiences, both deemed experiences of "impossibility," namely, the experience of one's mystical union with God's "absolute giving" and the experience of one's phenomenal exposure to death's "unconditional givenness." The impossibility of apophatic experience is determined by its being incommensurable with "the structures and categories of common experience"; heterogeneous with respect to the phenomenal range of "what we commonly know and express as experience," it is defined negatively in terms of absence.³ Apophatic experience is such that it cannot be phenomenally experienced, and yet, it provides the Euclidean axes, the α and the ω, of finite human existence.⁴

Within the coordinates of the apophatic tradition, the two experiences granted the pilgrim by Dante's negative poetics, both irreducible to and absent from common experience, fall under the rubric of the impossible. One simply does not experience, in time and space, the phenomenon of boundless charity or the phenomenon of irreducible finitude—or so it is being unanimously argued. But does the contemporary discussion on mystical and phenomenological impossibility, in its "most recent and most forceful treatments" by Jacques Derrida and Jean-Luc Marion, tell the whole story?⁵ Lucia Boldrini talks of Dante's "poetics of the ineffable" in order to express an analogous sense of experiential impossibility from the perspective of the reader's response. In the *Paradiso* Dante would have endeavored to represent "'a shadow' of the truth . . . so that [his reader] could . . . 'recreate' or re-experience [his] extraordinary journey into the world of eternity."⁶ The reader, if not the author, would have to move in a space of merely figurative experience.⁷

What if the shadows of nonreferentiality were to commingle in Dante with the irreducible givenness of human existence? What if an area of reciprocal permeation between two equally impossible experiences and two equally inadequate levels of representation—the nonreferentiability of the invisible and the irreducibility of human finitude—were to twist Dante's as well as his reader's experience away from the protocols of both realism and figurality? In these interrogations, I venture, lies the crux of Dante's influence on Joyce.

To his posterity, Dante's representation of the pilgrim's necropolitan journey constitutes the most comprehensive instantiation of his own existence. It is questionable whether the narration of the necropolitan journey brought Dante to an authentic recognition of his own self; it is debatable whether the intricacy of this journey expresses the authentic intricacy of his intentional consciousness. The biologic of the complex adaptive system that expresses either Dante's or any individual's intentional consciousness eludes our inquiry, and in my opinion is destined to elude it for many decades to come. But in the narrative of the necropolitan journey we have access to the distinctively existential instantiation of Dante's intentional consciousness. This narrative instantiates Dante Alighieri as a uniquely historical person vis-à-vis his fellow human beings.

The otherworldly pilgrimage is the existential datum, while Dante's documentable exilic life is merely the circumstantial process leading to it. One could say that existential instantiation overdetermines documentable biography. In the specific case of the necropolitan journey, then, the impossible experience of his own death attains existential priority over the phenomenal and conventionally meaningful experiences of Dante's factual life.

In the present study I shall discuss the influence of this Dantesque framework on James Joyce. I shall probe Joyce's writings for examples of instantiations where human existence is made eccentric to the domain of the phenomenally experience-able. More specifically, my inquiry shall address the secret impossibility intrinsic to the biographies of four among the protagonists of Joyce's works, namely, Gabriel Conroy, Stephen Dedalus, Leopold Bloom, and Shem, and justify why existential priority over the common facts of life is predicated on this very impossibility.

The Logic of Negative Representation

In Thomas Carlson's terminology, the experience of divine light in its uncondi-tional giving and the experience of human finitude in its indestructible givenness "belong inextricably to the constitution [of the self]," insofar as no conscious indi-vidual may dissociate their own existence from the question of their own prove-nance and destination. Even at the individual level, the history of human existence begins with archeology and ends with eschatology. Yet, origin and destination remain stubbornly beyond the self's conscious or intentional grasp, marking therefore the limits of knowledge and self-knowledge. While they play an essential role in the constitution of the self's finite experiencing, origin and destination remain irre-ducible to consciousness.[8]

Inherent in these apophatic views on mystical and phenomenal impossibility, however, is an allegorical attenuation of the Dantesque experience. The mystical and phenomenal experiences of the pilgrim in the afterlife would have to be reduced to the allegorical representation of *imitatio Christi*. The pilgrim would have to be understood as a merely figural double of the poet, his journey to the afterlife as a merely figural rendition of the biographical data of his exile—an allegorical exile from either the political life of Florence or the Christian life of grace, or both. Informed by the promise of Christian salvation, Dante's documentable biography would have to be understood as neither precursory nor engendered vis-à-vis its concentrated replay in the afterlife, but rather as the performative chain of events that Dante's poetic realism loaded with the allegorical meanings derived from the promise of salvation. In turn, his inexpressible experience of divine light in para-dise would have to be understood as the allegorical anticipation of the fulfillment of that promise.

The negative existence of the messianic self discussed in the present study goes beyond allegorical reduction and factual performance. The Dantesque experience of the afterlife does not consist of a merely allegorical *imitatio Christi,* but is rather predicated on the existential emulation of the Messiah, as described in Augustine's *Confessions.* After his death Christ descends to hell (*descensu*), compounding his visi-ble absence from the tomb (*discessit ab oculis*) with his immersion in the absence of grace.[9] The same journey is undertaken by the poet after the (negative) death that, as Freccero puts it, precedes his conversion.[10] On the part of the poet, Christ's emulation is existential rather than allegorical, and embraces the entire catalogue of messianic stations: *factis, morte, vita, descensu, ascensu*—from death to resurrection, from fall to redemption, from burial to manducation, from incarnation to transubstantiation.[11]

While the impossible experience of the apophatic tradition is negatively defined by absence, Dante's emulation of Christ's journey to the afterlife, equally impossible, hinges on the positive acceptation of absence found in Augustine's *Confessions*. As Freccero indicates in *The Poetics of Conversion,* Dante's experience of death in hell is "ontologically real," substantially permeated, no less than Augustine's experience of sin, by Satan as the radical absence of life, the "'degree-zero' of form and intelligibility."[12] Up to the moment of their respective conversions, the theological impossibility of death as ontological substance fills both Augustine's and Dante's existence with overwhelming and unquestionable plenitude.[13] As Phillip Cary has put it: "The soul fleeing from a God who is inescapably everywhere . . . stems from Augustine's sense that separation [from] God . . . is wellnigh impossible yet abominably real."[14] And this impossible condition of absence *from*—rather than *of*—an ever-present God is owing to the human soul's subjection to "the power of death."[15] Death is not a substance but a real existential possibility, made accessible to Augustine by an act of self-forgetfulness.[16] This Augustinian view, I venture, compels a critique of the apophatic scheme and its allegorical implications.

Augustine's "phenomenological region of lure and temptation . . . oscillate[s] between metaphysics and facticity," according to John Caputo, with Augustine's discussions of the self being "on the verge of a conceptual and categorical revolution of which they are never quite capable."[17] This unaccomplished revolution, in whose premises Heidegger identified an essential source for his existential hermeneutics,[18] may have already found its philosophical implementation in Derrida's and Marion's shared view that "experience is really experience when it is an experience of the impossible," as Caputo suggests.[19] Nonetheless, the existential implementation of this revolution calls for a radical questioning of the conventional norms of predicative, denotative, and referential representation of the self's individual experience.

"[Augustine is] the earliest writer to give memory a critical role in sustaining the [self's] personal continuity."[20] In choosing the genre of confession to report his journey from sin to conversion, Augustine adopts remembrance as the dominant mode of biographical narration. While his recollected experiences proceed from lure and temptation to his encounter with God at Ostia,[21] Augustine places "faith increasingly in interior discourse."[22] Since no sensory confirmation is afforded to his instant of divine intimacy at Ostia, Augustine is left with two sources of alternative confirmation for the authenticity of his impossible experience, namely, "the teaching and learning that take place entirely within [him], that is, in and by [himself]; and the sensory world that [he] recreate[s] by putting into words again what [he] know[s] by interior means."[23] It is at this juncture that Augustine finds himself on the verge of an existentialist revolution. Remembrance of the impossible encounter with God at Ostia is interpretative. Out of memory's contemplative silence,

Augustine extracts the recollections of God that he *intends* to express in words.[24] However, his mnemonic intention is metaphysical, entirely dependent for its validation on the external discourse of Scripture.[25] He is one small yet vital step away from opening himself entirely to the facticity of "all that [his] memory knows."[26]

The absence of the apophatic experience from the range of ordinary experience may turn out to be coeval with the history of the irreducible separation between the existential experience of factical life, defined by Heidegger in sections 10 and 22–24 of *Being and Time,* and the ordinary representations of human existence.[27] How does one recognize an instance of negative existence? How does one differentiate it from the ordinary domain of phenomenal experience? How does one express it in words? Jacques Derrida has debated this issue from his earliest writings. Is it possible to establish a "deep semantic anchoring" or "a system of prescriptions inscribed in language or in the continuum of a linguistic tradition" that would allow "translation, metaphorization, metonymization, exchange [of the impossible experience] with an ultimately homogeneous semantic circle?"[28] How does one bring linguistic representation to bear on the intentional instantiation of negative existence, without reducing the latter to an allegory that lacks existential concreteness?

Jean-Luc Marion addresses this concern with his phenomenological discussions of the miracle of the Crucifixion and its Scriptural representation in Holy Writ. As a phenomenon "beyond the limits of this world,"[29] the miracle of the Crucifixion is intended by Marion not as phenomenally factual but as phenomenologically hypothetical.[30] In and of itself Scripture's representation of the Crucifixion amounts to a phenomenal collection of "inert words and dead letters;" when sermonized in the Eucharistic site, however, this representation enables the Eucharistic community to experience an "original repetition" of the Crucifixion.[31] The theology of transubstantiation crosses "the gulf separating the text [of Scripture] from its referent." This crossing of the gulf, predicated on the requirement that the unutterable Word itself "saturate of absoluteness each one of the [dead] signs within His [i.e., the Word's] text," would warrantee the linguistic transduction of the factually impossible event of the Crucifixion onto its factical—ontologically and intentionally compelling—repetition.[32]

The problem with Marion's "original repetition" of the event of the Crucifixion is that it must be experienced in the guise of an episcopal performance. In other words, the repetition consists of the Word coming *prima persona* to instantiate itself in the sermon of the bishop. This self-instantiation of the Word requires that the "inert words" of Scripture be vivified by the miracle of episcopal liturgy, which consecrates the analogizing transduction from Holy Writ to its referent in the Crucifixion. Marion is implicitly positing the occurrence, about two millennia ago, of an analogously Pentecostal process, whereby the *original* analogizing transduction—from the phenomenon of the Crucifixion to its representation in Holy Writ—came to be executed (i.e., transcribed) in conformance with the original *verba* of the Word. Furthermore, the Pentecostal symmetry of this analogizing transduction —from the Crucifixion to Holy Writ and vice versa—must apply not only to the textual trace of the Crucifixion, whose composition by the neo-Testamentary scribes is assumed to have occurred in a regime of Pentecostal authenticity, but also to the liturgical interpreter, the bishop himself. The bishop's credentials, as the authentic *porte-parole* of the Word, rest on his legitimate election by the successor to Peter Pontifex. Only an absurd transposition of the history of the Church of Rome, inclusive of the Crusades and the Spanish Inquisition, onto a tale of Pentecostal legitimacy could endorse such genealogical succession.

My perplexity with regard to the current apophatic discussion is based on this consideration, that this discussion derives apodictically the incommensurability of two distinct orders of absence, that is, the direct experience of one's irreducible finitude and the direct experience of God's boundless charity, from their concordant position at one denotative and referential remove from ordinary or common experience. The notion of messianic self that informs the present study is based instead on the presumption that one may envisage an Augustinian order of presence bridging the cleft between these two distinct orders of absence. Carlson seems to suggest an analogous presumption when he argues that a collusion (which he calls "indiscretion") may bring distinct spheres of mystical and phenomenological negativity to points of convergence and shared resonance.[33] The space of instantiation for negative existence would be circumscribed by these collusions.

One may indeed envision the negative existence of a messianic self as engaged in open and polemical confrontation with the dictates of common experience—a messianic self that, to put it aphorismatically, experiences the phenomenon of its own death as collusive with the unconditionality of its own self-giving. In my discussion of archaic sacrifice in *Rituals of Literature,* I attribute to the participants in the primordial rite an analogous experience of self-dissipation, whose outcome I label "intimacy with the divine." This label is aimed at capturing the organic absorption in *horror religiosus* undergone by primitive worshipers, as well as the self-instantiation, indifferent to raw biographical data and irreducible to referential or allegorical representation, obtained by their existential identification with the sacrificial victim.[34]

The existential view of sacrificial experience promoted in the present study clashes with the doctrinal codification of the Eucharistic rite, found primarily in Aquinas's notion of transubstantiation.[35] The sacrificial tradition of Christianity is characterized by the separation between the doctrinal codification of the Eucharistic rite on the one hand and the synergy of its spontaneous, individual experience on the other. Pseudo-Paul, author of the Letter to the Hebrews, is traditionally considered the source of the hiatus separating, in the celebration of the Eucharist, the doctrinal understanding of the nature of Christ's death from the cathartic experience of the Crucifixion. However, the prevailing interpretation of Hebrews 10:8, according to which Jesus's death is the metaphoric and proleptic "true form" of a kingdom-still-to-come, is only one of two possible interpretations. The alternative interpretation promotes instead the understanding of the Crucifixion as the full actualization of the kingdom-to-come, that very factical actualization—ontologically and intentionally compelling—that is delineated, according to some interpreters, in Paul's Second Letter to the Corinthians (5:17, 6:16) or in Paul's Letter to the Galatians (3:23–29).[36] In the former case, the Crucifixion is intended as a once-for-all event, irrepeatable; the human experience of the covenantal sacrifice in blood is presumed to have reached its full fruition and ultimate closure in the historical event of the Crucifixion; the Eucharistic celebration of the Crucifixion is reduced to an act of commemoration and commiseration, consumed via the metaphoric ingestion of the sacrificial victim. In the case of the latter interpretation, Jesus's death affects the worshiper as an existential rather than virtual repetition, as the incorporation of a factical blood-shedding; intimacy with the divine is lived through in all its repulsive and irresistible concreteness, as an individual feat of organic theophagy.

In this latter perspective, the negative existence of the messianic self would result from the collusion of the two orders of absence discussed in the apophatic scheme, both absences—that of the experience of one's own death and that of the experience of unconditional giving—being mediated by one's existential incorporation of the messianic sacrifice. And the biography of this messianic self, being the offshoot of two compounded impossibilities, would unapologetically unfold at a second denotative remove from common and ordinary experience.

Joyce's Negative Hero

I was inspired to write this book by the earliest presentation in *Ulysses* of an impossible self at odds with common experience. In accusing Stephen Dedalus of being "an impossible person," Buck Mulligan is certainly unaware of the existential import of his accusation (*U*, 1:222). The conflict between Buck and Stephen centers on their different views concerning the respect due to the dead and the moribund.

Buck, a medical student, reproaches Stephen for his refusal to kneel at his dying mother's bedside. "[Death] is a beastly thing and nothing else. It simply doesn't matter. . . . To me it's all a mockery and beastly" (*U*, 1:206–10). Stephen takes personal offence. In his eyes, Buck's words represent an expeditious dismissal of his extraordinary and unconventional mourning. He has long been tormented by the special pain "frett[ing] his heart" after his mother's death and by the "bitter mystery" of the love that linked his mother to him. He struggles to reconcile the horrid decomposition of his mother's corpse, which in his most manic fantasies he feeds upon like a cannibalistic "chewer of corpses" (*U*, 1:103, 253, 278), with the transcendent destiny of her soul, doctrinally modeled by the Church on the commensality of Christ's transubstantiation—a sacramental commensality intolerant of the physiology of chewing, incidentally. But this struggle is nothing short of a struggle against the phenomenal dominion of personal and collective history. Stephen must redeem his own self from the ordinary rule of everyday existence and economic constraint, from the deterministic norms of cause-and-effect and even of molecular physiology (*U*, 9:376–78; see chapters 5 and 6), if he truly wants to redeem his mother's soul and become the messianic harbinger of her escape from the misery of annihilation and decomposition. For a Christian apostate (*P,* 247), quite an impossible task!

Stephen Sicari maintains that "the body of [his mother] signifies [Stephen's] connection to the past, to history, and to the body that lives in time."[37] Short of his own death, his mother's death constitutes Stephen's most vivid experience of radical finitude. Mary Goulding Dedalus shows herself several times to Stephen on June 16, 1904, either in the oneiric visions of her "wasted body within its loose brown graveclothes" (*U,* 1:102–10, 1:270–72, 2:145–46) or as the inauspicious apparition of a cadaver in advanced decomposition, "green with gravemould" (*U,* 15:4157–219). Stephen's entire day in *Ulysses,* as well as his frequent and mostly abortive episodes of poetic composition, are punctuated by his meditations on his mother's death. In this regard, Stephen's character seems modeled on Augustine's relation to his own mother, Monica, the remembrance of whose death triggers the autobiography of the *Confessions.*

Just as Stephen did at his mother's bedside, Augustine betrays no "sense of grief" (*sine sensu doloris*) in front of his friends on the day of Monica's death. Just as Stephen, the "unclean bard," fuels the rumor that he "makes a point of washing [only] once a month" (*U,* 1:472–77), so Augustine dismisses the efficacy of the waters from the bath (*balneis*), which "could not wash away the bitter grief [*maeroris amaritudo*] from [his] heart." Augustine's urgency to confess, informed by his hardly extinguishable debt to Monica, manifests itself as the need to probe in writing the intolerable depth of his bereavement. *Et nunc, domine, confiteor tibi in litteris.*[38]

There is a trace of the uncompromising protagonist of *Stephen Hero,* in Stephen's irreligious reaction to his mother's death. One could say that he is after a "vivisection" of the fact itself: he wants to reconstruct "the spectacle of [her] redemption" regardless of "presumptive Redeemers and Churches."[39] As though his struggle to purloin his mother's "wasted body"—his frequent remembrance of it, that is—from the dictates of natural decomposition were not symptomatic enough of a rebellion against the common experience of death (the experience that his fellow Dubliners submit to in a spirit of fatalistic resignation), there also surfaces from Stephen's bereavement an existential attitude that significantly complements this rebellion. One must factor in, on the one hand, Stephen's struggle against the inescapable identity of an impoverished and disenfranchised drunkard carousing all night long in the streets and disreputable neighbors of Dublin, and capable of writing only the four perplexing lines of his "Vampire Poem"—such a disappointing youth would be wise in conforming to the dominant customs regulating the conduction of funerals, vigils, and wakes in his hometown. On the other hand, one cannot ignore Stephen's tenacious self-affirmation as a legitimate successor in the line of descent of four among the greatest poets of the Western tradition, namely Dante, Blake, Yeats, and Mallarmé—significantly enough, four artists whose striving toward artistic creation is mirrored in their respective attitudes toward maternal nurturance. From his entrance on the stage of the Martello Tower to his farewell exit from the stage of Leopold Bloom's garden, Stephen appears actively engaged in the unrealistic reconciliation of his social disadvantages with his grandiose ambition to emulate these four precursors. The instantiation of his own biography in full disregard of his plebeian condition and even, perhaps, of his limited poetic talent, balances his rejection of the fatality of death.

To succeed as a poet, Stephen must then truly invent himself as an "impossible person," engaged in open and polemical confrontation with the dictates of common experience and social convention, earnest in his scandalous appropriation of the impossible experience of his mother's death. Not a living soul in Dublin would bet one penny on this intolerant and intolerable youth—except his creator, that is, Joyce himself, who chose to enact Stephen's own struggle against impossibility in his own scandalous elopement with Nora (an uncompromising challenge against the society of his and her time), in his own "underbred" writing endeavors (an uncompromising challenge against the status quo of intellectual privilege), and above all, in his epoch-making promotion of the vigil or the wake for the dead as the distinct toil informing the existential condition of the modern self (an uncompromising challenge against the secular value-makers of modernity).[40]

Not long before his mother's death, Stephen longed for the condition of a liturgical poet endowed with the generative powers of the "priest of eternal imagination, transmuting the daily bread of experience into the radiant body of everliving life" (*P*, 221). Already at this immature stage, evidently, the liturgical aesthetics of Yeats and Mallarmé are pervasive of Stephen's poetic ambition. He is eager to second Yeats in the titanic task of taking upon his shoulders "the burdens that have fallen from the shoulders of the priests"—a task that, as I argue in *Rituals of Literature,* counts Dante and Blake among its most authoritative promoters.[41] He is eager to undermine conventional religiosity by means of the Mallarmean poetics of "Immaculate Creation."[42] However closely attuned with the views of his favorite poets, though, Stephen's liturgical aesthetics is still derivative, reflecting the immaturity and lack of commitment of his youth. His only extant poetic composition at the time of his mother's death bears witness to it—a "eucharistic hymn" resounding with the unconstrained vitality and lustful self-complacency that saturate its compositional process:

> A glow of desire kindled again his soul and fired and fulfilled his body. Conscious of his desire she was waking from odorous sleep, the temptress of his villanelle. . . . Her nakedness yielded to him, radiant, warm, odorous and lavishlimbed, enfolded him like a shining cloud, enfolded him like water with a liquid life. (*P*, 223)

These lascivious bodily fluids, metaphorically congealed in the lines of Stephen's "Villanelle of the Temptress," will curdle, less than two years later, into the "snotgreen" waters of his mother's "bitter death" (*U*, 1:78, 3:329–30). At the time of his villanelle Stephen still needs to graduate from the empty formalism of poetic imitation to the authentic expression of his existential dilemma, whose maturity will be obviously manifest in his day-long wanderings in *Ulysses*. On June 16, 1904, instructed by his short-lived French exile, Stephen acts as the punctual foil to the "centripetal" Bloom-Odysseus of *Ulysses,* who celebrates his (more or less) felicitous homecoming at the end of the day.[43] Stephen embodies rather Dante's rebellious Ulysses—the second Ulyssean incarnation in Joyce's novel, hence—who travels away from home, church, and country in order to *seguir virtute e canoscenza* ("to pursue virtue and knowledge" [*Inferno,* 26:120]). It takes at first a flight to Paris, the city where Irish patriots hide, "spurned" and "forgotten" (*U,* 3:255, 3:263), and where Mallarmé's aesthetics reign unchallenged, for Stephen to go beyond the derivative sterility of his previous poetic endeavors. When his mother's death puts an end to this Parisian sojourn, calling him back to his family obligations, Stephen's complex attitude toward these obligations reflects the cultural richness of his recent maturation.

As the first-born son of a drunkard, Simon Dedalus, Stephen has social and financial obligations to his next of kin, left orphans and indigent by their mother's demise.[44] As the "yokefellow" of Irish expatriates (*U,* 3:228), he has obligations to Mother Ireland, the musaic figure much of Yeats's early work "draws heavily on."[45] As the escapee supported in Paris by his mother's "money orders" (*U,* 3:185), sent to him in all likelihood without his father's knowledge or consent, he has obligations to an absent creditor who could never be appeased with hard cash. As the ambitious artist who had planned to "forge in the smithy of [his] soul the uncreated conscience of [his] race" (*P,* 253), he has obligations to his own poetic vocation, no less *maternante,* as we shall discuss in chapter 6, than Yeats's and Mallarmé's respective muses.[46]

Should he swim or sing the "waters [of his mother's] bitter death?" Just as he "could not save her" from these waters, so his next of kin would probably "drown [him] with [them]," were he to try rescuing them from indigence (*U,* 3:329–30, 10:875–77). But he recalls having sung the "music" of these waters and its "wave-white wedded words" at the request of his dying mother. She had cried in response to the words that he sang "holding down the long dark chords;" she cried for "love's bitter mystery," as she put it herself (*U,* 1:246–53). Why should his mother's grateful tears be less authentic than the "hoarse loud breath rattling in horror" at the moment of her death, when her curse fell on him for refusing to pray on his knees? (*U,* 1:275–76). And why should his poetic labors in her memory be less valuable to his dear ones than the coins of his salary, "soiled by greed and misery" (*U,* 2:227–28)?

As we know, Stephen attempts to solve this existential dilemma with the pecuniary compromise of his teaching position at Mr Deasy's school, but this solution, evidently precarious, only stimulates his pathetic binging at night. An early poem by Mallarmé, *Aumône* ("Alms") adumbrates this conflict of Stephen's. Derrida's *Glas* devotes several brilliant pages to the illustration of the "entirely other organization of resources," elusive of ordinary experience as well as of the conventional norms of referential or denotative signification, which is promoted by the alms offered to the beggar in *Aumône.*[47] "Don't think I'm telling you foolish things / . . .

And above all, my brother, don't go buy bread," enjoins Mallarmé's speaker.[48] The poet *is* a beggar capable of squeezing a resounding feast of the imagination from the gift of a single glass of golden wine (*un lac de vin d'or*), from a little tobacco (*berceur d'une nuit éclaircie / Le tabac*), or a dose of narcotic (*l'opium puissant*). Nurturance of the imagination is his first concern, nutrition of the body his last. But is there room for reciprocity or altruism in inventiveness of this sort? Can the poet's well-honed words emancipate the needy, besides himself, from the unyielding dictates of material needs? Can Stephen's choice to be a poet rather than a breadwinner be honorable at all? It would be a matter, for Stephen, of identifying himself fully with the logic of negative existence. It would be a matter of undertaking first of all the poetic conveyance of his own messianic self. His own everyday self—positive, factual, prone to binge drinking—must blur in the mists of his mother's death and fade "into impalpability" (*U,* 9:148–49). Like the diligent disciple of Mallarmé that he is, Stephen must undertake the "long descent into nothingness" that enabled his French master "to speak with certitude."[49]

NEGATIVE EXISTENCE

Negative Interpretation

My aim in the present study is to write a Joycean chapter in the history of the irreducible separation between the existential experience of factical life and the ordinary representation of human existence. I show in my discussions of *Dubliners,* *Ulysses,* and *Finnegans Wake* that the mature Joyce's renditions of the "spectacle of redemption" fill some of the most banal, vulgar, prosaic, realistic actions of his protagonists with the negative core whereby human existence is made eccentric to the domain of the phenomenally experienceable. I show, more particularly, that Joyce bestows on his protagonists a distinct catalogue of messianic connotations, informed by the Christic stations of death and resurrection, fall and redemption, burial and manducation, incarnation and transubstantiation; this catalogue evolves gradually through Joyce's successive writings, enacted in its fundamental aspects by Gabriel Conroy's necropolitan journey at the end of "The Dead" (chapter 4); by Stephen Dedalus's Augustinian lapse in the "noise of common speech" (chapter 5), and his subsequent emulation of Dante, Blake, Yeats, and Mallarmé's poetry of the afterlife (chapter 6); by Leopold Bloom's dilemma—at once comic, erotic, and pathetic—between bestial decomposition and sacred manducation (chapter 7); and finally by Shem's logorrhoic incarnation of the messianic self (chapter 8). These are distinct case studies forming their own cohesive picture within the larger frame and greater internal complexity of Joyce's negative poetics.

Before undertaking this exegetic task, it remains for me to qualify the Augustinian connotations of the messianic self that were foreshadowed above, explaining what sets them in open and polemical confrontation with the dictates of common experience (see chapter 3), and how their existential negativity foregrounds a gesture of self-instantiation. The most emblematic event pertinent to this existential negativity consists of the repetition of Christ's journey unto death, and becomes, first in Dante and then in Joyce, the fulcrum of their respective negative poetics.

Even as I am aware of the scandalous challenge entailed by my resistance to figurative interpretation, I need to stress that this resistance, based on the hypothesis of an irreducible separation between ordinary experience and negative existence, also calls for an interpretive stance immune to the temptation of literalism. The figurative interpretation of Joyce is questionable *because* one lacks the literal referents for "figuration."[1] I have deconstructed the temptation of literalism in *Scriptural Poetics in Joyce's "Finnegans Wake,"* with special reference to the confusion between literal and typological expression, and between character amalgamation and naturalistic identity in the *Wake*.[2]

My resistance to figurative interpretation is more problematic to defend because contemporary Joycean interpretation seems almost entirely grounded on the tropological tenet that the Joycean *interpretanda* need to be "construed as a ground inhabited by discernible figures."[3] Among recent studies of Joyce's Dantesque and Christological influences, Stephen Sicari and Lucia Boldrini have contributed two of the most persuasive tropological approaches, both taking their initial orientation —granted the profound difference in their views—from Dante's transformation of the "allegory of the theologians" in the poetics of the *Commedia*. To Sicari "the allegory of Incarnation . . . solves all problems of interpretation and allows for a *belief* in the literal as well as its various levels of symbolic meaning."[4] To Boldrini, "[Dante's] allegory is not only restricted to words . . . but is also *in facto,* and the letter both corresponds *truthfully and faithfully* to the facts it describes ('literam') and also signifies *other meanings* ('significata per literam')."[5]

My resistance to the figurative interpretation of Joyce's writings is the pièce de résistance announced in the foreword to this book. This resistance is based on the thesis that Joyce's writings are disseminated with examples of individual instantiations of negative existence; these instantiations, in turn, brim over the experiential range of the literal referents indispensable to the "figurative coherence" of tropological exegesis.[6] The remainder of the present section and the next section are devoted to a meticulous discussion of the epistemology of this thesis.

In the present study the term instantiation defines the code-like document (from the Canonic Bible to the American Constitution, from a poem to the displayed bundle of my inherited and acquired characteristics) whereby an individual constitutes himself/herself as a person vis-à-vis another individual and/or a community. An instantiation may therefore be considered as the objectual and intentional datum resulting from the process whereby an individual comes to recognize its own subjective selfhood. An individual's self-constitution becomes an instantiation when it is intersubjective, that is to say, recognizable by an observer or destinee.

Recognition plays an essential role in the intrasubjective and intersubjective expressions of instantiation. As the etymology of the term recognition indicates (and recent neurophysiological studies on the interplay between recognition and episodic memory confirm),[7] a recognition depends primarily on the autonoetic reoccurrence or, more exactly, the mnemonic reactivation of a previous (act of) cognition. To the objection that no subject is autonomously or autonoetically cognizant of a formerly unexperienced phenomenon, the conventional rejoinder is rhetorical, based on the interplay between the episodic or autonoetic memory of punctual phenomena (in their literal factuality) and the semantic or noetic memory of acquired codes of communication (in their tropic discernibility): the mechanics of recognition would liken in sum a previously unexperienced phenomenon to a trope or a matrix of tropes that "our culture has made us familiar with."[8]

However, as argued in chapter 1 (in the subsection titled "The Logic of Negative Representation"), the phenomena to be dealt with in the recognition of an instantiation of negative existence are at a second denotative and referential remove from ordinary experience; as such, they do not provide any factual basis for either the neural mechanics of working-memory storage or the referential relation of tropic recognition.[9] And yet, the fact remains that in the context of apophatic discussions the negative experiences of impossibility are never addressed as mere fantasies or as mere fictions of truth.

How does one recognize that which is both factually uncognizable and tropically/allegorically irreducible? Are there procedures of mnemonic reactivation that are exuberant of the expressive norms of the literal and the figurative, of the episodic and the semantic? To cope with this problem, the linguistic dimension of the apophatic discussion must be factored in. The apophatic tradition is linguistically paradoxical insofar as it "remains on 'this side'" of language[10] (as the muteness of Augustine's mystical experience at Ostia clearly indicates),[11] and yet, it is compulsively, irresistibly logorrhoic. As Derrida has put it, "apophatic . . . discourse [is] interminable [since it] cannot contain within itself the principle of its interruption," which principle consists of the "absolute rarefaction" of its ineffable signified.[12] The paradox of apophatic discourse is that, irresistibly driven to "positive predication," it defers indefinitely the collusion with the signified that would silence the movement itself of predication.[13] Putting it in the Heideggerian lingo, even before there will have occurred an existential fruition of the apophatic experience of impossibility, I shall posit, the interminable discourse that precedes it will have articulated its predicative and denotative intelligibility.[14] The question then is, where does one find or experience or retrieve the referential ground for this always already available apparatus of intelligible predication/denotation of the apophatic experience?

Let me summarize the above remarks. The contemporary discussion of the apophatic tradition postulates that the two fundamental experiences of impossibility, that is, death's unconditional givenness and deity's boundless giving, "belong inextricably to the constitution [of the self]," yet are beyond the self's ordinary experiential grasp. On the side of linguistic signification, this discussion postulates that these two impossible experiences are unnamable, since they brim over the predicative reach of linguistic expression. Finally, this discussion recognizes in these two experiences the imprint of the Christic legacy.[15] Such apophatic scheme, predicated on certainties that cannot be factually experienced or linguistically signified, is no less transgressive of rhetorical conventions than my resistance to both literal and figurative interpretation. It suggests furthermore, in concert with my thesis of negative existence, that there exists a range of messianic, inscrutable, and linguistically inexpressible phenomena that are constitutive of our own self.

Unfit to manifest itself through either the literal immediacy of factual experience or the figural mediatedness of predicative discourse, and inaccessible as well to the tropic recognition of mnemonic retrieval, this range of phenomena instantiates itself in negative existence. Although exorbitant of linguistic signification, this range of phenomena is nonetheless talked endlessly about by way of retrospective reference and/or prospective anticipation. One could say that the contemporary debate on the apophatic tradition hinges on the tenet that we all know what it is that we are discussing: the *cognoscibile operabile,*[16] a something emerging out of our remote past that will have been germinating in our remote future. However, we cannot be authentically knowing it or even discussing it, since we never experienced it and it has never even been properly named. One might venture that such a logorrhoic discussion about an unnamable and unexperienceable cipher bespeaks the evidence of some unexplored sort of relational affinity between this cipher itself and the constitution of our discursive faculty.

Although their respective writings are emblems of linguistic self-instantiation, Augustine and Dante do not seem to share my opinion. Rather than a relational affinity, they postulate a radical separation between the experience of impossibility and the experience of human discourse. Augustine conceives of human speech as a noise (*strepitum*) silencing the crystalline silence of divine intimacy.[17] God is ineffable insofar as, "intelligible to the mind,"[18] It is not comprehensible by means of words.[19] Dante's afterlife experience is in turn exorbitant of his poetic vocabulary. When he tries to describe his "unrepresentable reality,"[20] his pen starts spitting ink clumsily and profusely (*la penna abborra* [*Inferno,* 25:144]), filling the page with redundant and unreliable impressions. In the *Paradiso* Dante's own words are "short-winded and whiny": of his supreme moment of intimacy with the divine he can tell us "less than little" (*Paradiso,* 33:121–23).[21] As Sam Slote has put it, the language of Dante's negative experience colludes with "a language of silence in order to access that which is inaccessible to language."[22]

One will have to wait for Joyce's messianic protagonists, and specifically for the influence of Vico's linguistics on Shem's characterization in *Finnegans Wake,* before the existential negativity of the messianic self may become fully and unmediatedly recognizable in its linguistic expression.

Vico's Vestigial Theory of Language

It is well known that in the *Scienza nuova* Vico postulates the historicity of language. Individual words are treasures of etymological sediments that, properly excavated, reveal the stratification of signifieds that subsequent historical periods have progressively attached to them.[23] It is usually taken for granted that this procedure of etymological excavation is performed by an investigator who treats language as a societal archive and has furthermore at their disposal the cultural apparatus of a communal tradition. By means of etymological study, this investigator draws a virtual one-to-one map, whereby distinct stages in the evolution of communal ideas, beliefs, and institutions are punctually related to their linguistic expressions, while their origin is provided with historical and cultural rationale. In this perspective, the "entire development of human history" may be said to be condensed in the history of language.[24]

Access to a specific tradition and apprehension of a specific language are two necessary but not sufficient conditions, however, to the Viconian performance of historical explication via linguistic analysis. Only very recently has this aspect of Vico's linguistics been paid proper scholarly attention, primarily by Marcel Danesi. To Vico language recognition is species-specific.[25] All classical and vernacular languages are informed by the same "mental vocabulary" (*dizionario di voci mentali*),[26] as the *Scienza nuova* calls it—a genetically transmitted neural endowment, to phrase it in biogenetic terminology, which "allows us to re-evoke the first experiences of conscious humanity."[27] This neural apparatus is antecedent to the process of linguistic apprehension that awakens it. Lorraine Weir defines it a "mnemotechnic and semantic field," the unconscious repository of etymological vestiges inherited from the archaic past of the species.[28]

Compounded with the individual experience of language apprehension, the genetic endowment of these etymological vestiges accounts for the historical and cultural character of human discourse. This aspect of Vico's linguistic theory agrees with Noam Chomsky's views about the ontogeny of belief systems. Almost forty years ago Chomsky maintained that our ability to recognize linguistic expressions derives from genetically determined neural networks that correspond to the deep structures of intentional language.[29] In a recent work he has relaxed the severe limitations originally imposed upon the "naturalistic inquiry into the language faculty,"[30] intimating that vestiges "from belief systems" can percolate inside the information embedded within these genetically wired structures.[31]

The convergence of Vico's and Chomsky's linguistics enables me to graft an autonoetic, evolution-bred extension on the conventional understanding of Augustine's notions of mental imprint and mnemonic functions.[32] As I suggested earlier, it is in his dissertation on human memory, in Book X of the *Confessions,* that Augustine comes closest to that "conceptual and categorical revolution" of which, according to John Caputo, his existential conception of the self is "never quite capable."[33] The premises for this revolution can be found in Augustine's awareness that memory—where his knowledge of God resides[34]—is a place of "hidden crevices" (*in cavis abditioribus*) wherein linguistic expression is "recognized" (*recognovi*) independently of literal reference and allegorical reduction. The "things themselves" of language (*res vero ipsas*), Augustine writes in the *Confessions,* "must have been in my heart even before I learned them, . . . already in my memory, but hidden away and crowded far back in its hidden crevices" ([*in meo cordi*] *erant et antequam ea didicissem, . . . iam erant in memoria, sed tam remota et retrusa quasi in cavis abditioribus*).[35]

"Looking forward to Vico," Brian Stock argues, "Augustine saw memory as the basis of culture."[36] In the light of the above discussion, I should go one step farther, and claim that Augustine's discussions of memory have set down the foundations for Vico's vestigial theory of language—which, one should recall, is being discussed here as the solution to the problem of recognition in the linguistic instantiation of negative existence. The analogy between Vico's *dizionario di voci mentali* and Augustine's "mental words" is striking to say the least. Just as Vico's mental vocabulary precedes the formation of classical and vernacular languages, so the "mental words" that Augustine discusses in *De trinitate* "do not belong to the spoken or written forms of specific languages like Greek or Latin. . . . They constitute . . . an inward expression of the heart, that is, a 'speech' of 'truth.'"[37] As Calvin Troup has put it, "Augustine recognizes the existence of a priori principles in [the human] mind."[38] Yet, as discussed in chapter 1 (in the subsection titled "The Logic of Negative Representation"), Augustine is incapable of pushing his conceptual and categorical revolution to its farthest existential consequences, because this revolution would lead him onto the uncharted territory of an innate, autonoetic, or genetically transmitted faculty of linguistic expression, independent from the transcendental signifier of the divine *Verbum*.[39]

Vico's vestigial theory of language provides the recent concerns about the "coevolution of genes and culture" with a linguistic framework.[40] Is there an evolutionary interaction between the human mind and cultural discourse? From the perspective of the present discussion the same question may be rephrased from an Augustinian viewpoint: What kind of interaction subsists between the vestiges hidden in one's memory's crevices and the external guidance one receives (from Scripture) in one's attempt to bring these vestiges to the surface of consciousness (*admonente aliquo eruerentur*)?[41] The Heideggerian viewpoint authorizes an even farther-reaching formulation: Is there an evolutionary interaction between the mind's intelligence of predicative discourse and language's autonomous articulation of predicative intelligibility?

The vestigial-theory answer to these questions is that language apprehension is simultaneous with the awakening of a genetically inherited substratum of linguistic vestiges, so that linguistic acquisition results from the dovetailing of nature and nurture. Both the vestigial endowment and the apprehended language are embedded with preordained and intelligible cultural values and belief systems that, being diachronic with one another, enter into an interplay of reciprocal influence in the course of language apprehension. Language acquisition could be said to result therefore from the phenotypal adaptation of a vestigial endowment to cultural or nurtural evolution.[42]

Vico's and Joyce's respective fear of thunder, for instance, can be related to the primordial linguistic identification of the word designating thunder with the name of an overpowering deity, and to the consequent attribution of a purposively malignant agency to the thunder-phenomenon.[43] If Vico and Joyce had been more Viconian, they would have identified thunder with an impersonal phenomenon subject to the predictable laws of electrical discharge, discriminating ironically between the signifier, wired to ancient belief systems, and its modern significance. This view of Vico's linguistic, promoted by Hayden White in *Tropics of Discourse,* is insufficient for our discussion of the apophatic experience, however, to the extent that it identifies fulfilled linguistic signification with the ironic reduction of signs to literal referents and/or to their symbolic/allegorical valence.[44]

In my opinion Vico's vestigial theory of language reaches much farther than ironic reduction. More precisely, it actualizes the archaic principle of augural and visceral interpretation by acknowledging the neurophysiologic pathways of recognition at play in cryptanalysis and symbolic code-breaking. "In Vico, the body is . . . an Orphic medium of civilizing sight and sound which incorporates its world and in turn articulates it in song and dance, in rituals and in poetry that pronounce the necessary illusion of a sacred world."[45] *Finnegans Wake* was arguably written to demonstrate the rootedness of etymological vestiges in the folds of individual memory, and their oracular effects on the apprehension of punctual phenomena and punctual linguistic expressions.

It is indicative of this peculiar thrust of the *Wake* that its patriarchal protagonist, Earwicker, is portrayed as engaged in a cyclical process of rebirth that entails a constant reawakening of linguistic memory. Earwicker's thought processes are "patternmind[ed]" and informed by "paradigmatic" procedures; they derive from a "receptoretentive" ability to hear (*recepto*) human speech and to retain it mnemonically (*retentive* [*FW*, 70:35–36])—a praeterhistorical autonoetic ability, judging from the analogy between this "receptoretentive" faculty and the colossal Ear of Dionysius in Siracusa, Italy, a petrified symbol of dictatorial omniscience. Moreover, Earwicker's linguistic talent of mnemonic retention is activated in the guise of an archeological excavation (*FW*, 19:8–9), and experienced as such in the guise of the autonoetic resurgence or upward "burrowing" of sedimental traces through the brain's fluid lobes ("equalobe" [*FW*, 599:18]), up to the "Uppercrust" of the cerebral cortex (*FW*, 78:11). This sort of recollection is Viconian in character, carrying with it "a socially organic entity" (*FW*, 599:15–16), or, as John Bishop aptly puts is, "a whole array of darkly drowned civil structures," which are "the civil structures of [Earwicker's] own unconsciousness."[46]

In order to validate the thesis that Joyce adopted a language rich in vestigial implications for the composition of *Finnegans Wake,* the next section applies vestigial cryptanalysis to a significant passage from Book I. The subsequent section argues in turn that vestigial remembrance plays a crucial role in the deployment and the recognition of instances of negative existence.

Vestigial Interpretation in *Finnegans Wake*

The "claybook" segment from *Finnegans Wake* provides the example of a simple sentence wherein neural vestiges are amalgamated with the evolution of typographic recognition:

> Thik is for thorn that's thuck in its thoil like thumfool's thraitor thrust for vengeance." (*FW*, 19:6–7)

The "claybook" episode illustrates an excavation of the linguistic vestiges buried within the human mind. The cited sentence is meant to exemplify the etymological potency inherent in the characters of the Old English alphabet being excavated. "Thik" stands for thicket, shrub, undergrowth, or a mass of low trees—the typographical landscape in sum of the archeological excavation taking place in this episode. In the expression "Thik is for thorn," the copula "is" signifies "stands metonymically [for]." In the term "thik" one finds th—, a sound that in Old English was designated through a single letter whose typographic symbol was surmounted by a thorn-like protuberance; this letter from Old English was called "thorn" because it looked like a spine and it sounded like the first uttered sound of the word "thorn."[47] Hence, amalgamated with the term "thik" one finds the typographic symbol of thorn, just as in a thicket or shrub one finds real thorns. Thicket stands metonymically for thorns.

Moreover, the text says that the thorn in the thicket is stuck (the spelling "thuck" repeats the metonymic amalgamation) in the soil ("thoil" insists on the metonymic amalgamation). The thorn stuck in the soil or ground is "thrust" ("th—" again) out like some fool traitor (the amalgamation of *some* and th— becomes "thum"; the amalgamation of *traitor* and th— becomes "thraitor"). This traitor lies in ambush "for vengeance." To recapitulate: *The tip of the thorn that is stuck in the soil underneath the thicket is thrust out of it like a traitor lying in ambush for vengeance.* In the experience of primordial human beings, a thicket would usually hide the thorns stuck in the ground underneath—sprouting perhaps out of an uncovered root. These thorns were perceived by primordial imagination as positioned in an attitude of ambush, and would be therefore given human-like attributes of intentional malevolence.

Only the reader whose reading skills are interfaced with the proper layers of etymological vestiges is equipped to attend properly to the broad signifying reach of the th— typography amalgamated by Joyce with the words "thik," "thuck," "thoil," and "thrust." In the Joycean acceptation of Vico's linguistics, the th— in the word "thicket" functions like a signal or a warning vestige that the evolution of Old English has posted within the very signifier denoting the thicket-thing. Denotation is always already connotative in the *Wake*.

Vestiges of Negative Cult

In the above example from *Finnegans Wake,* typographic recognition ("th—") comes first; it triggers etymological recognition (thicket, stuck, thorn, thrust, soil, traitor); in turn, etymological recognition predisposes the reader to the recognition of the text's broad linguistic intimations of ancient belief systems. Archaic men and women attributed human malevolence to the natural phenomenon of a forest bush, and this attribution came to be semantically incorporated—as the associative vestige of a primordial belief rooted in the human mind—onto the minimal linguistic units adopted to signify the forest's component parts. Joyce's text expresses with great typographic economy the Old English logic of this phenomenon by calling the reader's attention to the th— configuration of certain minimal linguistic units that are pertinent (in terms of consonance, assonance, resonance, acoustic contiguity, etc.) to this personification of nature.

The same closed-loop, adaptational interaction between vestigial heritage and linguistic recognition may be attributed to the experience of recognition I started this linguistic digression from. Even in the absence of literal reference and of tropological/allegorical reduction, the mind's vestigial endowment would be capable of recognizing certain phenomena pertinent to the history of culture—phenomena neither susceptible of strictly literal or of strictly allegoric/symbolic predication, yet susceptible of linguistic expression—whose sediments have been embedded in the mind's genetic endowment by the evolutionary process.

This is the solution I propose to the riddle of the relational affinity between the inexpressible messianic phenomenon and our discursive faculty to address and recognize it. Not only can one logically discuss (and signify) the illogical experience of apophasis by means of expressions endowed with predicative and denotative intelligibility, as we all do; one can, as Joyce is the first to show, instantiate and recognize the apophatic experience strictly within the linguistic dimension, through evolution-bred associative propensities that are beyond the conscious purview of literal and/or allegorical signification.

Based, as I said, on a relational affinity between the messianic phenomenon and the genetic constitution of our discursive faculty, the vestigial theory justifies a reconsideration of Émile Durkheim's thesis that a cross-generational interplay links "positive" and "negative cult." According to Durkheim's *Formes élémentaires de la pensée religieuse,* the civically responsible participant to the historical forms of "positive cult" is the indispensable offspring of the ascetic participant to the prehistoric forms of "negative cult."[48] Through their sacrificial exchanges with an intangible yet responsive divinity, primitive men and women gradually acquired a sense of responsibility, together with its interiorized, associative propensities toward solidarity and altruism. The contractual nature and the legalistic implications of the manducatory meal central to the modern rites—indirectly expressed in the recitation of prayers, chants, sortileges, and canonic formulae—would be the historical consequence of this evolution-bred sense of responsibility. In this perspective, one could infer that the positive cult of institutionalized religion reflects an adaptational stage in the evolution of the negative cult of archaic religions. Centuries and millennia of "renunciation, abnegation, self-detachment" would have embedded the vestigial imprint of the apophatic or "ascetic way" in the neural folds of subsequent generations.[49] Even in a social situation ruled by the norms of positive cult and social contract, these imprints or neural phenotypes would predispose the new generations to the expression and/or recognition of individual instantiations of negative cult. The moment when positive cult takes over in the determination of the predominant human condition, negative cult becomes the expression of an existential ideal, to be willed and achieved rather than passively lived through.

Our discussion of the messianic instantiation of negative existence, which is made recognizable through the matrix of its basic typal expressions (from death to resurrection, from fall to redemption, from burial to manducation, from incarnation to transubstantiation), is a subcase of this more general hypothesis.

MESSIANIC SELF

Augustine's Journey unto Death

Scholastic hermeneutics found the driving force of the Bible's teleology in the *analogia* and the *aetiologia* linking all previous and posterior types to the messianic type.[1] Subsequent studies have found the key to the Old Testament's teleology in the interplay between the vestiges of prevalent types and their "accretive evolution."[2] I have studied James Joyce's *repêchage* of this particular aspect of biblical typology in *Scriptural Poetics in Joyce's "Finnegans Wake."* This study persuaded me that Joyce offers his characters a chance of existence outside of the boundaries established by the norms of common and ordinary experience. Positioned at the threshold of the impossible experiences of death and of divinity, these characters' individual self manifests itself as an original instantiation of the messianic type. Moreover, their individual existence expresses the precarious balance between the conventional acceptation of the messianic type and the special adaptive circumstances of its revisionary evolution, as reflected in their instantiation of it.

I said above that the Augustinian repetition of Christ's journey unto death is the hinge of Dante's and Joyce's respective poetics. In the light of my previous discussion of the evolutionary patterns in mnemonic retention and discursive communication, one could say that the necropolitan journey, as *redemptive journey unto death,* is the adaptive phenotype intrinsic to Augustine's original instantiation of negative existence. The journey unto death pervades Augustine's narration of the negative experience whereby his selfhood manifests itself as messianic.

Impendente autem die, quo ex hac vita erat exitura . . . perambulavimus gradatim cuncta corporalia, et ipsum caelum . . . et adhuc ascendebamus, interius cogitando et loquendo et mirando opera tua, et venimus in mentes nostras et transcendimus eas, ut attingeremus regionem ubertatis indeficientis, . . . et ibi vita sapientia est . . . [E]t dum loquimur et inhiamus illi, attingimus eam modice toto ictu cordis; et suspiravimus, et reliquimus ibi religatas primitias spiritus, et remeavimus ad strepitum oris nostri, ubi verbum et incipitur et finitur.

[Not long before the day when (my mother Monica) was to die, we shared thoughts which led us to climb step by step the entire gamut of corporeal things, up to the heavens, and higher than that yet, as we mused, conversed, and

admired (God's) creation; we eventually arrived at our own minds, passed beyond them, and reached a region of perennial plenty, where life is wisdom. We
conversed awhile, longing for (wisdom), then we reached it and paused in it for
the peaceful duration of a whole heartbeat; then, with a sigh, leaving the sweetest breath of our souls bound to it, we returned to the noise of common speech,
wherein each word knows both of end and beginning].[3]

A long tradition of mistranslation has induced many scholars to mistake Augustine's
ecstatic experience of intimacy with the divine for a metaphor of sensible touch, a
discordant complement to Plato's metaphoric usage of the sense of sight.[4] Textual
translation is never a neutral practice devoid of interpretive agenda, of course. Philip
Schaff translates the climax of Augustine's journey thus: "We slightly touched [Wis-
dom] with the whole effort of our heart." F. J. Sheed translates: "With all the effort
of our heart we did for one instant attain to touch [Wisdom]." Rex Warner translates: "We did, with the whole strength of our hearts' impulse, just lightly come into
touch with [Wisdom]." John Ryan translates: "We attain to [Wisdom] in a slight
degree by an effort of our whole heart."[5] The reduction of Augustine's intimacy
with the divine to an instance or a symmetric reversal of Platonic discourse is predicated on a specific and deliberate assimilation of Augustine's existential coherence
in the *Confessions* with the rhetorical schemes of conventional neo-Platonism—an
assimilation that, notwithstanding his earlier adherence to Plotinus's neo-Platonic
views of asceticism, Augustine would not have encouraged.[6] I am persuaded that a
proper appreciation of Augustine's description of his communion with divine wisdom, as well as a correct translation of the pertinent passage from the *Confessions*,
call for a less conventional exegetic apparatus, responsive to the existential negativity of Augustine's experience, and grafted, as we shall see, on a drastic conversion of
Platonic transcendence.[7]

The dominant experience undergone by Monica and her son in the course of
their dialogue at Ostia is the journey, whose conclusion signals the reaching
(*attingimus*) of a safe destination in a dimension of "perennial plenty." Mother and
son undertake a journey *sur place* through "the entire gamut of corporeal things, up
to the heavens," until they are enabled to leave behind the realm of the sensible,
enter their respective minds, and through this gate achieve an instant of intimacy
with the divine. As illustrated by the long and detailed confessions of his previous
sinful life, guilty especially of lust and heresy, Augustine travels (back) to God via a
detour in the realm of evil, just the way the crucified Christ has done before him
according to Book IV of his *Confessions*,[8] and Dante will have done after him. Contrary to the trope of Plato's gaze, which is at one metaphoric remove from its object
(in the sense that the Platonic gaze perceives precisely that which is invisible to the
common experience of eyesight), Augustine's and Monica's "touching" of *sapien-
tiam* (*attingimus eam*) is at a second denotative and referential remove from its object.
The negative experience of touching expressed in Augustine's words does not refer
metaphorically to the sensible touching of a physical thing, in the way, for instance,
the trope of seeing in Plato's allegory of the cave refers, as a semantic paradigm, to

eyesight's enabling of the observer to the ordinary perception of a physical thing. Given the semantics of his *attingimus,* Augustine's experience of touching clearly refers, rather, to the figural touching of a destination (a harbor, a beach, a port of entry) at the completion of a journey, which in this specific case consists of a journey away from common and ordinary experience and through the gate of one's own mind. As such a figure of speech, whose objective referent is not a palpable object but a geographical location, Augustine's touching of the divine is applied in turn to a destination, the divine, which is itself impalpable and devoid of geophysical location.

It is not accidental that in the *Paradiso* Dante introduces the final leap of his necropolitan pilgrimage to God with an untranslatable neologism, *trasumanar,* expressive of a relocation of the self away from both ordinary existence and predicative/denotative language. Noteworthy in Dante's expression of choice is not just that he signifies in words the referent of an impossible condition (of intimacy with God) that "cannot be signified / in words" (*significar per verba / non si poria* [*Paradiso,* 1:67–70]), but also that this referent is shielded behind the denotation of an impossibly existential condition, trans- or dehumanized. As I suggested above, the biography of the necropolitan traveler unfolds at a second denotative and referential remove from common and ordinary experience.[9]

In depriving Augustine and Monica of the usage of their bodily senses, desensitization signifies at once the discontinuation of their factual and documentable biography, and their vestigial recognition, which no words or speech can signify with sufficient precision, of a phenomenally impossible condition. This is the paradox at the heart of Augustine's self-abandonment. By losing himself as a sensible being, a pursuer of factual experiences and a purveyor of allegories of sin, he finds himself as *interior self.* Through this introspective gate, which leads him to his innate "speech" of "truth,"[10] he achieves intimacy with the divine. This is the messianic conversion of Platonic transcendence that is inherent in Augustine's journey unto death. The metaphysical insight into the far-away elsewhere of the Platonic ideal is converted into the journey within the silence of Augustine's own interiority.

After their short-lived intimacy with the divine, mother and son leave behind their messianic self in its "sweetest expressions" (*primitias*), and journey back (*remeavimus*) to their phenomenal or sublunary self. At the conclusion of this return journey to the realm of sensuous activity and factual experience, they find themselves again in the spatial and temporal dimension from which they started their journey unto death. This is the factual dimension of human speech; here each single word, "know[ing] both of end and of beginning" (knowing both of space and time), comes to the life of significance, performing its customary functions (denotative and connotative, referential and tropic) through its contamination with the anthropology of death and procreation.

Dante will emulate this striking contrast between the sublunary self's phenomenal communion with language and the messianic self's wordless communion with *sapientia,*[11] but only to a partial extent. Dante's paradisal condition instigates the existential collapse of ontological distinction. While Augustine's mystical ascension corresponds to a gradual separation from the sublunary dimension wherein ordinary human beings spend their existence, the separation from common experience intrinsic to Dante's transhuman intimacy with the divine is coextensive with his global immersion in the biography of the universal other (*intuarsi* [*Paradiso,* 9:81]; see the detailed discussion of this aspect of Dante's negative experience in the next section and in chapter 4). The self-instantiation of negative existence on the part of the Dantesque pilgrim obliterates Augustine's separateness from the other's existential condition.

As we shall see, one of the greatest accomplishments of the mature Joyce consists in the overcoming of Augustine and Dante's respective suspiciousness toward the expressive potency of human language. To Joyce, the "sweetest expressions" of the journey unto death are not harvested at the instant of Augustine's final arrival (*attingimus* [*Confessions,* Liber IX, cap. 10]), nor in the instantaneous and fulminant coincidence of Dante's desire with divine love (*fulgore* [*Paradiso,* 33:140–45]), but throughout the instantiation of negative existence. In *Finnegans Wake* Joyce depicts Shem's negative existence as fully instantiated in the expression of human language. But this achievement, discussed in chapter 8, comes only at the apex of Joyce's literary career, as the conclusion of a long and tormented evolution punctuated by episodic adherences to Augustine and Dante's reductionist views of language.

In chapters 5 and 6 we shall see how Stephen Dedalus struggles with the inadequacy of poetic language. As remarked above, before his mother's death Stephen sees himself as a poet/priest of "eternal imagination," whose aim is the transubstantiation of ordinary experience into "everliving life" (*P,* 221). He then realizes that the life-giving ambition of his poetry, as transposed into his "Villanelle of the Temptress" and the compositional process leading to it (*P,* 217–23), is a pretext for the narcissistic self-indulgence of an aesthete.[12] The "liquid letters of speech," which he borrows from the poetics of Dante's *Vita Nuova* (see chapter 5) in order to "forge . . . the uncreated conscience of [his] race" (*P,* 223, 253), veil rather poorly, behind the smoke screen of a liturgical "praise," the onanistic imagery of his "chalice flowing to the brim"—a self-congratulatory image from a previous episode at Clongowes Wood College, incidentally (*P,* 217–23, 59). Stephen has come of age, after all, in the decade of the Narcissus, inaugurated in 1891 by Gide's *Traité du Narcisse,* Valéry's *Narcisse parle,* and Wilde's *The Picture of Dorian Gray.* This decadent "fascination of the mirror," prepared by the works of Pater, Ruskin, the pre-Raphaelites,[13] as well as by the escapism of Mallarmé trilogy of the *faune,*[14] is irresistible to the Stephen of *A Portrait of the Artist as a Young Man,* a youth still untouched by personal grief. He is lightheartedly confident that "the reality of experience" will be faithfully reflected in "the smithy of [his] soul." He is lightheartedly confusing the "roselike glow" painted on his cheeks by a wet dream[15] with the Dantesque "rose" of poetic inspiration (*P,* 217, 253).

It is only after his mother's death that Stephen undergoes a conversion comparable to the one that leads Augustine to write his *Confessions* and Dante to undertake his pilgrimage. The Stephen we meet in *Ulysses* is a fallen and dis-graced poet, a captive of the lapsed instrument of his own artistic craft. Gone is the self-enamorment of his sensuous drive to poetry. The "batlike soul" of womanhood, which Stephen chanted in his villanelle, is transmogrified into a "pale vampire" that sucks the juices of creative inspiration from the cadaver of his own mother (*U,* 7:524). Stephen's poetic vocation does not consist anymore in the liturgical expression of erotic, "dewy wet" complacency (*P,* 217), but rather in the redemption of a debt to the dead that seems bound to compound itself in time. We shall see that Stephen, at a loss vis-à-vis his material obligations toward his next of kin, looks now for guidance in a poem by the twenty-three-year-old Stéphane Mallarmé, *Don du poème,* wherein the French poet, devastated by his inadequacy as husband and father, turns poetic utterance into a self-forgetful gesture of altruism. However, Stephen's fascination with the "liquid letters" of his previous poetry leaves him virtually speechless in his new poetic quest.

Negative Biography

Augustine's messianic experience grounds the poetics of Dante's epic enactment of the necropolitan journey. Although the journey to the underworld was an essential paradigm of the classic epic tradition, inherent in this epic journey was a paradox that only Dante could solve. The paradox is most strident in Homer himself. Having come back home after the journey that renewed and transformed him, giving him a post-Trojan sense of purpose, Odysseus claims his old identity, his old throne, his old nuptial bed back: a new King, then, for an old, unchanged kingdom? An analogous paradox is encountered in the biblical epos narrated in Exodus. How could the Hebrews responsible for pagan worship at the foot of Mount Sinai possibly envision the implementation of a monolatric homeland for themselves? How could they possibly envision this Promised Land as hospitable to an unredeemed, idolatrous Israel? Both Homer and the Torah solve the dilemma with the expedient of sacrificial extermination, that of the suitors in the *Odyssey,* that of the idolatrous generation in Exodus. A fumigated and sacrificially purified—hence, renewed —*oikos* welcomes back its born-again master, Odysseus. In turn, the wilderness extinguishes the older generations of the Hebrews; only a literally and generationally renewed Israel enters the Promised Land.

The paradox at the heart of the epic tradition bespeaks the contradiction between the restoration of the old covenant and the revolution of the new. As I have shown elsewhere, the contradiction between restoration and revolution is found at the heart of the Thomist hermeneutics of the Bible, whose Messiah is caught in the typological paradox of a "non-originary novelty."[16] It would seem that for the ancient Greeks and Hebrews a sanguinary compromise submitting humane justice to cultic bloodshed was a viable solution to the reconciliation of the old with the new. Not so for Christianity, which seeks the solution in the "impossible" characterization of messianic selfhood.

In enacting a Paschal imitation of Jesus's journey unto death after crucifixion, and garbing at once this imitation in the literary conventions received from the classical epic tradition, Dante highlights the typological elements inherent in Jesus's journey. It is a restorative journey insofar as it repeats the classical, redemptive scheme of the hero's journey away from home, his reversal or conversion of direction, and the cultic culmination of his adventure in homecoming. It is also a utopian and innovative version of the typical journey, though, insofar as, contrary to the classical scheme, the converted hero journeys back to a converted home; Dante-the-pilgrim is not so much reclaiming the identity of his old self and his old Florentine homeland as affirming his true, cryptic self within an impossible sphere of imperviousness to sensible experience, among the maculae of fellow human beings.[17]

Every apostle (but Thomas) could recognize in the resurrected Jesus the carpenter's son, who had come back in a formidably regenerated persona, that of the Anointed One, because in his absence (and because *of* his absence as well) every apostle had been anointed too. In turn, every soul in paradise can recognize in Dante the wanderer of the *selva oscura* who has come to intimacy with the divine, because everybody in paradise shares that impossible intimacy. How simple it becomes, in this light, to understand why the Joycean Odysseus, having departed from his wife Calypso in the morning, will have come back home at night, a changed man for a new wife, Penelope.

The literary tradition of Christian epics, whose Dantean and Joycean aspects I discuss in *Rituals of Literature,* is inaugurated by Dante's negative *imitatio Christi.* The reenactment of the journey unto death gives expression to the protagonist's individual self by means of the typological repetition of his messianic predecessor's negative homecoming. Leopold Bloom comes back home, to Penelope, as a type of Homer's Odysseus; his identity is converted by his twenty-hour centripetal journey through the streets of Dublin. By the same token, being offered the opportunity of a shelter for the night and virtually a surrogate domestic abode by Leopold, Stephen Dedalus rejects the opportunity of this prosaic homecoming and chooses perennial wandering instead; as he does so, he converts to his true self (or at least to the quest of it) by means of the typological repetition of the fate of the Dantesque Ulysses.[18] Like the Ulysses of Canto 26 of the *Inferno,* Stephen is at home—is his messianic self, that is—only in this centrifugal wandering away from his hometown.

It is important to stress that the poetics of the journey unto death, installed at the very heart of the messianic experience, is properly inaugurated by Dante's single-handed invention of Christian epics as a distinct literary genre. Two conflicting modalities of selfhood are simultaneously at play in the *Paradiso.* One is the mimetic selfhood of historical subjects, endowed with the prerogative of irreducible individuality. The other is the negative selfhood of paradisiac saints, who are invaginated in a celestial rose so antagonistic with individual, subjective separateness that not even the *fonte* (source, fountain) of the rose itself, God, nor the *fonte* of the rose's imagic representation, Dante-the-pilgrim, may be kept distinct from it. The saints and the pilgrim are *indiati,*[19] "in-numenated"—invaginated onto a *numen,* or god, that is indistinguishable from this very motion of universal invagination.

Dante's notion of in-numenation is indicative of an existential collapse of ontological distinctions. In the *Paradiso* the logic of in-numenation is especially expressed by means of three reflexive verbs whose infinitive forms are: *indiarsi* (to in-nume-nate oneself, to transduct one's self onto God [*Paradiso,* 4:28]), *intuarsi* and *inmiarsi* (to transduct my own self onto yours, and, respectively, to transduct your own self onto mine [*Paradiso,* 9:81]). These three neologisms are predicated on a linguistic principle of *trinitarian reflexivity.* They consist of verbal forms that, in denoting the reflection of the subject's act of consciousness on the subject itself, incorporate alterity as the etymological source and destination of the subject's very act of self-consciousness. Existential separateness from the other is reflexively obliterated in Dante's notion of in-numenation. In invaginating verbal reflexivity, that is to say, in turning it inside out, Dante's paradisiac neologisms are, to put it in Freccero's lingo, "immobilized in literalisms that are ironically irreducible."[20]

Dante's revolution in the configuration of consciousness dictated a literary revolution. In turning individual biography into the negative experience of the necro-politan journey (at a second remove from the objectively documentable and verifiable facts of one's stations through earthly life), literature embarks on the "abandonment of all reference."[21] In the *Paradiso* the Augustinian model of the self—a soul (i.e., an interiority endowed with free will) signified by the presence of a living body—is substituted by corporeal iconicity; the rosiform fusion of all blessed spirits, being unrepresentable to human imagination, is imaged by recourse to the presence of that which is not there, that is to say, the mere macula of human corporeality. "Media-tion is turned back upon itself and reified in the letter of the text."[22] Via invagina-tive mediation, the literary text becomes its own iconic referent.[23]

Dante's poetry positions the fulcrum of individual self in a necropolitan dimen-sion. His epic journey to the afterlife is the journey that everybody will have under-taken in order to engage in a future-perfect repetition of Christ's death. According to Augustine's *Confessions,* as well as to both Nicodemus's apocryphal Gospel and a 1215 article of faith,[24] after his crucifixion and before ascending to heaven Christ descended to hell, experiencing thereby the intimacy with radical evil that is typo-logically repeated in the first part of Dante's own journey—just as the rest of Dante's journey repeats Christ's ascensional return (*ascensu*)[25] to the Father. Only the immer-sion in the totality of evil and in the totality of charity endows Augustinian free will with the *cognitio causae* of its own moral choices, hence, with its boundlessly salvific potency. (Without the outlet of *cognitio causae* free choice, deprived of con-textual responsibility and moral imputability, is paralyzed, as Augustine indicates in *De libero arbitrio* and Dante suggests in the *Paradiso.*)[26] Christ's necropolitan journey delineates therefore the universal biographical model intimated and enacted in Dante's *Commedia.* Through this messianic biography, which eludes all laws of fac-tual determinism and literal experience, the Augustinian self comes into its own, having reached the coincidence of its desire with divine will (*Paradiso,* 3:70–87).

Insofar as the self's achieved intimacy with the *numen* entails the obliteration of individual separateness from the other, one could say that Dante's messianic biog-raphy entails the dissolution of that very self it serves to affirm. The stage of the homecoming at the conclusion of the necropolitan journey coincides with the end of the self's irreducible individuality. The invagination of all individual travelers into a unified, paradisiac Christ-type does not bring about a loss of individual distinction, however, but rather a universalization of individual fate—the very constitution and persistence of Dante's celestial rose is essentially dependent on the exceptional singularity and extraordinary historical importance attributed to every single individual by Salvation History. The miracle of Crucifixion, as Dante sees it and Joyce will duplicate it, is that each and every individual becomes the hinge, the sine qua non condition of possibility for cosmic salvation. Hence, Dante's existential poetics of irreducible finitude, whose effectiveness of naturalistic mimesis was much admired by Auerbach, is never completely dispelled by the poetics of non-referentiality.

The Crisis of Irony

It goes without saying, however, that the narrative coordinates of Christian epics reduce naturalistic mimesis to a marginal condition, because those very facts that naturalism records, relates, and faithfully reproduces are but the phenomenal attractors to the adaptational phenotypes intrinsic to the instantiation of negative existence. The individual journey unto death must be left intact in its unrealistic garments; literal and allegorical decodification must not be applied to its plot, nor to the distinct catalogue of its Christological stations (i.e., death and resurrection, burial and manducation, fall and redemption, incarnation and transubstantiation), if one wants to appreciate the existential tenor of its negative valence. The poetic rigor required of such a surrender to messianic instantiation on the part of the reader cannot be overstressed.

Of the four fundamental tropes of literary discourse discussed by Vico in the *New Science* (metaphor, metonymy, synecdoche, irony), irony is, according to Hayden White, the "metatropological" decoder of the other three.[27] Irony is the trope that allows one to read figures of speech as tropes, and not to confuse them with naturalistic representations. According to White, only an ironic reader is capable of discriminating between the self-referential, affective, and codifying function of a trope, and the predicative, communicative, and expressive functions of the representation inherent in the same trope.[28] Ironic interpretation seeks the ultimate foundation for literary expression in literal referents that are analogous with it; the documentable and verifiable facts (objects, events, sensations, opinions, speeches, etc.) orbiting the fantastic realm of literary invention would therefore be the stable, historic, analogic referents that substantiate literary figures.

An example of ironic interpretation emerges for instance from Margot Norris's apprehension of Maria's "soft wet substance," the clay never explicitly named except in the title of Joyce's short story "Clay." Rather than some far-reaching intimation of impending mortality or civic disintegration, the concrete, slimy contact of Maria's hand with the clay freshly dug from the garden lingers in more domestic figural latitudes according to Norris, suggesting first of all its own immediate, repulsive sensation. As a trope, this clay figures just what it is in reality: dirt, the brutal signifier that Maria's "only 'family' . . . treats her like shit."[29]

This kind of naturalistic or ironic reductionism feels limited and dissatisfactory, though, in Joyce's case. Even when technically impeccable, as in the case of Margot Norris's epoch-making exegesis of "Clay" (whose merits are discussed in chapter 4), the denotative and prosaic transduction of this or that episode, of this or that figure from Joyce's writings to a stable, circumscribed body of literal signifieds turns out to be, more often than not, inadequate with respect to the aesthetic latitude informing Joyce's work—this being especially true when Joyce's intentions are clearly divergent from the naturalistic tradition, as is the case with the negative poetics inherent in many sections of *Ulysses* and most sections of *Finnegans Wake*.

The first and fundamental Dantesque trope that needs to be taken un-ironically coincides with the very notion of the necropolitan journey. Dante expects us to embrace the story of his triple journey to hell, purgatory, and paradise as existentially compelling—not so much, in Charles Singleton's lingo, as a "fiction . . . that is not a fiction,"[30] but rather as the tangible instantiation of his negative existence. To assist us in this readerly feat, exuberant of both literal reference and symbolical/allegorical interpretation, he entirely reshapes the classic epic tradition of the hero's visit to the underworld by subsuming it under the existential aegis of the messianic self.

"I am not Paul," he declares at the *incipit* of *Inferno,* and "I am not Aeneas" (*Inferno,* 2:32). It goes without saying that he is not Virgil either, a second-time visitor to the afterlife (*Inferno,* 9:22–30), whom he is addressing as his guide. In order to add his own name to the illustrious list of epic personages who undertook the two-way journey to the underworld, Dante must first submit the otherworldly journeys previous to his own to a sort of Christian homogenization.

What kind of human being is allowed to come back from the underworld? Jesus Christ, for one, whose "harrowing of hell" (*Inferno,* 12:31–45) opens the way, figurally and typologically (as well as topologically, at the entrance to the seventh circle of hell), to Virgil and Dante. Then comes St. Paul, whose supernatural journey/vision, narrated in 2 Corinthians (12:1–7) and in the apocryphal "Apocalypse of Paul," is a constituent part of his saintliness and apostolic authority. Then comes Aeneas, Virgil's hero, the founder of the empire that will provide the secular foundations to the Church of Rome. Then comes Virgil himself, who, as expert a guide to the underworld as the Sibyl was in his *Aeneid* (6:564ff), was earlier on dragged to the very bottom of Hell by Eriton, according to Dante's version (*Inferno,* 9:22–30).

Dante reluctantly inscribes his own name at the end of this list. His name (introduced by the double negation "I am not . . . I am not . . ." as an allusion, I venture, to the negative individuality of the Homeric Noman, Nobody, or Everyman) stands for the individual multitude of humble Christians whose free-willed choices have become, after Jesus's sacrifice, pivotal to the unfolding of Salvation History. The centrality of these multitudes, more historically pivotal in the last two thousand years than the feats and deeds of the aristocratic protagonists of the classic epic tradition, bespeaks in turn the elusive yet tenacious impact that the paradigms of existential Messianism have exercised over time on the conventional acceptation of phenomenal experience.

It might appear that one crucial name, Odysseus's, is still missing from the above list. But the name of Odysseus is a name, from the classic list of the epic travelers to the underworld, that Dante cannot afford to include among his predecessors. The story of Odysseus's voyage is a pagan fiction and a Christian incongruity, allegorized as "the archetype of the presumptuous philosopher" by Augustine, who adumbrates in the *De beata vita* the doctrinal necessity of Odysseus's fated shipwreck.[31] Odysseus's implausible, supernatural return from Hades is the key story from the classic tradition that relegates the entire epic genre to the narrow limitations of fictionality. From Dante's and Augustine's Christian perspective, a pagan can journey back from the underworld only in a regime of fictionality—only as a pure pretense or a fictional trope. And this is why Dante, although probably aware of the homecoming that closes the *Odyssey*,[32] feels compelled to reverse Homer's ending into Ulysses's shipwreck in front of the mountain of purgatory (*Inferno*, 26:130–42).

In the medieval scheme of things, a pagan cannot be allowed to perform the return from the afterlife graciously afforded the Christian epic hero. (Aeneas and Virgil figure at this juncture as the *traits d'union* between the pagan and Christian worlds.) The inclusion of Odysseus in the list of preternatural travelers would plunge Dante's readers back into the narrative realm ruled by the ironic paradigm, and force them therefore to decode Dante's own journey as a merely fictional invention that means *something else*.

Logorrhea of Messianism

The movement of filiation linking Augustine to Dante to Joyce is hinged on the existential stance inherent in the journey unto death. In the transition from one author to the next, this filiation manifests itself as revisionistic, in the specific sense, here, that each author, engaged in a restoration or retracing of the predecessor's voyage or quest, "inscribe[s] within the intertext [his] negotiation . . . of his own place within the literary tradition."[33]

Both Augustine and Dante understand apophasis literally, as an experience that is intrinsically impossible to speak of (ἀποφάναι). When Dante's Francesca surrenders to adultery, turning the finitude of a kiss into its eternal repetition, she closes the treacherous book that she and Paolo were reading together: "That day we read there no further"[34] (*Inferno*, 5:138). When Augustine reaches the safety of conversion, turning his renunciation to lust into ineffable bliss, he closes the book of Scriptures: "No further would I read; nor needed I."[35] Silence brackets the inexpressible dimension in both authors; in both authors phenomenal experience is literally an intertext,[36] bridging the negative experience of irreducible finitude and bountiful plenty. Not so for Joyce. At the threshold of the "dividual" collapse of ontological distinction, there where Dante's language would be silenced by the inexpressible truth of paradise (see chapter 4) and his senses dulled by the lightning bolt of God's will (*Paradiso,* 33:141), Joyce's Shem from *Finnegans Wake* turns himself into an open book: "[He] wrote over every square inch of . . . his own body," transforming himself thereby into a Scripture in the "present tense"—"common to all flesh, human only, mortal" (*FW,* 185:35–186:6).

With *Finnegans Wake* Joyce's revision of the Christian epics of the journey unto death acquires distinct autonomy from the fundamental stages of departure (from sin) and arrival (to grace or intimacy with the divine), while its deepest significance, as an instantiation of negative existence and the self-expression of a messianic self, becomes eminently linguistic, and closely identified with the experience itself of the journey.[37]

As we discussed, the climax of Augustine's journey unto death is predicated first upon his gradual separation from the inertia of human language, second, upon his gradual separation from the existence of ordinary human beings, and third, upon his silent moorage to the state of mystical intimacy with the divine. Dante's intimacy with the divine, obtained at the end of the journey unto death undertaken in the *Commedia,* coincides with his catholic-universal fusion with the negative existence of all other human beings. Yet, Dante's dialogue with the paradisal saints consists of a merely "condescending" performance, instrumental to the limitations of his sensory apparatus (*Paradiso,* 3:13–14; see chapter 4).[38] Without the succor of the divine *Verbum* as transcendental signifier, Dante's instantiation of his otherworldly biography would be devoid of sense. And this *Verbum* escorts him beyond the expressive power of language at the instant of his fulminant experience of the divine (*Paradiso,* 33:140–45).

It is noteworthy, however, that Dante's journey unfolds preeminently as a voyage *in* language—"to the extreme reaches of the language," as Boldrini effectively puts it[39]— rather than away from it. Dante travels *in* a vernacular language, on the one hand, expressive of the messianic condition as *katholikós* or universal, and *in* a poetic textuality, on the other hand, whose reenactment of Jesus's journey amounts to a novel instantiation of Holy Writ. This latter aspect inscribes his poetry of the afterlife in the Pauline tradition, which, according to Brook Thomas and Stephen Sicari, brought Scripture itself to the "climax" of a revision of the historically canonized *Verbum.*[40]

One might therefore say that Dante's linguistic expression of his apophatic experience in the *Commedia* bridges the gap between the unconditional silence of Augustine's episode of intimacy with the divine and, as we shall see, the unrestrained eloquence or logorrhea that expresses analogous apophatic episodes in Joyce's *Finnegans Wake.* However, the Dante of the *Commedia* is not the only Dante we are acquainted with, just as *Finnegans Wake* is not Joyce's only literary work. Sam Slote refers to the poetry of Dante's *Vita Nuova* as a poetry of uncompromising silence. Stricken by an apophatic and unutterable vision,[41] Dante discontinues abruptly the composition of this work and becomes the poet "who cannot write," willingly submitting "to the economy of the interval [of silence]."[42] This is correct, as long as one does not forget that before the rapture of Dante's vision the love poetry of the *Vita Nuova* is far from frugal or restrained in its expressions; it unfolds in smooth and unconcerned versification and commentary, supremely confident in those very "liquid letters of speech" that, as I show in chapter 5, Stephen Dedalus borrows for the sake of his own poetic endeavors.

I do not agree with Slote's thesis that Dante's apophatic silence, inaugurated in the *Vita Nuova,* informs the *Commedia* later on without any significant solution of continuity.[43] But I do agree with his view that it is the incommunicability of the apophatic experience that silences the poetic utterance of the *Vita Nuova.* The transition from the uncompromising silence that interrupts this earlier work to the cautiously linguistic expression of the apophatic experience in the *Commedia* is paralleled in the transition from Stephen Dedalus's adoption of the "liquid letters of speech" and subsequent poetic silence in *Ulysses*—a silence that turns his biography into a perplexing epic of existential gestures—to Shem's logorrhoic incarnation of the Word in *Finnegans Wake.*

The poet who is protagonist of *Ulysses,* Stephen Dedalus, is a most laconic writer. His only extant composition in *Ulysses,* the so-called "Vampire Poem" (*U,* 7:522–25), compares poorly with his previous "Villanelle of the Temptress." Besides, can one call this quatrain truly a poem, after all? It has been deemed, rather, "an early model for a poem-to-be."[44] The completion of this poem-to-be is never presented to the evaluation of the reader, and remains very likely unachieved by the end of *Ulysses.* However, this unachieved poem, whose four-line fragment is a mere parody of a stanza from Douglas Hyde's translation of a Gaelic song, "My Grief on the Sea,"[45] rests on an imposing compositional architecture; its innumerable components surface gradually in the "Proteus" and "Aeolus" episodes of *Ulysses,* as we shall see in chapter 6—compositional elements that, intertwined with Stephen's frequent, inexpressible visions of his mother's cadaver, reveal a network of literary influence and intertextual allusion linking Stephen's creative process with four great poets of the apophatic experience, namely, Dante, Blake, Yeats, and Mallarmé. In his refusal to translate his existential and aesthetic ruminations into punctual poetic expression, Stephen goes out of his way to embrace the linguistic principles promoted by Dante in the *Vita Nuova.* This adhesion turns him into one of Slote's poets "who cannot write."

In *Finnegans Wake* James Joyce takes a titanic step forward with respect to both Dante and Augustine, as well as to the laconic vocation of Stephen Dedalus. As I have suggested in my previous considerations on the vestigial potency of linguistic expression, the biography of negative existence does not need to be left uninstantiated, nor does it need to be instantiated in the language of literal reference and allegorical significance. If Augustine in the *Confessions,* Dante in the *Vita Nuova,* and even Joyce's own Stephen Dedalus in *Ulysses* appear to confirm Blanchot's views about silence being "the ultimate possibility of human speech,"[46] in *Finnegans Wake* Joyce trespasses this frontier. He adopts from his two predecessors the condition of intimacy with the divine as the crucial predicate of the journey unto death, yet discards deliberately from this condition the instant of silent separation from language.

While Augustine and Dante have displaced to the self's interiority everything that, according to the previous metaphysical tradition, pertained to the transcendental *elsewhere,* in the *Wake* Joyce displaces to logorrhea everything that to Dante and Augustine pertains to the contemplative silence of this interiority. While both Augustine and Dante have traveled, each in his own terms, beyond the limits of history, tradition, and human language, toward the instant stillness at the culmination of their journey unto death, Joyce expands *ad libitum* the linguistic boundaries of the Canon of Revelation—which is the eminent Western archetype of history, language, and tradition—by turning Holy Writ into the epic vessel of everybody's journey unto death.[47] As discussed in chapter 8, in *Finnegans Wake* Holy Writ becomes a body, a sacrificial corpus even, the sepulchral embodiment of our vestigial familiarity with negative cult and negative existence. Everybody can excavate this tomb the way one excavates archeological monuments, because it is buried in the deepest recesses of our own memory. The instantiation of one's negative biography, as the existential model proposed by Joyce to his contemporaries, finds a validating ground in this excavation.

As we have seen, the term instantiation defines in the present study the implementation of a code (scriptural, mental, or genetic) whereby an individual constitutes himself or herself as a person vis-à-vis another individual and/or community. The process of recognition plays an essential role in this intentional process. We have also seen, in reference to the messianic self engaged in the journey unto death, that the occurrences pertinent to the individual instantiation of negative existence may be reduced to a catalogue of basic typal expressions (from death to resurrection, from fall to redemption, from burial to manducation, from incarnation to transubstantiation).

The second part of the present study examines the unfolding of one such catalogue of typal expressions in the corpus of Joyce's writings. Among the several examples of messianic instantiation disseminated in Joyce's works, I have chosen to substantiate my hypothesis with the sustained and highly circumstantial discussion of five case studies, selected from *Dubliners, Ulysses,* and *Finnegans Wake.* These distinct discussions feed on one another, contributing an interconnected picture of the typal catalogue that articulates the notion of Joyce's messianic self.

In my opinion, the network of existential relations circumscribed by the following discussions unveils a substantial fragment of Joyce's program for the intentional consciousness of the modern self. On the other hand, however rich in nuances and distinctive features, it is far from exhaustive of the visionary horizon progressively embraced by Joyce's negative poetics. Based on my persuasion that Dante's negative poetics informs Joyce's artistic agenda since his earliest critical dissertations on the Ibsenian modernity of Dante,[48] the next five chapters consist of ad hoc inquiries into five subsequent implementations of this agenda, each one easily distinguishable from the others in light of its specific connotations. The objects of these five inquiries do not share an identical poetics, in sum, although there is enough overlap among them to sustain a cohesive debate, and especially to chart the pattern of gradual emancipation of Joyce's negative poetics from Dante's and Augustine's constriction of human language within the dimensions of literal and figurative expression.

As we shall see in chapter 8, the journey unto death undertaken by Shem in *Finnegans Wake* is neither a journey of separation from language nor a journey unfolding in language, but rather a journey within the corporeality of language—one might define it as a journey away from both ordinary reality and allegoric/symbolic representation, and toward the negative incarnation (incorporation, instantiation) of a Scriptural corpus. To paraphrase the Paul of Galatians 6, Shem is virtually crucified to the language of Holy Writ.

I discuss Shem's body as the simulacrum of a consecrated corpse. His skin is minutely tattooed with the script of his journey unto death, the way Egyptian mummies were wrapped in bands inscribed with the spells and incantations from the Book of the Dead. Shem's skin is turned into the envelope or integumentum of the "sacramental vocabulary,"[49] which at one and the same time narrates and sustains his voyage toward his chosen fate and messianic condition, away from the prose of the everyday, and unto death. The inscription on his skin is executed by his own tongue, the appendicular prolongation of his vestigial memory, muted however, turned into a style or stylus that is dipped into his liquid and solid waste—as a proleptic metaphor, since his spontaneously putrefying corpse will have eventually coalesced with the Word of the crucified and buried Messiah, thrown down into the pit of hell. No instant of transcendentally ecstatic intimacy with the divine is reserved for Joyce's Shem, no passively awaited Parousia, no eschatological triumph of grace, but rather a lifelong incarnation of the Word and impersonation of its sepulchral catharsis—a lifetime of messianic enactments, disregardful of "presumptive Redeemers and Churches."[50] To him the journey unto death is not a means to an end but the end itself, the interplay wherein the past tradition he comes from and the future realization he aspires to meet feed off each other, instantiating in the process the negative experience of his messianic self.

As conventional in the literary tradition inaugurated by Augustine and consecrated by Dante, Shem's existential experience is universal yet distinct, individual yet "dividual" (*FW,* 186:4–5), sacrificial yet freely chosen. Bizarre, monstrous, eccentric, a physiologic impossibility, Shem is in this world of common and ordinary experience, but certainly not of it. He has accomplished that very emancipation from both molecular biology and personal history that Stephen Dedalus aimed at since the inception of his artistic vocation. If one recalls that Joyce completed *Finnegans Wake* in 1939, it comes as no surprise that by the intercession of Shem's ministry, the raw matter of individual self-instantiation can only transubstantiate itself into feces.

PART TWO

Joyce's Negative Protagonists

GABRIEL CONROY'S
NECROPOLITAN JOURNEY

Necropolitan Matrix

"Throughout *Dubliners* people are jostled by incarnations of what they would like to be, or really are, or never were."[1] Twenty or so years after making this remark, Hugh Kenner asked himself what defines the literary style required to articulate these complex sort of "incarnations." He elaborated the influential notion of the "Uncle Charles principle," whereby he described a naturalistic style, mainly a variant on Flaubert's free indirect speech, that reveals what the principal characters of *Dubliners* would like to be, portraying at the same time, by naturalistic intimation, what they really are or never were.[2] As Margot Norris's description of the narrator of "Clay" shows persuasively, Kenner's principle is based on the stylistic mimesis of a character's mannerisms of self-validation. Maria, the protagonist of "Clay," projects "the fictitious embodiment of [a] wished-for narrative voice," the personification of the idealized narrator by whom she would like her mimicry of a true lady's demure and serene comportment to be reported.[3]

In *Joyce's Voices* Hugh Kenner remarks that the first line of "The Dead" introduces a character's (Lily's) mannerisms of self-validation through the stylistics of the "Uncle Charles principle."[4] These mannerisms are contagious. They affect even the principal validator of Lily's self-image, Gabriel Conroy, who happens to be the totemic father figure—hence, the master validator for most of the characters in the story. Gabriel is soon seen projecting all around himself a carefully crafted self-image, that of the complacent, socially integrated, well established professor of letters. Most of the characters targeted by his mannerisms of self-validation are eager to grant him the legitimacy of his own status, since it is in his social validity that they find a manner of vicarious legitimization for theirs. From the carving of the goose to the after-dinner speech, from the confidence generated in the other women at the party (all unmarried, incidentally) by the presence of his charming (and successfully wedded) wife, Gretta,[5] to the confidence generated in the two professional drinkers of the party, Freddy Malins and Mr Browne, by his taking of "long draught[s] of stout" ("The Dead," 197–98), Gabriel plays his role of patriarchal column and

arbiter of legitimacy vis-à-vis the Misses Morkan's microcosm through an imposing spectrum of self-validating mannerisms.

The transparent dynamics of this kind of outward self-projection and its backward reflection or backfiring in inverted, fragmented, distorted, undermined ways
have informed a great deal of recent criticism of "The Dead." Such an interpretive
angle is partially misdirected, though, because the mannerisms and stylistics of self-
validation, however masterfully displayed in the naturalistic scenes describing the
dinner party at the Misses Morkan's residence, are abruptly dismissed by the narrator at the story's climax, when Gabriel and Gretta leave the party and reach their
hotel room. Here Gabriel has no more audience to charm with the projection of
his self-image of bourgeois complacency. His conversation with Gretta is strained
and sterile, more a soliloquy of hers punctuated by his laconic, diffident, mostly (not
always) tactful questions than a dialogue. When Gretta conveniently falls asleep,
Gabriel, left to the resources of his own interior monologue,[6] experiences not so
much the backfiring of his outward self-projection as a transcendental reshaping of
his own selfhood. This is where Dante's poetics kicks in and the "Uncle Charles
principle" loses predominance.

In the hotel room Gabriel is facing two mirrors, the cheval-glass in the room
and the glass of a window. Since the room is in total darkness and receives the light
from a street lamp outside, the glass of this window is turned into a virtual mirror,
reflecting the person in front of it, yet not occluding the outside view. Florence
Walzl may have been the first critic to underline the reflecting property of this window and its Dantesque aura.[7] As we shall see, this window functions metaphorically
as the gate introducing Gabriel to Dante's necropolitan journey.

At the end of "The Dead" Gabriel Conroy is arguably afforded a visionary stasis analogous with the one experienced by Dante at the culmination of his ascent
to the celestial spheres. This transcendental effect is achieved by Joyce—as a coda to
the previous naturalistic episodes—via a systematic duplication of that very "negative poetics" whereby Dante, as John Freccero pus it, "represent(s) the impossibility of representation" pertinent to a paradisiac experience.[8] Gabriel's two mirrors
may therefore be said to signal, respectively, the culmination and the collapse of the
naturalistic strain of "The Dead."[9]

In the cheval-glass Gabriel recognizes his own narcissistic reflection as that of the
man who sought self-validation at the dinner party; a bit later, after Gretta's revelation of her juvenile romance with Michael Furey, this self-reflection is reversed
into Gabriel's imagination of himself as "a ludicrous figure, . . . a pitiable fatuous
fellow" ("The Dead," 120). The real mirror in the room reflects one image but intimates the opposite of it. Gabriel has, then, spontaneous recourse to the other mirroring device in the room. He walks to the window. If the cheval-glass stands for
the pitfalls of a sort of narcissistic consciousness, the transparent mirror provided by
the reflections in the window stands, I shall maintain, for the demise of the Augustinian paradigm of phenomenal identity.

In archaic iconology, Narcissus dies because he does not understand that a conventionally mirroring surface can only show the mirrored self and not the other

from it; he dies so that the principle of irreducibly individual distinction (of the self from the other, or the non-self, as described by Nietzsche in *The Birth of Tragedy*) may impose itself unquestioningly upon archaic culture.[10] The Augustinian paradigm of phenomenal identity is on the contrary the indispensable premise to the Dantesque obliteration of the self's separateness from the other in the afterlife. As a collusion of spiritual interiority and carnal exteriority, of *ego interior* and *sensus corporis*,[11] the Augustinian self affirms itself through the exercise of free will.[12] By subduing the body's innate propensity to sin, described in Book VIII of Augustine's *Confessions*,[13] the self's will power gains admittance to the necropolitan matrix that corresponds, before the Second Coming and the resurrection of the flesh, to its own authentic abode. This necropolitan matrix is best exemplified in Dante's paradise: the individual self comes into its truest own in a place without extension, a time without duration, where the persistence of its good intentions is not limited anymore by the temporal dimension of human will, as it was before death.[14]

In this paradise of self-completion, the distinct selfhood of the individual is obliterated via a process of depersonalization. Having achieved full intimacy with the god (the *numen*), the individual self finds shelter within the invagination of an undifferentiated multitude of blessed subjects, all of which have reached the same stage of complete self-extinction—or in-numenation, if you will—in their divine source.

Dante-the-pilgrim provides the primary model for the fading away of Gabriel's individual identity. Dante experiences the dissolution of the Augustinian self when he enters paradise. Perceiving the faces of the blessed as though reflected in "polished glass" (*vetri tersi*) or "limpid and calm waters" (*acque nitide e tranquille* [*Paradiso*, 3:10–18]),[15] Dante, a novel Narcissus (*Paradiso*, 3:17–18), mistakes at first the nature of the medium in front of him. This mirroring surface reflects the faces of the saints standing behind him, he thinks, but not his own face. Soon he recovers from this misapprehension, though. There is no mirroring surface. The blessed—who are standing in front of him, rather than behind—are enacting a "condescending" performance to the benefit of his limited sensory apparatus;[16] having recurred to feebly "surface tracings" (*postille debili* [*Paradiso*, 3:13–14])[17] in order to manifest themselves in a manner compatible with and condescending to the limitations of Dante's senses, and having appeared therefore in the bodily guise of several distinct individuals of both genders, they represent themselves by representing their very impossibility of being naturalistically represented.

Yet, being the destination and, as it were, the source itself of the performance, Dante is not excluded from it, instead he is at its very fulcrum. Rather than a separate individual, effaced, as he thought at first, from the reflected image of the saintly individuals, Dante discovers that he is the reflecting medium itself. His sensitive apparatus constitutes the ultimate criterion of verisimilitude for the self-manifestation of the blessed spirits. The blessed spirits' atomic disaggregation bespeaks by inversion, as an inside-out figure from Dante's negative poetics, the obliteration of their individual separateness from each other and from Dante himself—the latter being, in the paradox of this necropolitan fiction of conventional verisimilitude, their very *author.* This celestial invagination of saints suffers Dante's gaze and mirrors it back to him as the saints' own reflection, just the way the celestial rose, infused and empowered with the ray of God's "light" or *lume,* mirrors it back to Him as though it were the rose's own independent emanation (*Paradiso,* 30:100–114).

Back in 1965, Virginia Moseley sensed the Dantesque aura in an analogous performance enacted in "The Dead," condescending in this case to Gabriel Conroy's sensory limitations, and—quite aptly in this specific case, as we shall see—referred the reader to Canto 4 of the *Paradiso.*[18]

Joyce positions Gabriel Conroy at the threshold of Dante's paradise through a cumulation of intertextual intimations, stroke after stroke after stroke. Warned by the "fading out" of his identity while his reflection in the window merges with the refractions from the flurry of snowflakes, Gabriel is enabled to recognize the shades pushing against the glass as a beneficial visitation ("The Dead," 223). The "hosts of the dead" have assumed the tremulous appearance of a tempest of snow flakes because the incidents and allusions distributed throughout the previous, naturalistic segments of "The Dead" are brusquely transposed, in these snowflakes "falling obliquely against the lamplight," each flake separate and distinct from the next, to the necropolitan dimension of a paradisiac vision ("The Dead," 223).

The blessed of paradise manifest themselves frequently to Dante in configurations of atomic disaggregation, as though the very multitude inherent in the images of dusty corpuscles floating in a sun ray (*Paradiso,* 14:109–17), of minute stars crowning the sun in the sky (*Paradiso,* 23:28–30), or of birds flying with the fastness of tiny sparks (*Paradiso,* 18:70–78), were to intimate, by the inverted figurality of a negative poetics, the obliteration of their individual separateness. It is when the blessed, parting ways with Dante, discontinue the artifice or negative poetics of their "signaling" to him (*per far segno* [*Paradiso,* 4:39]) and fall (or rise) back home, to the Empyrean—the home that, as Dante knows, they never actually left, except in the artifice of their condescending performance—that they manifest themselves in the guise of myriads of snowflakes.

> *Sì come di vapor gelati fiocca*
> *in giuso l'aere nostro, quando il corno*
> *de la capra del ciel col sol si tocca,*
> *in su vid'io così l'etera adorno*
> *farsi e* fioccar *di vapor triunfanti*
> *che fatto avevan con noi quivi soggiorno.*
> *Lo viso mio seguiva i suoi sembianti,*
> *e seguì fin che 'l mezzo, per lo molto,*
> *li tolse il trapassar del più avanti.*
> [As, when the horn of heaven's Goat abuts
> the sun, our sky flakes frozen vapors downward,
> so did I see that ether there adorned;
> for from that sphere, triumphant vapors now

were flaking to the Empyrean—
returning after dwelling here with us.
My sight was following their semblances—
until the space between us grew so great
as to deny my eyes all farther reach.][19]

(*Paradiso*, 27:67–75, my emphasis)

The blessed spirits flow, or "snow," triumphantly back onto their permanent (and never discontinued) condition of "in-numenation"; the "vaporous" multitude of their staged disaggregation fades out in the obliteration of its artificiality. The necropolitan *ensemble* of paradisiac invagination reconstitutes itself in the celestial rose.

The rest of the present discussion will be devoted to illustrating the emergence and prominence of this negative poetics in "The Dead."

Sepulchral Adumbrations

The stories collected in *Dubliners* provide the reader with a rich catalog of modulations of Flaubertian naturalism. Modulation is perhaps too prudent a term. Joyce seems bent on testing the degree of flexibility of Flaubert's stylistic paradigms by stretching, twisting, and twining them with the ingenuity of a most lively imagination. How much figural latitude can they accommodate? "The Dead" constitutes the culmination of this narrative strategy; it is much longer than the other stories, more eloquent, more fully characterized and emplotted, woven with a uniquely minute texture of historical detail and psychological symptom. This story's naturalistic tapestry is so craftily assembled that it diverts much of the reader's attention toward stylistic instances of self-validation—what does this or that character think they are, and who is the real person hiding behind their mannerisms? Gabriel Conroy's public views of himself and their self-promoting mannerisms, in particular, erect a diversionary façade around the epiphanic (seasonally and metaphorically speaking) significance buried in Gabriel's own experience at the end of the story.

Much of the criticism devoted to "The Dead" seeks in fact to break through this naturalistic façade in order to scrutinize the down-sized persona Gabriel is reduced to by the revelation of Gretta's preemptive betrayal. Reformed by his humbling experience, Gabriel will turn perhaps into Garry Leonard's psychological stoic, John Paul Riquelme's social anticonformist, Florence Walzl's moral impotent or, alternately, passionate humanitarian, Donald Torchiana's former opportunist, lastly, converted to the cause of Gaelic revivalism.[20] If not, he will just remain that which he has personified all along according to Hugh Kenner, that is to say, an "anticommunal" messenger of death.[21] The diagnosis of the sordid truth behind the protagonist's carefully crafted self-image disregards, in turn, the glamorous change of register brought about by the story's closing section. This is perfectly understandable, insofar as the "Uncle Charles principle" lends itself to interpretive approaches radically distinct from (and hardly reconcilable with) those called for by Dante's negative poetics.

The aesthetic difference between the story's naturalistic figurality and the Dantesque poetics of its closing section turns out to be therefore fundamental to a proper understanding of Joyce's overall intentions. The naturalistic figurality of "The Dead" is user friendly; it provides the critic with the advantages of a remarkable malleability vis-à-vis the ideology inherent in this or that interpretation. On the contrary, the closing section's poetics result somewhat impenetrable, a diamond-smooth shield impervious to the critic's own ideological persuasions—or, as Margot Norris warns self-reflexively at the end of "Narration under a Blindfold," a shiny mirror (scoured bright perhaps, like Maria's boilers in "Clay," by Joyce's "scrupulous meanness")[22] showing the critic an "unflattering self-image."[23]

In my interpretation of "The Dead" I shall leave aside, with three exceptions, the naturalistic events and incidents relating to the long sections devoted to the dinner party at the Misses Morkan's house. I shall focus instead on the negative poetics —that is, the representation of the unreal and unrepresentable, and the exegetic protocol inherent in it—that informs the story once Gabriel Conroy and his wife Gretta leave the house and reach the Gresham Hotel, where they will spend the night before going back home to Monkstown. Two of my three naturalistic exceptions (Gabriel Conroy's encounters with Lily and with Molly Ivors) relate to the stylistics of self-validation inherent in the "Uncle Charles principle," the third to the scene describing Gretta Conroy as she listens to Mr Bartell D'Arcy singing "The Lass of Aughrin." These three episodes have provided the "critical template" common to a majority of past and recent interpretations, as David Higdon has astutely observed.[24]

The stylistics of self-validation emerge as a prominent narrative mode of "The Dead" from the first line, as Hugh Kenner brought to universal attention in his discussion of the "Uncle Charles principle."[25] In a *tourbillon* of comings and goings, Lily the maid finds solace from her strenuous work thanks to an imaginary narration of her generous attitude. Far from being "run off her feet" *literally*, she projects on the imaginary mirror of her self-validation the amiable picture of a *figuratively* omnipresent, tireless Mercury. Validation for her self-styled trope is found in the gratitude expressed by hosts and guests alike; however, only the arrival of Gabriel provides the ultimate and unquestionable validation Lily is craving for. Being the "favorite nephew" of the Misses Morkan, as well as the proxy for the absent paterfamilias (his aunts and their niece, Mary Jane, being all unwed), Gabriel figures in the story as the master validator for the social legitimacy and mundane success of the Morkans' yearly dinner party.

Contrary to the prevalent opinion, I shall venture that Gabriel's predictable validation of Lily's self-image materializes in his gift of a coin to her. This gift does not bespeak a symbolic act of prostitution, as variously argued in Leonard's and Riquelme's censorious critiques.[26] Such a gift or Christmas bonus was customary of old Europe, a constituent part of the salary for a dependent in Lily's position, never formally hired of course with a regular job contract; its equivalent is found nowadays in the tips given to American waiters, which constitute a substantial part of their income. As the proxy for the absent paterfamilias, Gabriel is expected to express his appreciation of Lily's functions in the Morkan family with an informal yet substantial monetary contribution. In Lily's case, validation of status boils down to a socioeconomic phenomenon.

The unease provoked in Gabriel by Lily's "bitter and sudden" allusion to "palaver," whereby young men may have on occasion talked her into trading favors that a good Catholic girl should never consider trading, translates probably into a more-or-less-generous-than-usual gift from Gabriel ("The Dead," 178–79)—which must have translated, in turn, into Lily's perception of a more or less genuine authentication of her self-crafted image on his part. Which is which, Joyce chooses not to tell. (He chooses to modulate instead, at this rather uncomfortable juncture, the echo of the gold coin at the end of "Two Gallants," creating thereby an ambiguous interplay between the economics of workers' compensation and the metaphorics of human exploitation.)

One of the single women at the party, Molly Ivors, refuses to play her assigned womanly role, and challenges Gabriel's authority. Her challenge is based on political grounds—Gabriel writes for the *Daily Express,* a pro-English publication, while Miss Ivors is a Gaelic revivalist. I find it strange how most readers tend to take Miss Ivors at her word (just as they tend to take at face value Gretta's romantic cliché of a love-story previous to her encounter with Gabriel), neglecting to pay attention to the emphatic flirtatiousness of her attitude toward Gabriel. She provokes him and accuses him of being a "West Briton," then declares she was "only joking," then invites him (and Gretta, a pious afterthought) to join her and her friends on a month-long vacation to the West of Ireland, then accuses him of neglecting his own country and language, then looks at him "quizzically" until he smiles, then insults him again: "West Briton!" If Gabriel should ever opt to undertake this patriotic journey westward in the company of Molly Ivors and her friends (as Donald Torchiana believes he will, placing Gabriel on the footsteps of St. Patrick),[27] it is to be expected, I venture, that he and Molly would end up in bed together.

The tension between the two grows out of control, and Molly thinks wiser to make herself scarce. As a result of her departure from the party, a phrase carefully calibrated by Gabriel as a retort against this female member of the "new and very serious and hypereducated generation that is growing up around us" ("The Dead," 192) will lack its intended audience during his after-dinner speech; it will fail therefore to validate whatever sensuous self-image Gabriel was trying to craft with this declaration.

"The Dead" abounds with symptomatic situations of this kind, luring one into the ironic exegesis of their underdeveloped motives. Some circumspection is required of the critic, though. As my brief discussion of Gretta's romance with Michael Furey will confirm, the deterministic analysis of clear-cut symptoms whose implications Joyce chooses not to develop may lead to paralyzing vistas. Hugh Kenner calls this phenomenon a "reshuffling of associations,"[28] whereby Joyce first deals the (naturalistic) cards and then changes the (figural) rules. Florence Walzl refers to Joyce's dissemination of symptomatic imagery in "The Dead" as "shifting patterns of mean-ing";[29] the symptoms are clear-cut, their aggregation prismatic.

I have already alluded to the third scene I intend to illustrate before we follow Gabriel and Gretta out of the Morkan residence. Gretta is the last and most impor-tant in the tercet of women who, the analogues of Dante's Maria, Lucia, and Be-atrice, are going either to keep Gabriel well wrapped inside himself, as Garry Leonard aptly puts it, or unwrap him altogether.[30] Gretta is in the shadow on the stairs lis-tening to D'Arcy singing. Gabriel looks at the panels of her skirt, whose architec-tural impression on his senses (the "terracotta and salmonpink panels" appearing "black and white" in the shadow ["The Dead," 209]) makes her appear in the guise of a cenotaph. What is she a symbol of? he wonders. This moment in "The Dead" has triggered the most unanimously symbolistic responses from the critics. As I have shown in a study of the Mariology inherent in Stephen Dedalus's "Vampire Poem," Mallarmé's and Dante's respective influences are crucial to the more mature Joyce of *Ulysses*.[31] But Dante's negative poetics is clearly foundational and of primary importance with respect to French symbolism, when it comes to Joyce's earlier fic-tions. The artifices of French symbolism hit the young Joyce via the mediation of the sensuous mysticism of the early Yeats, the pictorial Dantism of Dante Gabriel Rossetti, and the lapidary aestheticism of Walter Pater; it is a symbolism imbued through and through with Dantesque poetics.

What is Gretta a symbol of? Gabriel wonders—superfluously enough, in my opinion, since his sculptural impressions of her are evident adumbrations of a tomb, Michael Furey's, in "the lonely churchyard on the hill" that Gabriel will halluci-nate at the climax of his paradisiac vision ("The Dead," 223). More elliptically speak-ing, Gabriel's impressions may also be intended as the adumbrations of an empty tomb—the corporeal monument hiding Gretta's soul's vacancy (temporary, far from irremediable, I think) from her marriage and her long-lasting love for Gabriel.

Later Gretta will tell Gabriel the story of her juvenile romance with Michael Furey, a delicate boy enamored of songs about unrequited love and of the cruel death this kind of love often provokes. As in the case of Molly Ivors's provocations, it is somewhat conventional to take Gretta's version of her love story at face value. If one were to look deeper into the disconcerting delusions inherent in its numerous clichés, one might be tempted to wonder whether Gretta's name ought not to be intended according to the Italian valence of its double "t"—the Italian *gretta* stands for "petty, narrow-minded." Gabriel seems inclined to pursue this line of inquiry when he wonders, "Perhaps she had not told him all the story" ("The Dead," 222). Everyone gets the Beatrice they deserve. Busy perhaps paring his fingernails,[32] Joyce chooses not to orient the reader within this conjugal maze. The critic steps into its symptomatic intimations at their own risk.

Negative Biography

The bracketing of individual consciousness within its own historical contingency is one of the great virtues of Dante's *Commedia*. Dante's adoption of a negative poetics in order to represent the otherworldly unrepresentable (and unimaginable) is a move of the greatest consequence, insofar as it inaugurates the suspension of the phenomenal primacy that St. Augustine attributed to the sublunary self. This may best be seen in Dante's naturalistic representations of historical individuals, emphatically praised by Eric Auerbach[33]: the souls encountered in the *Commedia* are irreducibly placed under the sway of a praeterhistorical condition.[34]

As I suggested above in the illustration of Dante's initial misapprehension of the blessed spirits' self-manifestation in paradise, two conflicting modalities of selfhood are simultaneously at play in the *Paradiso*. One is the naturalistic selfhood of historical subjects, endowed with the prerogative of irreducible individuality. The other is the necropolitan selfhood of paradisiac saints, who are invaginated in a celestial rose so antagonistic with individual, subjective separateness that not even the rose's two distinct sources, that is, God on the ontologic side and Dante on the representational side, may be kept distinct from it. The saints and the pilgrim are invaginated onto a *numen* that is indistinguishable from this very motion of invagination. The former, or naturalistic, modality of selfhood is susceptible to the ironic interpretation advocated in Hayden White's studies of Vico's tropology;[35] documentable facts, causes, and effects may be identified behind the *figura,* as Auerbach would put it. The latter or necropolitan modality of selfhood is impervious to irony, instead; no documentable and verifiable referents may factically substantiate paradisiac disindividualization.

Dante's poetry relocates the fulcrum of the individual self in the necropolitan dimension. His epic journey to the afterlife is the journey that everybody will have undertaken in order to engage in a future-perfect repetition of Christ's death and descent to hell. It is through the negative biography of one's necropolitan journey, descriptive of an experience that is factically unexperienceable and exuberant of allegorical representation (the textual instantiation of the traveler's negative existence, elusive of the norms of factual determinism and literal causality consistent with the "Uncle Charles principle") that the Augustinian self comes into its own.

As foreshadowed in the introduction, this negative biography brings about the dissolution of that very self that it serves to instantiate, though, as evidenced in the semantics itself of Dante's reflexive neologisms—*indiarsi, intuarsi, inmiarsi*—denotative of the collapse of ontological distinction. In the *Paradiso* Augustine's sublunary model of the self—a soul (i.e., an interiority endowed with free will) signified by the presence of a living body—is substituted by corporeal pointillism; the rosiform fusion of all blessed spirits, being unrepresentable to human imagination and unexperienceable to sensory perception, is imaged by recourse to the presence of that which is not factically there, that is, a multitude of corpuscles, each endowed with his or her own distinct identity. "Mediation is turned back upon itself and reified in the letter of the text."[36] Via invaginative mediation, the literary figure becomes its own referent[37]—a referent impervious to the ironic decoding of its literal and/or allegorical meaning, insofar as neither a literal ground of validation nor a referential ground of allegorization is compatible with the necropolitan dimension.

Epiphany of Negative Self

Mortified first by his reliance on the narcissistic self ("a broad, well-filled shirt front") and then by his awareness that to the prosperous, external self "he had caught a glimpse of in the mirror" corresponds the sordid interiority of "a ludicrous figure . . . idealizing his own clownish lust," Gabriel Conroy rejects both narcissistic and naturalistic self. He walks to the window, choosing to expose himself to a different kind of reflection. Having done so, he stretches himself cautiously beside his wife. "One by one they [are] all becoming shades," he considers bitterly. And "generous tears fill . . . [his] eyes" ("The Dead," 218, 220, 223).

Lucia Boldrini suggests that "some form of redemption . . . come[s] nearer to its realization with the[se] 'generous tears.'" This form of redemption is Dantesque in kind: "Gabriel's tears and the general pattern of revising one's position . . . point to an analogous process that takes place throughout the whole of Dante's journey in the other world." Boldrini's argument is unimpeachable, so far as it goes; and it does go farther, admittedly, than most of the critics discussed in the present essay do, insofar as it brings Gabriel near "the concealed implication of a positive outcome" and distances him from the failings and psychological ailments diagnosed by so many naturalistic interpretations.[38] But an extra step remains to be taken in order to acknowledge the negative thrust of Gabriel's existential stance.

Boldrini's contribution to the apprehension of Gabriel's necropolitan journey is no less fundamental a stage, however, than Dante's descent to hell to the ultimate realization of his celestial homecoming. One could not overstress, in fact, the dark side to Gabriel's epiphanic revelation, duly remarked by Boldrini. Being seized by "a vague terror" at Gretta's revelation of her inconsolable love for Michael Furey, Gabriel has the impression that "some impalpable and vindictive being [is] coming against him" ("The Dead," 220). Gabriel's feelings function as an intertext at this stage, signaling the analogy of his situation with "Dante's difficult predicament in the first canto of the *Inferno*."[39] Faced with such evident intimation of incumbent despair, one might feel inclined to object that not even Joyce's propensity toward the reshuffling of associations could afford to elevate Gabriel from the vestibule of hell to the threshold of paradise in the space of the few paragraphs it takes the story to end. It takes three canticles for Dante himself, after all, to accomplish such a reversal.

Yet, it is not difficult to establish that the literary type of instantaneous transition from infernal to paradisiac vision is exquisitely Dantesque—furthermore, Joyce adopts it more than once.[40] The origination of this type may be ascribed to the canzone *Donna pietosa e di novella estate,* from section 23 of the *Vita nuova.* In the narrow space of an eighty-four-line poem, Dante's autobiographical narration establishes the literary type of instantaneous transition from the abyss of hellish despair to the bliss of paradisiac release. This song is particularly relevant to the present discussion because the imagery informing the following three of its lines is considered the most immediate literary antecedent to the figure of saints flowing back to the Empyrean in the guise of snow flakes (used by Dante, as we saw, in *Paradiso,* 27:67–72).[41] My introductory remarks in the subsection titled "Necropolitan Matrix" stressed the intertextual collusion between this Dantesque imagery from Canto 27 and the merging of Gabriel Conroy's reflection with the flurry of snowflakes behind the hotel window.

> *Levava li occhi miei bagnati in pianti,*
> *e vedea, che parean pioggia di manna,*
> *li angeli che tornavan suso in cielo . . .*
> [I raised my tearful eyes,
> and saw, in the guise of a rain of manna,
> the angels going back to the high heaven.]
>
> (*Vita nuova,* 23:25–27, my translation)[42]

Having realized that one day Beatrice will die, Dante imagines a group of women telling him that one day he will die, too. At the words of these women, Dante's fantasy shows him an apocalyptic scene: the sun is eclipsed, the stars cry bitter tears, the birds fall dead from the sky, and the earth is shaken by quakes. Then Dante imagines a friend of his bringing him the news that Beatrice has actually died. He starts crying, "not only in his imagination but . . . filling [his] eyes with real tears"—as Gabriel does when he lies down in bed beside his wife. But looking up at the sky, Dante has now the luminous vision of angels "going back to the high heaven" while singing *Osanna in excelsis* and carrying with them the "very white cloud" of Beatrice's soul. The angels appear to him in the guise of "a rain of manna"—an "inverted rain" falling skyward, as Singleton phrases it, and inverting, in its reverse directionality, the mode of Dante's hellish desperation.[43]

> The tears gathered more quickly in his eyes and in the partial darkness he imagined he saw the form of a young man standing under a dripping tree. Other forms were near. His soul had approached that region where dwell the vast hosts of the dead. He was conscious of, but could not apprehend, their wayward and flickering existence. *His own identity was fading out* into a grey impalpable world: the solid world itself which these dead had one time reared and lived in was dissolving and dwindling. ("The Dead," 223, my emphasis)

What is Gabriel's fading identity going to dissolve into? The paradisiac destination of his self-fading is emphatically delineated by the pervasiveness of intertextual referentiality. The dissolution of the individual self and the self's corollary assumption onto the heavens, via the poetic artifice of superposed pointillist reflections, is a Dantesque type dear to Joyce's imagination.

Evidence of this may be found in a crucial episode from *A Portrait of the Artist as a Young Man*. Although rendered with better dramaturgic skills than those available to Joyce in "The Dead," this episode duplicates faithfully the Dantesque progression of Gabriel's in-numenation. Having identified himself with Daedalus, "the fabulous artificer," Stephen Dedalus wades through a rivulet left behind by the sea tide. The reflections and refractions of the water are mirrored in the chiasmatic style of Stephen's inner emotions and sensations.

The water of the rivulet was dark with endless drift and *mirrored* the highdrift-ing clouds. The clouds were drifting above him silently and silently the seatan-gle was drifting below him. . . . *Where was the soul* that had hung back from her destiny [of priestly duties], to brood alone . . . in faded cerements . . . ? Or *where was he?*[44]

Evocative of Dante's absent reflection from the imaginary "limpid and calm waters" of Canto 3 of the *Paradiso* (3:11), Stephen's own reflection is excluded from that of the "highdrifting clouds" above his head, whose moving image mingles with the refraction from the colorful "seatangle . . . drifting" at his feet. A bit later Stephen, whose soul is still robed in the "cerements" of its death to the priesthood (the "graveclothes" of his "boyhood"),[45] encounters his famous "seabird" girl, who, white and blue like the Virgin Mary, functions as allegoric correlative of personal rebirth: she is the "virgin womb of [an] imagination" born to the sacerdotal duties of the artist—"her thighs, fuller and softhued as ivory," figuring a profane proxy to the virginal "Tower of Ivory" of the Church.[46] As Richard Ellmann and Mary Reynolds have both recognized, Stephen is ripe for his visionary assumption onto the self-dissolution of the heavenly spheres.[47] He lies down to welcome it:

He felt above him the vast indifferent dome and the calm processes of the *heav-enly bodies;* and the earth beneath him, the earth that had borne him, had taken him to her breast. . . . His eyelids trembled as if they felt the vast cyclic move-ment of the earth and her *watchers,* trembled as if they felt the strange light of some new world. *His soul was swooning into some new world,* fantastic, dim, uncer-tain as under sea, *traversed by cloudy shapes and beings.* A world, a glimmer, or a flower? . . . An opening flower, it spread in endless succession to itself. . . .[48]

In the case of both Gabriel Conroy and Stephen Dedalus, Joyce's Dantesque allu-sions suggest that a fourth option, allegorically and literally unreferentiable, is offered his protagonists, beyond the ontological options of being what "they would like to be, or really are, or never were."[49] This option, elusive of the traditional primacy of ontology over human existence, corresponds to the Dantesque condition of in-numenation. The full range of Gabriel Conroy's "incarnations" (to use Hugh Ken-ner's diction),[50] made available to the critic by the ironic interpretations informed by the "Uncle Charles principle," is not broad enough to enclose this fourth pos-sibility. As Lucia Boldrini maintains, it is only by paying due attention to the "ves-tigial traces" of Joyce's relationship with Dante that one is enabled to probe "the symbolic and semantic web" at the proper depth.[51]

The terminological analogy between Boldrini's "vestigial traces" and the vesti-gial theory of language described in chapter 2 is coincidental, of course. Nonethe-less, it comes to my succor in the completion of the extra step necessary to assess the negative thrust of Gabriel's existential stance at the end of "The Dead." More to the point, Boldrini's understanding of *Finnegans Wake*'s literary relation to Dante's poetics in terms of "vestigial traces" may be extended to our intertextual under-standing of "The Dead." The Dantean intertext's symbolic and semantic web is cryptically disseminated in Joyce's story, too—not only to signify the discordant resemblance between a Dantean and a Joycean use of allegory,[52] but especially to indicate the points of contact between two distinct instantiations of negative existence. From the perspective of character's intentionality, it is legitimate to assume that vestigial sediments from what Durkheim describes as the "ascetic way" of negative cult are adaptively at play both in the case of Dante's pilgrim and of Gabriel's experience, determining, together with a more deliberate range of intentional gestures, their respective self-dissipation in the negative dimension of nonreferentiality. The reach of this symbolic and semantic web is put to the ultimate test, of course, by the image of Gabriel's "journey westward."

> A few light taps upon the pane made [Gabriel] turn to the window. It had begun to snow again. He watched sleepily the flakes, silver and dark, falling obliquely against the lamplight. The time had come for him to set out on his journey westward. ("The Dead," 223)

Gabriel's journey westward belongs to the biblical, epic, and Dantesque tradition of the postexilic homecoming. Yet, it is not, as I anticipated earlier, the coming-back-home of the Homeric hero; to be geographically precise, Monkstown, Gabriel's own "Ithaca," is located in the south side of Dublin Bay, five miles southeast precisely —hence, not certainly *west*—from the center of Dublin. Neither should Gabriel's journey be simply reduced to the traditional figure for Gabriel's physiological journey "westward into death," as Chambers puts it;[53] nor, I venture, should it be simply reduced to the figure for Gabriel's patriotic journey back to the Galway root of authentic Irishness, as predicted by Donald Torchiana;[54] nor, again, to the journey away from Gabriel's delusional and disintegrating ego, leading, according to Garry Leonard, to the Galway root of genuine existentiality that thus far Gabriel "has refused to acknowledge."[55]

All of these interpretations, reflective of various exegetic affiliations, are far from wrong, per se; they do find different degrees of legitimacy in the interpretive practice conforming to the "Uncle Charles principle." It is not for me to differentiate or classify them in light of their respective plausibility or rigor. But their explicative power is limited by their common disregard for the hybrid mix of naturalism and negative poetics informing the first and second part respectively of Joyce's story. Granted our discordant views on the explicative reach of allegorical representation, my discussion of "The Dead" concords with the Lukacsian accent of Sicari's study of *Ulysses.* The operational presence of naturalism is undeniable in "The Dead." In Sicari's lingo, one could argue that naturalism "reduces [Gabriel's] will to impotence;" negative poetics assumes the role that Sicari attributes to modernist allegory, in providing Gabriel's will with the means of "escape from the real [existence] from which it is alienated."[56]

If one must map out the allegorical latitude of Gabriel's journey in terms of its longitudinal motion, one ought not to neglect, therefore, its intertextual evocation of Dante's journey *through* paradise, which, in light of Dante's precise account of it, results to be evidently westbound. (At the passage from the Heaven of the Fixed Stars to the Crystalline or *Primum Mobile,* Dante measures the longitudinal distance covered by him and Beatrice through the eighth planetary sphere as equivalent to 90° westward.)[57]

Gabriel Conroy shares his name with Gabriel, the amorous angel, *angel . . . innamorato sì che par di foco* ("the angel so much in love that he looks fiery" [*Paradiso,* 32:103–5]), who is most often mentioned in the *Paradiso.*[58] For the duration of his youthful courtship of Gretta, Gabriel's soul was consumed by a tenderly flaming condition, analogous with the celestial "fire of the stars" ("The Dead," 213). His fiery-hearted devotion moved Gretta, too, to play gently with fire—of all fires, the literal one from a "roaring furnace" ("The Dead," 213). Michael Furey shares his name instead with Gabriel's angelic partner, Michael, who, agent of divine revenge, is virtually absent from the *Paradiso; [M]ichele fe' la vendetta di superbo strupo* ("Michael revenged [Lucifer's] proud rape" [*Inferno,* 7:12–13]).[59] When Richard Ellmann talks of a "'Furey' quality of the [Irish] west," one is tempted to pun on the "Furey" overtones of the *furious* west of Gaelic anticolonialism,[60] "the full glory of [whose] passion" is being offered Gabriel Conroy tonight as alternate or perhaps complementary opportunity to his brief interval of negative existence ("The Dead," 223).

Yet, to be true to the negative thrust prevalent in the closing section of "The Dead," one must complement Ellmann's metaphor with that of the *fiery* and celestial West of celestial dis-individualization, where Gabriel Conroy, paradisiac pilgrim, will have encountered and merged with his flaming counterpart, *angel . . . di foco.*

It seems to me that Seamus Deane strikes a most truthful note when he writes, regarding Gabriel's tracking of the snow westward, that ". . . everything is dissolved . . . into an evocation of a world elsewhere, that of the aesthetic moment, in which conflict is annulled and the distinction between deathly paralysis and total liberation is designedly and with great virtuoso skill canceled. It is one of Joyce's finest fine moments."[61] A fine moment indeed, yet Deane risks praising an old-fashioned aestheticism that does not do justice to the negative poetics probed by young Joyce at the closure of "The Dead." Deane's "world elsewhere . . . of the aesthetic moment" feels disquietingly analogous with the marginal influence of William Butler Yeats's "aristocratic insolence," "pre-Raphaelite poise," and "Faustian glamour," deservedly stigmatized by Hugh Kenner in *Dublin's Joyce.*[62] If echoes may be heard in the "concluding details of 'The Dead'" of the visions from Yeats's *Stories of Red Hanrahan,* as John Paul Riquelme has observed,[63] Joyce clearly invests these languid visions with the robustly redemptive spectacle of Gabriel's necropolitan "journey westward."

Florence Walzl suggests that "the directional symbolism" of the westward journey must be associated with Gabriel's final vision of the graveyard.[64] "Falling through the universe . . . like the descent of their last end, upon all the living and the dead," the snow, joined with the Christological imagery of "crosses . . . spears [and] thorns," would be the intentional allegoric correlative of Gabriel's necropolitan journey

("The Dead," 223–24). However, one must not simply think of Gabriel as the sacrificial victim of the epiphanic meal at the Misses Morkan's dinner party. Gabriel is
not a crucified scapegoat, nor does he personify the wooden cross or inert totem
instrumental to that sacrifice. It would be erroneous to assume simplistically that in
Joyce's view "[a Christ-like] sacrifice of self is the condition of [Gabriel's] revival."[65]

Such a Christological angle would, once again, confuse negative poetics with ironic
interpretation, unduly transposing Gabriel's paradisiac, unreferentiable experience of
dis-individualization to a literal or allegorical repetition of the Eucharistic rite.
Although repetitive of Christ's emblematic biography, and notwithstanding "the
imagery of Calvary" playing over it,[66] Gabriel's necropolitan journey must be intended as immune also from the referentiality intrinsic to patristic typology. If, in
Stephen Daedalus's words, Gabriel's journey could be said to "reconstruct the *spectacle* of redemption,"[67] it would have done so by transposing this "spectacle" to the
exquisite unreferentiability of Dante's negative poetics. We are facing here an instance
of literature's autonomy from other discursive and rhetorical forms (all conventionally susceptible to ironic interpretation), not excluded the rhetorics of church liturgy.

At the beginning of his literary career, Joyce takes upon himself the task of reha-
bilitating Dante's original poetics. As he already intimated in his youthful lecture,
"Drama and Life," the artist's true goal is to displace the repetition of "mythus"
from church liturgy to literary reenactment. "Struggl[ing] back to [drama's] right-
ful place," the power of the necropolitan journey is claimed back from church
liturgy and made "coeval," in "The Dead," with the instantiation of Gabriel's existential predicament; it is turned into a negative biography "aris[ing] spontaneously"
out of Gabriel's own life.[68] The unfolding of Gabriel's necropolitan journey constitutes therefore the occasion for his most genuine biography. It is through the eli-
sion of factual determinism and literal facts, through the dismissal of naturalistic
referentiality and the fading away of phenomenal identity, that Gabriel, on the night
of the Epiphany, will have come into his genuine self.

STEPHEN DEDALUS'S
SILENCE IN PROGRESS

Are you not weary of ardent ways,
Lure of the fallen seraphim?
Tell no more of enchanted days.

A Portrait of the Artist as a Young Man, *217, 223*

In the previous section we discussed the vision that leads Stephen to his mystic self-dissolution in the heavenly spheres. It is provoked by the appearance of a cranelike girl on the beach, an image of the Virgin Mary, white in complexion and blue in garb, made unconventionally sexy and rather suspicious in allegoric significance by her naked legs and "darkplumaged" bosom (*P*, 171–72). This ambiguous vision is followed by an encounter with Emma, Stephen's sweetheart. Recollected by Stephen after the nocturnal emission[1] that initiates him to the "ecstasy of the seraphic life" (*P*, 217), this encounter induces Stephen to write the "Villanelle of the Temptress." Stephen's muse is an ambiguous figure, both "dark fall [and] brightfall,"[2] both angelic source of poetic inspiration and demoniac source of existential abjection.[3] And because of this ubiquitous inspiration, his verses fail in the attempt, not devoid of poetic intelligence, to emulate the erotic language of mystics and saints. The barely veiled onanistic imagery of his "sacrificing hands uprais[ing] / The chalice flowing to the brim" is indeed a poor transposition of his devoted liturgical elevation (". . . the smoke of praise / Goes up from ocean rim to rim" [*P*, 221, 223]). It reminds one of the child protagonist of "Araby," who falls victim to an analogous carnal infatuation, imbued with liturgical overtones.[4]

On the eve of his departure for France and his self-imposed exile from "nationality, language, [and] religion" (*P*, 203), Stephen appears disenchanted about his artistic accomplishments. In the journal entry reporting his final skirmish with Emma, he scorns his own poetic mannerisms by comparing them to Dante's "spiritual-heroic refrigerating apparatus" (*P*, 252). For the expression of the vision of the temptress who was supposed to open him to "all the way or error and glory" (*P*, 173), he had adopted the "liquid letters of speech" of this Dantesque apparatus. But the resulting verses confused erotic mysticism with nocturnal emission, overflowing with the not-so-metaphoric fluids of his exuberant sexuality.

On June 16, 1904, we meet a different Stephen, reformed by the demise of his mother, whose absence informs the entirety of his existential tension and poetic ambition, turning him into a poet of the afterlife. His attempted repudiation of the tongue and faith of his fellow country people induced him to burn all bridges, both literally and metaphorically—one cannot help comparing Stephen's exile with James and Nora's irreversible elopement to Italy. After the homecoming forced on him by bereavement and indigence, Stephen is the pathetic personification of the "disappointed bridge" he jokes about in his classroom (*U*, 2:39). His intimate disappointment consists first of all in having come home as "a jester at the court of his master," the "servant of two masters," Church and State (*U*, 1:44, 1:638), who recants the abjuration that had shaken "the wings of [his] exultant and terrible youth" on the eve of his short-lived French exile (*P*, 252). But an even graver disappointment lies in this: that only by bridging the immense gap separating his present life in Dublin from his mother's afterlife—a far more radical leap than the distance separating Newhaven from Dieppe (*U*, 9:952–54)—could his poetry ever fully extinguish his debt to the dead.

With his escape from Dublin, Stephen dreamt of awakening from the nightmarish paralysis of Irish history, but now the nightmare is more effective than ever. As Sicari intimates, the "demands of history," made irremediably concrete by his mother's death, whose decomposing body "signifies his connection to the past," are giving Stephen their "back kick" (*U*, 2:377, 2:379).[5] All of Stephen's youthful sanguineness seems sucked away by the incubus of his "Vampire Poem," on which he ruminates all day long in *Ulysses* (*U*, 7:522–25). As we shall discuss in the next chapter, this incubus fills Stephen's day with the torments of a sterile, fatigued poetic inspiration. The promiscuous, "batlike soul" of the temptress met by his friend Davin had called "the stranger to her bed" in the guise of a reincarnated Jael from the Bible (*P*, 183, 221),[6] and had awakened to "the consciousness of itself" in Stephen's poetico-onanistic fantasies.[7] This "batlike soul" has now transmogrified into the "pale vampire" of *Ulysses*, his mother's messenger from the afterlife. Is Stephen finding his artistic voice at long last, by addressing this repulsive creature, which gnaws all day long at the very fabric of his existence?

Stephen's incubus symbolizes death itself, and the death of his mother particularly.[8] It symbolizes the sterility of a death that the Catholic excesses of maternal fecundity brought prematurely upon Mary Goulding Dedalus.[9] It symbolizes the vampire of the menses, as I have argued elsewhere, whose whimsical visitations— "nourisher and bloodsucker"[10]—may bring a verdict of either life or death to the "womanhood of his country" (*P*, 221).[11] It is a figure, furthermore, of the reversal of maternal fecundity into deliberate abortion, an experience alluded to in "Oxen of the Sun," which a multitude of Catholic women in Dublin were secretly accustomed to (*U*, 14:242). But the ultimate instantiation of this incubus, capable of bestowing the gift of sterility but also of impregnating its victim "mouth to mouth" (*U*, 14:243–44), is Stephen himself, as Vincent Cheng suggests, in his necrophilic attempt to feed his poetic imagination on his own mother's cadaver.[12] In the final analysis, I venture, the theme of the "Vampire Poem" assimilates Stephen's poetic endeavor in *Ulysses* with a mimicry of abortion. It precipitates our young poet, who in *A Portrait of the Artist as a Young Man* hovered over the illusionary peaks of mystic self-gratification, down into the abysmal weariness of personal history. A significant parallel may be drawn with Joyce's description of his own mother's death: "My mother was slowly killed, I think, by my father's ill-treatment, by years of trouble, and by my cynical frankness of conduct."[13]

Stephen does not write poetry in *Ulysses,* nor has he written any dignified poetry since his apostasy from church, family, and country. What is he waiting for? As we saw in chapter 3, Augustine and Monica (and Dante as well) return from their short-lived intimacy with the divine through a lapse back into the phenomenal dimension of denotative and predicative language, which pertains, in turn, to the maternal domain of death and procreation. In chapter 3 we also discussed the concordant position prevalent in contemporary discussions of the apophatic experience, according to which the impossible experience of the divinely bountiful cannot be expressed per se in a vocabulary adequate to its ineffable significance.

Does the abortive silence of Stephen in *Ulysses* indicate his new awareness of the limits of poetic language? Does his poetic sterility, hidden behind the mask of a garrulous chatterbox,[14] indicate a new level of existential maturity on his part? Is his newly adopted artistic restraint, so reserved when compared with Buck Mulligan's extemporary verses (*U,* 1:584–99), gaining him membership in the club of the "disempowered poets" of the silence-in-progress, such as Dante and Mallarmé, whose ultimate goal would be, according to Sam Slote's perceptive definition, "to inachieve writing" and express thereby apophasis?[15] Or is Stephen simply a fallen and dis-graced poet of the afterlife, a sterile captive of the lapsed instrument of his own craft, misguided by Dante's "liquid letters of speech?" In the current chapter and the one that follows, we are going to discuss the amalgamation of factors and influences that guide Stephen in his new-found vocation as a poet of the afterlife.

Christic Poet

Around 2 P.M. on June 16, 1904, Stephen Dedalus engages in conversation with an audience composed of real Dublin intellectuals and fictional characters at the National Library. The conversation will soon turn into the famous soliloquy, interspersed with interior monologues, of "Scylla and Charybdis," whereby Stephen articulates his Sainte-Beuvean views on the relationship between authorship, biography, and creation. I have analyzed elsewhere the aesthetic implications of Stephen's discussion of Shakespeare's *Hamlet*.[16] In this chapter I intend to probe the laconic motives of Stephen's poetic vocation as they unfold in the course of his "Scylla and Charybdis" conversation, soliloquy, and interior monologues. I intend to ascertain to what extent may Stephen's sterility be considered a manifestation of the silence-in-progress whereby, according to Slote, the apophatic experience is expressed by Dante, Mallarmé, and Joyce through the disappearance or "inachievement" of literary enunciation.[17]

The stage of "Scylla and Charybdis" represents a progression with respect to the Christic stage reached by Stephen's self-identification as a poet in "Aeolus." In the latter episode Stephen's poetic persona is endowed with Christ-like attributes via his own narration of the "Parable of the Plums." As the reader will recall, this parable is told by Stephen as a parody of professor MacHugh's recitation of a 1901 polemical speech delivered by John Taylor in defense of "the revival of the Irish tongue" (*U*, 7:796).[18] Let us scrutinize the delineation of Stephen's Christic stance in this specific case, before moving on to a discussion of the "Scylla and Charybdis" episode.

In drawing an analogy between the enslavement of the ancient Hebrews by the Egyptians and the colonial oppression of the Irish people by the English, John Taylor had suggested that the revivalists' resistance against the hegemony of the English language shared some affinity with young Moses's rejection of the greatness of the Egyptian culture and military power. The key paradigm informing Stephen's fabrication of his "Parable of the Plums" is the analogy between Moses, as the national liberator of the Hebrews, and Horace Nelson, the one-armed admiral whose statue rests on top of a column in the heart of Dublin, in an attitude similar to Moses on the peaks of the Pisgah ridge, yet personifying colonial rule and foreign oppression.[19] This discordant analogy suggests to Stephen the sterile image of two elderly "vestals" sowing a fist of plum pits (two dozen plumstones exactly) on the inert soil at the foot of the Nelson column; this image is to be coupled, in turn, with the onanistic image of the "onehandled adulterer," the prospect of whose manipulation in "diminished digits" seems to tickle the erotic fantasies of the two ladies (*U*, 7:923, 941, 1018, 1069).

In this perspective, the "Parable of the Plums" suggests an intentional fusion of the biblical story of Onan with Matthew's parable of the good sower.[20] Stephen is suggesting to his two listeners, Professor MacHugh and Myles Crawford, that the rhetorics of liberation conveyed by John Taylor's speech—the flatulent version, by all means, recited in the pseudopatriotic, complacent climate of the *Freeman's Journal* by MacHugh—must be intended in an upside down or inverted way, as politically sterile and allegorically onanistic, when applied to the political and linguistic liberation of the Irish.

If we engage in the definition of Stephen's poetic persona, the key figure of Moses in Taylor's speech acquires special significance. In Taylor's words, Moses is a young man who refuses to bow his head, his will, and his spirit before the arrogant admonitions of the high Egyptian priest (*U*, 7:863–64). I submit that this is the passage in Taylor's speech that triggers Stephen's resentment against MacHugh and his listeners.

The journalists, intellectuals, and loafers congregated in the offices of the *Freeman's Journal* after Patrick Dignam's funeral have embarked upon a celebration of the greatness of Ireland and of her most prominent citizens. But in Stephen's eyes it is mediocrity and complacent narrow-mindedness—intellectual, spiritual, emotional —that actually dominates the scene. Like whitened sepulchers, these philistines are willing to accept Moses's conventional greatness, as well as his *non-serviam* challenge of the Egyptian priesthood and powers-that-be, because they take the notion of such greatness as a historical or mythical given—a prewrapped package of biblical lore. Yet, none of them would dare imitate the biblical hero—just as none of them would be willing to acknowledge Stephen's own *non-serviam,* and his refusal to bow in front of his church's, his family's, his country's authority. Stephen's resentment toward his audience manqué does not fail to suggest, obviously, a concordant rancor toward his own failure to enact the full consequences of his existential stance.

Stephen's refusal to obey is perceived reductively by all the men he meets and has dealings with on June 16, 1904 (with the possible exception of Leopold Bloom), as the typical rebellion of a youth who has not yet given tangible proof of his right to rebel against authority and dominant mores. Buck certainly does not take Stephen's rebelliousness too seriously, nor does his father, Simon Dedalus, nor do the men in the offices of the *Freeman's Journal,* nor, lastly, do, a few hours after the episode in the offices of the newspaper, the Dublin intellectuals and the various fictional characters who listen to his soliloquy on Hamlet and Shakespeare at the National Library.

As I said, the "Parable of the Plums" is delivered by a Christ-like Stephen. He tells his thoughts about the two "Dublin vestals" in the genre favored by Jesus in his ministry. And the interpretation of these thoughts requires, in turn, that the listeners have intertextual familiarity with a specific parable from Matthew's gospel, namely, the parable of the good sower, together with Onan's vetero-testamental story. Stephen's resentment does not subside at all in the next few hours; by the time he reaches the National Library, in the episode of "Scylla and Charybdis," Stephen is ready to identify himself, more radically than earlier, in the figure of the unrecognized poet, the rebel against sanctioned authority, the unacknowledged messiah of national pride. All he lacks to substantiate this self-identification is the evidence of his poetic talent.

Poet of Maternal Absence

Stephen, the ubiquitously passive "server of a servant" from the "Telemachus" episode (*U,* 1:312, 1:638), is now actively modeling his poetic commitment on the figure of the absent mother. At the beginning of the day his divided loyalties had made Stephen an ubiquitous server: a server to Buck Mulligan in the first place, who is in turn a metaphorical servant to Haines, the personification of the British empire; a server, secondly, to the Catholic Church, which operates politically as a servant of the British empire; and a server, thirdly (as a latter day personification of Noah's rebellious son, Ham), to Japhet, Noah's second born, who is in turn a servant (and resident in the tents, according to the Bible) of Noah's first born, Shem.[21] In the "Scylla and Charybdis" episode, Stephen's divided loyalties are reversed, and his servitude turns Augustinian in character, molded upon the model of Augustine's mother, Monica, who becomes after her death the paradigmatic *serva servorum* ("server of servants") of the *Confessions.*[22]

I am going to show presently that there pertains to Stephen's poetic commitment —the way he perceives and apprehends it—a mystic and maieutic potency analogous with the matrix of truthfulness that Augustine identified in his own mother, Monica, and specifically in the Socratic dialogue that Monica exchanged with him at Ostia.[23] (This is the well-known dialogue, discussed in chapter 3, leading both participants to an instant of ecstatic communion with God.) This view is intimated by various pointers strategically distributed throughout the text of *Ulysses.*

By the time the reader reaches the "Scylla and Charybdis" episode, they have begun to suspect that there is a clear-cut Augustinian side to Stephen's artistic personality. At the beginning of the "Proteus" episode, for instance, Stephen's abdication to the succor of his sense of sight and simultaneous decision to "shut [his] eyes and see" (*U,* 3:9), may be taken as a rather deliberate echo of Augustine's transposition of the terminology of sensory perception to the language of theological noesis. Monica and Augustine achieve the instant of their intimacy with God by opening "the lips of [their] hearts to [God's] heavenly stream," thereby apprehending "that life which no eye has seen [and] no ear has heard."[24] Stephen, in turn, needs to close his eyes in order to properly "see" the waves that, "marching" toward him in "acatalectic tetrameter of iambs," bring him the memory of his communion with his mother, "silent with awe and pity" (*U,* 3:21–24, 1:251).[25] Given that Augustine's experience of intimacy with God comes, as mentioned, in the course of a Socratic conversation with Monica, another analogy between Stephen and Augustine may be detected in the recurrent visitations, alternatively inspirational and distressful, that the cadaver of Stephen's mother pays him from early morning to late at night on June 16, 1904.

One of the most explicit instances of Stephen's Augustinianism is encountered, in my opinion, in the "Aeolus" episode, during MacHugh's recitation of John Taylor's speech in defense of the revival of the Gaelic language. The first three lines of the section entitled "From the Fathers" (an obviously playful allusion to the Fathers of the Church) deploy a flash of consciousness, whereby we learn that Stephen has suddenly been hit by the recollection of a passage from Augustine's *Confessions.* This passage is cited *verbatim* in the text: "It was revealed to me that those things are good which yet are corrupted which neither if they were supremely good nor unless they were good could be corrupted" (*U,* 7:841–43; *Confessiones,* Liber VII, cap. 12). This citation indicates not only that Stephen listens to MacHugh's recitation in an Augustinian frame of mind, the frame of mind of the *serva servorum,* capable of Monica's dialogic delivery of truth, but also, still in specific reference to the contents of book 7, chapter 12 of the *Confessions,* that he is, for reasons that will be clarified shortly, reflecting on Augustine's transcendental notion of the *incorruptibilis substantia* (incorruptible substance) of the created universe.[26]

In "Scylla and Charybdis" Stephen expresses his opinions on the modalities of poetic utterance by means of his complex discussion of the relationship between authorship, biography, and creation in Shakespeare. This discussion's Sainte-Beuvean premises on the reciprocal encroaching of artwork and artist's biography were no less intolerable to Joyce, I venture, than they would have been to Marcel Proust, whose views *contre* Sainte-Beuve are deservedly famous.[27] Yet, the premises of this discussion help Stephen draw a rigorous distinction between, on the one hand, his own Augustinian views regarding the poet's craft and, on the other hand, the views expressed by George William Russell (AE) at the beginning of the episode (*U*, 9:46–53). Stephen sets the poetic craft in a dynamic relation of crossbreeding with the phenomenology of time and space, of duration and extension, within which, according to Augustine, human speech makes sense, while Russell attributes to poiesis the neoplatonic task to represent "formless spiritual essences."

In the "Nestor" episode Stephen's understanding of the poet's task was set in a relation of contiguity with Blake's illustration of the mnemonic gift of the muses.

> Fabled by the daughters of memory. And yet it was in some way if not as memory fabled it. A phrase, then, of impatience, thud of Blake's wings of excess. I hear the ruin of all space, shattered glass and toppling masonry, and time one livid final flame. What's left us then? (*U*, 2:7–10)

At the opening of the episode climaxing with Stephen's declaration (to Mr Deasy) that history is a nightmare that he must struggle to awake from (*U*, 2:377), Stephen's stream of consciousness superposes three distinct allusions to Blake's poetry with one another—one of these three allusions, "Fabled by the daughters of memory," is derived from *A Vision of the Last Judgment,* and the other two, conflated in the phrase, "Blake's wings of excess," from two of the proverbs from *The Marriage of Heaven and Hell* (*U*, 2:7–10). Even if Sicari is correct in attributing to Stephen's messianic rebellion against the dictates of human history a "more patient aesthetic" than Blake's ebullient one (the character of this patient aesthetic is discussed in the next chapter),[28] Stephen finds a crucial point of convergence with Blake's vision of history in their shared apocalyptic outlook.

The thematic thrust of his Blakean collage intimates that Stephen is entertaining here a reflection, inspired by Aristotle's *Metaphysics,* on the distinction between historiography (". . . it was in some way . . .") and poetry (". . . if not as memory fabled it . . .").[29] It is noteworthy that this meditation occurs in the middle of a classroom lecture on the figure of Pyrrhus, wherein historical fact and legendary anecdote are liberally mixed, and which leads Stephen to entertain a few thoughtful considerations apropos of Aristotle's views concerning factuality and potentiality, singularity and multiplicity of event (*U*, 2:48–52). Stephen appears to be persuaded that historiography is the reconstruction, via direct and indirect observation, of facts that actually took place (". . . it was in some way . . .") at some specific time and at some specific location. However, this reconstruction is always guided and informed by an act of interpretation (". . . as memory fabled it . . .") on the part of the historian, chronicler, or reporter. Different historians adhere to different interpretive paradigms and promote therefore different interpretive versions of the same fact. In Stephen's reflection, historiography turns out to be therefore the embryonal or proliferative discipline that transforms the singularity of an instant in time—via the examination and elaboration of available memories and testimonials—into a proliferation of alternative versions of it.

The difference between the historian and the poet, as framed in Stephen's meditation, appears to consist in the following consideration: history takes its departure from the germ of a single fact and differentiates it into a proliferation of possible, alternative versions; poetry, on the other hand, takes its departure from a boundless array of possible and mutually exclusive facts and/or ideas, and creates out of them a self-contained, unified, and, above all, *authoritative* version of (the *incorruptibilis substantia* of) truth. In the above passage containing the Blakean allusions to the Muses, for instance, the phrase "shattered glass and toppling masonry" may engender plural, conflicting versions of historical phenomena when referred to a specific event. The reoccurrence of the same phrase in "Proteus," in fact, alludes to a specific act of terrorism in England, namely, the 1867 Fenian attempt to blast a wall of the Clerkenwell prison in London—an act whose concrete results and historical responsibilities remain debatable to this day (*U,* 3:245–49).[30] But when the phrase "shattered glass and toppling masonry" is "fabled by the daughters of memory"—when it is poeticized, that is, and unmoored from factual, predicative singularity—it becomes a generic type of historical disaster, crisis, or revolution that, as Blake himself would put it, "has nothing to do with memory" in the narrow sense of the word;[31] it promotes rather, in the adaptive landscape of our Blakean allusions, an understanding of human history informed by an overarching, apocalyptic teleology.

Stephen's definition of his own poetic persona and artistic tasks is strictly related to this meditations on history, historiography, and poetry. At the time of his mother's death, the nightmare of historical necessity hits his poetic persona in self-gratifying exile with a vengeful "back kick" (*U,* 2:379).

> Her glazing eyes, staring out of death, to shake and bend my soul. On me alone. The ghostcandle to light her agony. Ghostly light on the tortured face. Her hoarse loud breath rattling in horror, while all prayed on their knees . . . (*U,* 1:270–76)

I have shown in *Scriptural Poetics in Joyce's "Finnegans Wake"* that the phrase "On me alone" (*U,* 1:273–74), describing the direction of the moribund's "gaze of accusation, indictment, and punishment,"[32] indicates that Stephen, just returned from Paris, identifies himself in the abject condition of Samuel Taylor Coleridge's "ancient mariner." As the breeze of redemption comes too late for Coleridge's Christic mariner, blowing on the deserted ship after his murder of the albatross brought a pestilence upon all his shipmates ("On me alone it blew"),[33] so Stephen, his lips sealed while "all [present] prayed on their knees" by his mother's deathbed (*U,* 1:275–76), is sentenced to a condition of Christic expiation by his mother's eyes: "On me alone . . . on me to strike me down" (*U,* 1:273–76).[34]

During his mother's wake Stephen recalls the lines from Yeats's poem, "Who Goes with Fergus?" whose song version (from *The Countess Cathleen*) he had sung for her, "holding down the long dark chords" (*U,* 1:250) It is from the "marching" of Yeats's "acatalectic tetrameter of iambs" that he will be inspired, from the "Proteus" episode onward, in his poetic quest—aborted or inachieved by the end of the day—of a poetry of the afterlife (*U*, 3:23–24). It is this inspiration, in turn, triggered by the spectacle of the bosom of the sea, "our great sweet mother" (*U*, 1:80), that twists his existential concerns on June 16, 1904, drastically away from the phenomenal prose of the everyday, turning them into an uninterrupted, impossible dialogue with the cadaver of his mother.

One must never forget that Stephen's (as well as Joyce's) choice to devote his time, talent, and energies to literary endeavors is not the lighthearted decision of a child of privilege, as was the case with many symbolist and modernist poets. His mother's death leaves Stephen's brothers and sisters in dire straits, as made evident in Stephen's encounter with his sister Dilly in "Wandering Rocks" (*U*, 8:800–880). He cannot adhere to the dictum of Villiers de L'Isle-Adam—"As for living our servants can do that for us"—because, contrary to Yeats and AE, both charmed by L'Isle-Adam's words, he has no servants to ask that favor from, nor does his family (*U*, 9:186).[35] Yet, Stephen struggles throughout *Ulysses* to persuade himself that his poetic outcome will eventually obviate the apparent selfishness of his artistic predilection. The escapism of Blake's apocalypticism is an irresistible refuge from such an oppressive sense of historical and material responsibility, but not the solution yet to Stephen's genuine obligation to the memory of his mother. As a poet, Stephen cannot simply exorcize or obliterate his debt to his mother's absence. Only by making his memory of her something "more than a [Blakean] storehouse of images," he could "transform . . . the present," as Sicari phrases it.[36] But this transformation of the present depends on the reversal of the factual responsibilities of his documentable biography onto the extraordinary obligations of negative existence. The lesson of Augustine's phenomenology of subjective memory comes to Stephen's succor now.

Augustinian Poet

Stephen's poetic evolution reaches a moment of culmination relatively early in the "Scylla and Charybdis" episode, precisely at the occurrence of the two following lines:

> I, I and I. I.
> A. E. I. O. U.
> (*U*, 9:212–13)

In order to apprehend the intentional sense of these two lines, one must put them in relationship with line 9:89 ("Hold to the here, through which all future plunges to the past."), with line 9:205 ("I am other I now. Other I got pound."), as well as with the implications of Stephen's previous meditation on book 7, chapter 12 of Augustine's *Confessions*—which chapter, as intimated earlier, deals with the contrast between permanent substance and the impermanent, accidental predicates of earthly things and beings. Arguably, Stephen's quadruple repetition of the "I" at 9:212

portends a pause of Augustinian meditation. In order to appreciate not only the Augustinian but also the naturalistic, historicospecific meaning subtending simultaneously this meditation of Stephen's, we will have to relate it also to the two lines immediately preceding it: "I that sinned and prayed and fasted. A child Conmee saved from pandies" (*U,* 9:210–11).

Having mapped this adaptive landscape of Stephen's interdependent pronouncements, I maintain that the first "I" in the quadruple repetition of the first-person grammatical subject at line 212 ("I, I and I. I") may be taken to indicate the intentional subject in the present time. As it conflates onto an "other I" (*U,* 9:205) the predicates, recollected from a historically past time, of its own selfhood or persona, this intentional subject projects the predicative expectations regarding its own selfhood or persona onto a future, third "I." These three individual I's (past, present, and future), pertaining to the same agent and sharing the (different, evolving) attributes of temporal predicates, get lastly transducted onto the perpetual and incorruptible substance of the "I" kept apart from them by a full stop. This fourth "I" may be taken to figure the praeterhistorical, disembodied and *incorruptibilis* substance holding together the accidental, temporal predicates of these three I's, that is, respectively, the subject's *memoria* of its own past condition, the subject's *contuitus* or instantaneous awareness of its own present condition, and the subject's *expectatio* of its own future condition.[37] This fourth "I" stands for the substantial conglomeration of the three other I's, in sum.

Stephen is probably thinking, at this juncture, of a passage from book 10 of the *Confessions,* where Augustine assesses the mnemonic potency of human interiority by means of a triadic or trinitarian formulation of the self: Ego *interior cognovi haec,* ego, ego *animus per sensum corporis mei.*[38] (I as inner man knew this, I, I as soul knew this by means of my bodily senses.) The present self-awareness of the Augustinian subject is in the *esse* (being) of *contuitus;* its past self-awareness is in the *nosse* (knowledge) of *memoria;* its purposeful self-awareness is in the *velle* (volition) of *expectatio.*[39]

In naturalistic, historicospecific terms, this juncture in *Ulysses* depicts the scene of Stephen remembering the misadventure of his younger self from *A Portrait of the Artist as a Young Man,* "saved from pandies" by Father Conmee. This was the self of Stephen's "that" sinned and prayed and fasted; Stephen's preference for the impersonal pronoun "that," instead of the personal pronoun "who," indicates that he is inclined to depersonalize or objectify his own boyish selfhood, reducing it to an agglomeration of accidental predicates from the past. In naturalistic, historicospecific terms, again, the two phrases "I am other I now. Other I got pound" may be related to Stephen's owing money to AE. But even in this case, there is a more substantially comprehensive meaning to the passage.

In phenomenological terms, the repetition of the first three grammatical subjects, "I, I and I," may be taken to allude to Stephen's previous considerations about Blake's "daughters of memory" (*U,* 2:7), insofar as the transition from one temporal "I" to the next is informed by remembrance and temporal progression; the addition of a fourth "I," separated from the previous three by a sign of full stop, may be taken to allude, in turn, to the interconnection posited by Augustine between *corruptibilis* and *incorruptibilis substantia* (corruptible, and incorruptible substance), the former relating, in the specificity of this Joycean intertext, to the Aristotelian notions of recollection (in time) and multiplicity (in space), the latter to the Aristotelian notions of imperishable potentiality and singularity (*U,* 2:48–52).

Immediately before Stephen's quadruple repetition of the "I" takes place, his stream of consciousness reinforces the allusion to analogous concerns by recurring to Aristotelian jargon: "But I, entelechy, form of forms, am I by memory because under everchanging forms" (*U,* 9:208–9). In this adaptive landscape of interconnected passages, the same criterion applied by Stephen in the "Nestor" episode to the relationship linking punctual history to historiography, as well as multiplicity to singularity, is now applied to the distinction and reciprocal encroaching of body and mind; it sets molecular transience on the one hand ("Molecules all change") and mnemonic reconstitution on the other ("I am other I now") in a reciprocal rapport of cross-breeding with, respectively, substantial permanence and incorruptibility on the one hand, and mnemonic potency on the other (*U,* 9:205).

To give full articulation to Stephen's intentional concerns about his own poetic vocation, one must have recourse again to St. Augustine, specifically to the passage from *De immortalitate animae* whose paraphrase juts out in clear relief from the adaptive landscape of Stephen's interdependent pronouncements:

> For what is done needs expectation, that it may be done, and memory, that it may be understood as much as possible. And expectation is of future things, and memory is of things past. But the intention to act is of the present, through which the future flows into the past.[40]

Stephen's intersecting pronouncements reflect the influence of this Augustinian view about time and intentionality. Reminiscence (of the past) out of memory, understanding (of the present) out of intellect, foresight (of the future) out of the will-to-act (all categories that fall under the Augustinian rubric of self-knowledge)[41] have become the foci of Stephen's poetic mission. "The intention to act is of the present, through which the future flows into the past," writes Augustine. Stephen faithfully echoes this statement at 9:89 with the words: "Hold to the now, the here, through which all future plunges to the past."

We are facing in Stephen a youth who is resentful of the incomprehension bestowed on him by everybody he meets or engages in conversation with, and is unwilling as well to sacrifice his artistic vocation to his and his family's subsistence. He assumes on the one hand a self-effacing, kenotic, servile attitude, modeled on a submissive dialogue with the memory of his absent mother, while on the other hand invests himself with the magnificent task of a repetition of the past, a repetition bound to bring about a future renovation—in a priestly *anamnesis,* or celebration of sorts, that, in these specifically thematic circumstances, is aimed at an ambitious rehabilitation of the Irish national and artistic pride. The "priest of eternal imagination" from *A Portrait of the Artist as a Young Man* (221) has grasped, it seems, the Augustinian character of his artistic identity:

> In the intense instant of imagination, . . . that which I was is that which I am and that which in possibility I may come to be. So in the future, the sister of the past, I may see myself as I sit here now but by reflection from that which then I shall be. (*U*, 9:381–85)

Stephen's meditations have transformed phenomenal time into an Augustinian, triadic personification—past, present, future—of Blake's "daughters of memory." And this triad, which acts as "the source of permanence that [Augustine knew] to exist apart from the transitory constituents of our understanding" of the self,[42] finds in turn existential validation in the *convitato di pietra* represented by Stephen's mother. To Stephen's self-instantiating vocation as a poet, his mother's proximity has never been as punctually intense as it is now that her presence eludes all temporal dimensions.

It remains for Stephen to define the linguistic apparatus that should enable him to instantiate this artistic identity.

Dantesque Poet

The cryptic sequence of vowels, "A. E. I. O. U." from "Scylla and Charybdis" is often attributed the naturalistic and historicospecific meaning based on the formulaic translation of the segment "I. O. U." into the phrase "I owe you"; this line of interpretation may find causal validation in the fact that the sequence of vowels appears shortly after Stephen remembers his conversation about money with Mr Deasy (*U*, 9:202). In this perspective, the first two vowels in the sequence, "A. E." would be taken to suggest that Stephen is reflecting on his "one guinea" debt to George William Russells (*U*, 2:257); as I mentioned earlier, the latter character, known as AE in theosophical circles, takes part in the conversation of the "Scylla and Charybdis" episode at the National Library. The "other I [who] got [a] pound" from AE (Stephen's memory is not too precise regarding the exact amount of his own debt) would therefore be a separate incarnation of Stephen's—of the four I's from the quadruple repetition discussed above, this money-borrowing "I" would correspond to the specific self that Stephen's memory presently recollects from the past. This interpretation is only relevant to the present discussion insofar as it provides it with a naturalistic substratum. However, the Dantesque and Augustinian dimension of the five-vowel sequence "A. E. I. O. U." unveils a more significant aspect of Stephen's self-instantiation as a poet. Let us discuss the details and the premises of this aspect.

Jean-Michel Rabaté and Lucia Boldrini have both remarked that the sequence "A. E. I. O. U." is a citation from Dante's *Convivio*.[43] It is in the *Convivio* that Dante describes the poetics of the *aueio* or "musaic"[44] word-binder, which is the kind of poet Dante identified himself with at the time of his composition of the *Vita Nuova*. With the abandonment of the *Vita Nuova,* Dante chose to reject this kind of poetic craft because in his view it deployed a lesser authority with respect to the genuine and "authentic"[45] authority of the philosophical thinker.[46] The latter is an *auctor,* whose writings "augment" (*augeo*) the reach of our knowledge of truth, while the poetic author is an *autor,* whose writings constitute a mere fluid "binding" (*aueio*) of words and typographic characters. According to Dante, the verb *aueio* itself is emblematic of the poet's binding of letters, since in it each single vowel may be plastically reshaped into another, the first into the second, the second into the third, etc.,[47] the result of this process constituting the sequence: "A, E, I, O, U"—not a word anymore (since the word Dante started from was composed by a different sequence of vowels, i.e., a, u, e, i, o), but the "image of a figure, . . . the figure of a bind" —the very sequence (a, e, i, o, u) that emerges, as an evident and deliberate allusion, from Stephen's stream of consciousness in "Scylla and Charybdis" (*U,* 9:213).

Dante concludes thus:

> And since the term *autor* [poetic author] derives from this verb, *aueio,* whose concatenation of letters images the figure of linguistic concatenation, [*autor*] is a term to be applied especially to those poets who, with musaic art [i.e., with the help of the Muses], bind their words to one another.

Notwithstanding its figurative factitiousness, not to mention its arbitrary etymology, Dante's faith in the ultimate Christian truth of this linguistic-typographic argument will turn out to be contagious for subsequent students of the mnemonic or musaic arts. In his 1322 treatise, *Forma Praedicandi,* for instance, Robert of Basevorn will recur to the sequence a, e, i, o, u as a mnemonic aid in the composition and delivery of sermons whose arguments lend themselves to five subdivisions, as in the case of the Passion according to Matthew 27—as many subdivisions, that is, as the number of vowels in the alphabet and the number of Christ's wounds.[48]

Dante's argument concerning the poet's work of letter concatenation is evidently informed by Augustine's approach to time and intentionality. Implicit to Dante's argument is the Augustinian tenet, discussed previously, that a relation of analogy ties human language to God's immutable and adimensional Word—the former functions, making meaning and recording facts, in time and space, but receives its condition of possibility from the immutability of the latter. In order to describe his and Monica's return to the imprecision and limited mnemonic range of human conversation after the instant of their silent, ecstatic intimacy with God, Augustine writes in book 9 of the *Confessions: Et remeavimus ad strepitum oris nostri, ubi verbum et incipitur et finitur.*[49] Each human word begins and ends in the noise (*strepitum*) of its own dissipation, while God's Word, *permanens verbum,* never grows old because, being permanent, is unaffected by temporality and impervious to human forgetfulness, and makes furthermore all things, as well as all of human speech, new and significant (*innovanti omnia*).[50]

In light of Augustine's treatment of the faculty of memory, both in the passage cited earlier from *De immortalitate animae,* in book 10 of the *Confessions,* and in the other relevant passages mentioned in chapters 1 and 2, this statement from book 9 of the *Confessions* signifies the mortality of human language. Each word, and to an even greater extent each single letter of the alphabet, is no earlier born in time and space, as sound or sign, than it dies away, to be resurrected or retrieved in the memory of the speaker, or listener, or reader, when the next word or letter follows it, both the word and the letter needing to be compounded in turn, to make meaning, with the words and letters preceding and following them.[51] But human memory is not self-sufficient in the performance of its assigned task.

Granted the reciprocal crossbreeding, at this juncture in Joyce's text, of Augustine's linguistics of noise and forgetfulness with the linguistics of plastic binding from Dante's *Convivio,* one might say that each individually scripted letter is nothing but a special liquid reshaping of the same basic typographic materials shared by all other letters of the alphabet. These are the "liquid letters of speech" that Stephen has inherited from the *Vita Nuova.* The signifying potency of each individual letter is not intrinsic to the letter itself but the result, as Stephen himself had put it in *A Portrait of the Artist as a Young Man,* of the "flow[ing] forth over [our] brain" of a mnemonic process of prospection and retrospection (*P,* 223). Unfortunately for the success of his journey unto the death of his absent mother, Stephen inherits from his two predecessors, Augustine and Dante, a linguistic apparatus whose condition of possibility is not found in the autonoesis of human memory but in the noesis authorized by the divine *Verbum.* Augustine's failure to deploy the existentialist revolution that, as discussed in chapter 2, was potentially intrinsic to his understanding of memory and mental words displays here some of its long-lasting effects.

Abortive Poet

Mary Reynolds attributes to the Joyce of *Finnegans Wake* the adoption of both the Dantesque principle whereby "ideas survive . . . because of [the] verbal art," and the Viconian principle (which, she claims, Vico learned from Dante) that "through the study of language . . . we recover a past reality."[52] The present discussion indicates that one does not have to wait for *Finnegans Wake* to find traces of this specific, Dantesque influence. An adoption of Dante's linguistic principles, together with their pertinent, Augustinian as it is, understanding of human history as a phenomenology of temporality, is already at play in the maturation and articulation of Stephen's poetic vocation. The Christic poet of the "Parable of the Plums" from the "Aeolus" episode, protagonist of a Luciferan *non-serviam* since the days of his short-lived exile in Paris, whose rebellious authority none of the men present in the offices of the *Freeman's Journal* is willing to acknowledge or recognize and whom none of the intellectuals gathered at the National Library a couple of hours later lends a benevolent ear to,[53] confirms in "Scylla and Charybdis" his vocation for the Dantesque (and, not to be forgotten, Ulyssean) self-imposed exile of the true seeker of *virtude e canoscenza* (*Inferno,* 26:120); and assigns himself, in so doing, the special authority of Dante's *autor* or *aueio,* whose diction contains *in potentia* the entire expressive apparatus of the divine *Verbum* itself.

After the evangelical stage of his "Parable of the Plums," after the various stages of his servile (albeit ironic) attitude toward Buck, toward Haines, toward the Roman Church, toward the British Empire, Stephen has reached—or rather, is adjudicating himself—the Augustinian identity of the authoritative and maieutic *serva servorum* who knows how to speak *ore cordis,* with the truthful "lips of the heart."[54] However capable of boundless loquacity, the lips of Stephen's heart remain sealed when it comes to uttering poetic verse, though. His poetic vocation is not displayed by means of any concrete instantiation on June 16, 1904, so that the assessment of his artistic commitment is left to the inferential analysis of intentional consciousness and literary influence, as we shall see in the next chapter. It is only from Stephen's eloquent yet cryptic pronouncements that one may somewhat infer the *probable* thrust of the poetry that he refuses or is unable to write.

As we have seen, Stephen has undertaken the quest of a poetic self-justification from the dead. However, his plebeian origins impose on his artistic vocation a punishing set of practical considerations. To Stephen (and to no lesser extent to Joyce himself), writing entails the neglect of his practical obligations toward his dear ones. How should he redeem himself from the rule of everyday existence and economic constraint? The poetics of self-forgetfulness—which Derrida attributes to the apophatic gestures of another plebeian poet, Stéphane Mallarmé,[55] and which characterizes as well Stephen's Christic stance as a poet—is not sufficient to achieve this mundane sort of redemption. Only the radical choice of negative existence, which entails a groundbreaking reversal in one's conception of human biography and individual history, would provide a viable solution to Stephen's predicament. But this choice cannot find its proper ground of validation in the language of either common and ordinary experience or of transcendental signification—neither language is equal to the task of instantiating the impossible condition of negative existence.

As the Joyce of *Finnegans Wake* is aware, and as Augustine failed to grasp fully in his probing of the "hidden crevices" (*in cavis abditioribus*) of human memory,[56] it is in the recesses of the mind, rather than in the dictates of documentable history or transcendental metaphysics, that one finds the vestigial sediments that unhinge the apophatic experience from the tyranny of ordinary experience, of predicative/denotative/referential expression, and from the divine *Verbum* as paradigmatic meaning-maker as well.

When Joyce declared to Paolo Cuzzi that Freud had been anticipated by Vico,[57] he had probably in mind not so much the *Scienza nuova*'s contribution to the social history of language as the Viconian intimation that there pertains to linguistic self-expression an autonoetic dimension that exceeds the codified norms of denotative and predicative signification. The mnemonic activation of vestigial sediments permits the linguistic instantiation and/or recognition of that which is historically and referentially, predicatively and denotatively, unrecognizable. This phenomenon, in turn, makes superfluous and anachronistic the metaphysical presumption that an original *Verbum* constitutes the foundations of all human *verba*. Dante's "liquid letters of speech" anticipate Vico's vestigial linguistics, since all the alphabetic characters and all the words of the language are vestigially contained in the fluid metamorphoses of the elementary signs of writing adopted in the *Vita Nuova*. Documentable history and received tradition are only secondary determinants in the deployment of

human writing's expressive potential. Of primary importance is the inherent rec-
ognizability of each single letter, each letter consisting of an assemblage of primitive marks that are congenitally familiar to the human mind. Yet, the linguistic valence
of these "liquid letters of speech," which are instrumental to Stephen's poetic
efforts, is deplorably perceived by both Dante and Stephen as ultimately authorized
by the divine *Verbum,* rather than by the autonoetic endowment that the vestigial
theory attributes to our discursive faculty.

Stephen is unable to make this radical leap in the direction of a nonmetaphysical language truly emancipated from the ordinary and common experience of his
historical condition. In the next chapter we shall see how his rebellion against the
constraints of the historical condition, lacking an adequately expressive outlet, inachieved at the level of poetic utterance, depletes itself in an array of abortive insights
into the irrepressible fecundity of death. Stephen's scrupulous reticence-in-progress
is his most genuine claim to poetic genius.

STEPHEN DEDALUS'S
POETRY OF THE AFTERLIFE

On swift sail flaming
From storm and south
He comes, pale vampire,
Mouth to my mouth.

Ulysses, 7:522–25

The Sepulchral Muse

The inspiration to write a new poem, the so-called "Vampire Poem," comes to Stephen Dedalus around midday on June 16, 1904, while "noon slumbers" (*U,* 3:216) and he takes a stroll on the Sandymount Strand (*U,* 3:397–402). After his conversation with Mr Deasy, which the school principal turned into a praise of moral rectitude (*vias rectas*) and historical realism, Stephen has withdrawn to the beach and communed with the maternal sea,[1] in search of means of escape from the nightmare of history. If to Stephen the love of/for his absent mother (*amor matris*) is "the only true thing in life" (*U,* 9:839–43), then "Deasy's business" was, as John Gordon puts it, "to kill it."[2]

Stephen's mother has been dead for almost a year. The "pain" that has "fretted his heart" at each visitation of her "mute, reproachful" ghost "is far" while Stephen strolls on the beach (*U,* 1:102–10, 3:444). The "faunal noon" of the surrounding "burning scene" gives him the Mallarmean aftertaste of his Parisian days. How can Stephen evade the nightmare of personal history? Mr Deasy's "banknotes" are in his pocket (*U,* 3:404). Does not his debt to his mother's memory consist primarily of the obligation to support his brothers and sisters? Should he extinguish it with hard cash? He fears that such practical considerations are self-defeating. Just as he "could not save [his mother]" from "bitter death," so a few hours later, on Bedford row, he will anticipate that Dilly, one of his sisters, would "drown [him] with her," if he ever attempted to save her from indigence (*U,* 3:330, 10:875–77).

The sun is "southing" and Stephen scans "the shore south" (*U,* 3:270, 3:442), nostalgic for the meridional escapism encouraged by the thirty-four-year-old author of *L'après-midi d'un faune*. He has long been acquainted with this special Mallarmean vein,[3] which emancipates the poet from his haunting phantasms simply by journeying closer to the tropical oceans, where even birds are "drunk" (*ivres*) with irresponsibility.[4] In "the tawny hour," Mallarmé's Faun "succumb[s] / to the proud silence of midday," and, "wide-mouthed to the wine-fostering sun," enacts the poetic gesture of giving up writing.[5] Overpowered by his own "sexual impregnation,"[6] Mallarmé's Faun "has nothing left to say,"[7] as its creator himself indulges, if only for a brief interval, in the summery escape of a "dream of happiness."[8]

A reformed escapist, a prodigal son come back home on the occasion of his mother's funeral, Stephen may still cherish the sweet memory of his short-lived adhesion to this Dionysian philosophy; it led him to the French "home of furlough" for Irish drifters and "forgotten" patriots (*U,* 3:163, 3:263). But this self-enamored, limiting hedonism is not for Stephen any more. As we shall see, he admires also a different Mallarmé, a poet as young as himself, the author of "Gift of the Poem" (*Don du poème*); at twenty-three Mallarmé was a struggling poet who, made sterile by family obligations and by his own abortive writing, envisaging himself as "an old man, finished,"[9] chose to contract rather than extinguish a debt with motherhood.

Stephen's homecoming as the prodigal son was not one of unconditional, Bible-like rejoicing. Far from being "welcome as the flowers in May" (*U,* 3:440–41),[10] he had to endure his mother's dying stare, meant "to strike [him] down." He now considers that the tidal life of the "winedark sea" facing the strand is "moondrawn," like the cycle of menstrual fertility, yet it appears to be "westering . . . in her wake," as though patterned upon his mother's all-too-prolific, westward journey onto the land of the dead (*U,* 3:393). He follows in his mother's moondrawn footsteps—"bridebed, childbed, bed of death" (*U,* 3:396)—and soon finds himself on Blake's familiar, apocalyptic territory.

David Hayman remarks in *Joyce and Mallarmé* that symbolistic and Blakean poetry had an analogously performative effect on Stephen's previous literary incarnation, as the protagonist of *Stephen Hero.* In the words of the narrator of *Stephen Hero:* "He read Blake and Rimbaud on the values of letters and even permuted and combined the five vowels to construct cries for primitive emotions."[11] Stephen, the musaic *aueio,* or word-binder, performs now one such set of permutations and combinations: "His lips lipped and mouthed fleshless lips of air: mouth to her moomb. Oomb, allwombing tomb. His mouth moulded issuing breath, unspeeched: ooee-hah . . . " (*U,* 3:401–3). The result of this freewheeling scansion, centered on the amalgamation of moon, womb, and tomb, is a crossbreeding of Mallarmean and Blakean associations.

Stuart Gilbert was the first to point out the "Blakean associations" implicit in this passage, derived, according to him, from Blake's *The Gates of Paradise.*[12]

> The Door of Death I open found
> And the Worm Weaving in the Ground:
> Thou'rt my Mother from the Womb,
> Wife, Sister, Daughter, to the Tomb,

> Weaving to dreams the sexual strife
> And weeping over the Web of Life.[13]

The moon-tomb-womb amalgam suggests that Stephen may be also thinking of two verses from Blake's "The Everlasting Gospel," whose implications fit equally well with Stephen's strive to achieve genuine poetic inspiration in *Ulysses:*[14] "[The God of this World] took on Sin in the Virgin's Womb, / And put it off on the Cross and Tomb. . . ." I have argued the Christological implications of this intertext in *Pruning the Genealogical Tree.*[15] If one recalls the Christic core of Stephen's poetic self, the Blakean overtones of his moon-tomb-womb amalgam entail four significant analogies: the analogy between the debt that Stephen contracted at birth with the maternal womb and Christ's surrender to sin and mortality in the Virgin's womb; the analogy between the life-giving womb of Stephen's mother, which figures as the indispensable and unexperienceable origin (*arche*) leading to her son's indispensable and unexperienceable destination (*telos*) in death, and Christ's tomb, which figures as an indispensable consequence of God's incarnation; the analogy between the womb of virginal conception and the praeternatural fecundity of poetic inspiration; and the analogy, discordant with the previous one, between the womb of seminal conception and the finitude of poetic utterance. Together with these four analogies, grafted on the dialectical interplay between natural and supernatural conception, one must factor in an essentially sociohistorical discrepancy, crucial to Stephen's personal history, namely, the discrepancy between the generative potency of maternal fecundity and its mortification in clandestine abortion. To a young twentieth-century Irishman, Blake's image of woman's lifetime procession—". . . Mother from the Womb, / Wife, Sister, Daughter, to the Tomb . . . "—was bound to evoke the clandestine practice familiar to a large number of Catholic women in Dublin.

Literary Influences

The quadruple analogy sketched above, modeled on the convergence of deity and putrefaction, is evidently informed by an Augustinian scheme of the poetic self. Stephen's physical body, conceived in the maternal uterus, would be sustained in its artistic inspiration by an interiority engendered within a spiritual matrix, and capable of bridging the separation of factual experience from spiritual expression, of the "noise of common speech," delivered in volatile syllables (*syllabas . . . transvolare*), from the divine *Verbum* as the transcendental signifier, whose instantaneous permanence "never passes away" (*non discedit*).[16]

Stephen's "fleshless lips of air, . . . unspeeched" are still an echo of the Faun's "wide-mouthed," midday silence in *L'après-midi d'un faune*. In order to instantiate his own poetic self in the flesh and blood of speech, exorcising thereby the silence—the *n'avoir-rien-à-dire*—of Mallarmean escapism, Stephen must turn his mouth into a womb. He must glue his "mouth to her moomb," surrendering thereby to the gravitational pull of the moon, to the cycle of uterine fertility, to the sepulchral destiny of all mortal creatures conceived of genital impregnation. Even if poetic inspiration may come and subsist in the praeternatural silence of a virginal conception, the gesture of poetic utterance entails the inception and subsequent delivery of speech, with its Augustinian lapse into the common speech of maternal finitude, entombment, and decomposition.

Earlier in the morning, standing on the roof of the Martello Tower, Stephen had heard the "wavewhite wedded words shimmer . . . on the dim tide" and scan the "twining stresses" of a Pre-Raphaelite song by Yeats, "Who Goes with Fergus?" Shortly before her death, Stephen's mother had listened to him sing this song for her, "crying in her wretched bed," moved by Yeats' image of "love's bitter mystery." Hearing "[a] hand plucking the harpstrings, merging their twining chords" at the iambic pace of Yeats's "lightshod hurrying feet," Stephen sensed the presence of Yeats's muse on the tower by his side (*U,* 1:239–53). Later, on the strand, the tide's "rhythm begins" again in his ears; the "acatalectic tetrameter of [Yeats's] iambs march . . . " (*U,* 3:23–24) at the poetic cadence of the tidal life of the sea. Yeats's muse, by his side again, clings to Stephen's soul like "a woman to her lover clinging, the more the more" (*U,* 3:421–23). Her maidenly feet, hurryingly spurning the foamy "mirror of water" (*U,* 3:344), are a metric measure, too, an allusion to "the measure of her flying feet" from the final poem of Yeats's *The Rose* (1893), which "made Ireland's heart begin to beat."[17]

As Stephen listens to this music, the trope of the hand plucking the harpstrings makes of Yeats's muse the twin sister of Dante's poetic inspiration, who "rises" as well (*surga* [*Purgatorio,* 1:9]) to the task of plucking the chords of her lyre,[18] and who, having sung of love's conspiracy against the sterility of death,[19] takes her leave as well, in each of the three canticles of the *Commedia,* at the appearance of the "stars" —this coincident trope being intimated by the unmistakable signifier adopted by Yeats at the closure of "Who Goes with Fergus?": "For Fergus rules . . . / . . . all dishevelled wandering stars"[20] (*Inferno,* 34:139; *Purgatorio,* 33:145; *Paradiso,* 33:145). The evidence that Dante affects Stephen's poetic inspiration on the beach emerges with greater clarity an hour later, in the offices of the *Freeman's Journal;* having recalled the verses he scribbled on the beach, Stephen probes at this juncture the alternative of various rhyming possibilities ("mouth, south . . . pout, out, shout, drouth" [*U,* 7:713–14]), which are especially inspired by three rhymes from Francesca's speech in the *Inferno* (*U,* 7:717–19).

> . . . . *la tua pace* (*Inferno,* 5:92)
> . . . . *che parlar ti piace* (*Inferno,* 5:94)
> *Mentre che il vento, come fa, si tace.* (*Inferno,* 5:96)

Robert Adams Day suggests that Stephen is dissatisfied with the gloomy, "leaden-footed" tone or pace of his quatrain. He will look for experimental relief from his verses' heavy foot by inviting Yeats's muse to pluck the strings of Mallarmé's harpsichord (*clavecin*), introducing thereby, as I shall discuss at greater length in the subsection titled "The Muse from the Crypt," a further crossbreeding branch to the lineage of his immaculate and nurtural muse.

Mary Kinzie maintains that Yeats learned how to move "among the shades in broad day" from Dante, whose negative mode of being-in-the-world "saturates Yeats's thinking and development."[21] Yeats's praise of Dante's "spectral image"—the poetic/biographic construct whereby the Florentine poet instantiates himself as a radically distinct being from "the man [whom] Lapo and Guido knew"—bespeaks Yeats's own propensity toward a necropolitan manner of negative existence, antithetical with conventional biography and factual experience.[22] Later at night, in a room of the National Maternity Hospital, it will emerge that Stephen, himself an eager guest of the abode of the dead ("Houses of decay" [*U*, 3:105, 3:319]),[23] himself a former if caustic devotee of Dante's "refrigerating apparatus" (*P*, 252), holds a similar view concerning Dante's influence on Yeats—which explains the crossbreeding of these two poets' otherworldly vision, complementing the Mallarmean and Blakean motifs in Stephens' inspiration on the Sandymount Strand.

Jennifer Margaret Fraser remarks that Stephen's stupefied words in the "Oxen of the Sun" episode, where he talks of "desire's wind blast[ing] the thorntree" till it becomes "a rose upon the rood of time" (*U*, 14:290–92), reveal his awareness of Yeats and Dante's intertextual contamination of influence.[24] The "rose upon the rood of time" represents the well-known poetic muse from Yeats's *The Rose,* the "measure of [whose] flying feet"—a metric paradigm—Stephen scanned in the morning. Yeats's rose represents in turn Dante's ultimate source of poetic inspiration, namely the Virgin Mary, "the rose in which the divine word / made itself flesh,"[25] whom St. Thomas allegorizes in Canto 13 of the *Paradiso* as the rose of salvation that/who supersedes Eve, the thorn of perdition.[26] As we saw in chapter 4, the inspirational potency of this muse pertains to Dante's negative poetics of nonreferentiality; it reflects God's light with such vividness that the poet may mistake this light for her own independent emanation (*Paradiso*, 30:100–114). Stephen seems confident that his "leadenfooted" rhyme in the "Vampire Poem"—"mouth south"—will be properly enlivened once bathed "underdarkneath the night" of this muse, where the tomb of mortal finitude rhymes with the womb of virginal procreation. We are back to Blake's "Virgin's Womb." We are back, more specifically, to the virgin-mother figure from the Catholic tradition.

In his appropriation of the pagan trope of musaic inspiration, Dante came gradually to identify the guidance supplied him by poetic inspiration with the guidance offered to his troubled soul by the Virgin Mary. His muse in the *Vita Nuova* was Beatrice, the pure disincarnate girl he passionately loved in Florence. His muse in the *Convivio* was the philosophical persona of Mary, the "mother of everything" (*di tutto madre*), immaculately conceived in order to show him the way to salvation via intellectual noesis (*per voi drizzare, in vostra similitudine venne a voi*) (treatise 3, 15, lines 15–18). His muse in the *Commedia* is again the Virgin Mary, personifying this time the Augustinian reconciliation of intellect and desire,[27] who sends Beatrice as her paradisiac envoy to Dante. Beatrice's mission in the *Commedia* is to nurture the instantiation of Dante's impossibly necropolitan biography, providing praeterhistorical justification, in the process, to Dante's political rectitude. Grafted on the gallantry of Dante's early adherence to the *dolce stil novo,* his firm devotion to the principles of the Catholic faith turns his poetic muse into the doctrinal paradox of a fecund and attractive virgin, the precursor of innumerable romantic, symbolistic, Pre-Raphaelite, and decadent identifications of maidenhood and maternal nurture.

Stephen encountered one such identification in his early exposure to Yeats's aesthetic and political agenda.[28] The discordant pair of maidenhood and maternity reflects in Yeats's poetry the intersection and reciprocal crossbreeding of nature and culture, of history and transcendence, and of poetry and politics.[29] "A metaphor on which Yeats draws heavily [since] his early work,"[30] Mother Ireland is perennially and praeternaturally young, as he defines her in "Into the Twilight."[31] The landscape of human and social desolation surrounding her children and the urgency to console them "for the colonial calamities"[32] turn her into this impossible, maidenly mother figure—a Sphinx continuously revitalized by the life-draining effects of gestation, procreation, and nurture. The natural force of her prolific youth is empowering to the poet's creative energies, which are made as insatiable as a nursling by her embrace. At the same time, the physiological work of her nurturance is, paradoxically, one of cultural transmission. It is her task to feed a tradition and a historical conscience to her child, which she does by disclosing not only the symbolic order of the status quo, according to the accusation leveled at the Catholic iconology of the virgin-mother by Julia Kristeva and Nina Auerbach,[33] but also the urgency for the subversion of that same symbolic order. As Jennifer Fraser puts it in the context of an analogous discussion, the poet "learns from the mother herself how to transgress and thereby escape her."[34]

Yeats's virgin-mother is a captive of the very order that her child needs to subvert on her behalf and on behalf of his own survival. This captivity is contagious to the participant in the culture that constructs and contains the oppressed figure of Mother Ireland; from a sociopolitical standpoint, the participant is "implicated," Diane Stubbings remarks, "in the consequences of [her] nurturance."[35] A responsible citizen and public man,[36] the poet becomes the mouthpiece of this contradictory mother figure. When facing the permanence of his country's historical tragedy, he claims for the victims the ineffable dignity of a rectitude indifferent to the vindication of social justice.

> Too long a sacrifice
> Can make a stone of the heart.
> O when may it suffice?
> That is Heaven's part, our part
> To murmur name upon name,
> *As a mother names her child*
> When sleep has come
> On limbs that had run wild.[37]

In *Ulysses,* Stephen's muse of poetic inspiration is ambivalent. She is Luke's erotically reticent handmaid of the Lord,[38] the sensuous, "whiteheaped corn" (Song of Songs

7:3) of her "belly without blemish" representing the fecund condition of immaculate conception. Her physical body carries the legacy of Eve's "womb of sin," though, her "naked wheatbellied sin" evoking the biblical curse of the moon-driven, periodic alternation of sterility and fertility (*U,* 3:43–45, 9:541).

As Stephen's figure of musaic inspiration, however, the virgin-mother is stripped of the political attributes that are essential to both Yeats and Dante's poetic mission. To Stephen the virgin-mother is manifest in the Madonna, the Church's icon of mass manipulation, "which the cunning Italian intellect flung to the mob of Europe" (*U,* 9:839–40). From a political viewpoint, the Madonna contributes to the transmission and perpetuation of the very patriarchal tradition that constructed and codified her cult. Her doctrinal function consists of keeping a self-engendered deity uncontaminated by woman's flesh and by human history—a function ultimately mortifying and demeaning to womanhood. Her multiple affinities with the Marian cult deprive the virgin-mother muse that inspires Stephen as a poet of the capacity for political inspiration that is intrinsic to Yeats and Dante's art.

These considerations explain to a considerable extent Stephen's secular dilemma. His poetry cannot negotiate at once Yeats's and Dante's two diametrical predispositions, namely, that of negative existence and that of positive, civic engagement. If Stephen is to write poetry at all, if he is to extinguish his debt to his mother in the soft cash of poetry writing, he cannot rely on any positive effect—be it political liberation or financial emancipation—being exercised by his poetry on the lives of his dear ones. The muse of inspiration that Stephen adopts from the coordinated influence of Dante, Blake, Yeats, and, as we shall see, Mallarmé, is strikingly ineffective when it comes to coping with day-to-day experience.

In twisting Stephen's poetic gift abruptly away from the responsibility of domestic and historical obligations, however, the virgin-mother's impregnation of Stephen's imagination still holds the power to translate his inspiration into the language of irreducible finitude; subsequent to her receiving the Holy Spirit's gift at the Annunciation scene,[39] the Virgin's gift to the Word itself consisted after all of a sepulchral destiny of irreducible finitude. The Blakean associations of the moon-tomb-womb amalgam find in fact a relevant complement in the concurrence, remarked by Diane Stubbings, "of 'womb' and 'tomb' across a number of Yeats's works."[40]

Death and the Maiden

Stephen sits down on a rock, scribbles four lines of verse on a scrap of paper, and crams them "into a pocket" (*U,* 3:406–7, 3:437–38). In the "Aeolus" episode his interior monologue will eventually reveal the text of this quatrain, which is cited as the epigraph to the present chapter. It reads like a sepulchral song of death by consumption. Stephen's composition is a pastiche[41] from the last stanza of Douglas Hyde's translation of the song "My Grief on the Sea,"[42] included in Hyde's collection of popular songs, *The Love Songs of Connacht.* The two complementary crossbreedings of Mallarmé and Blake's influence on the one hand, and of Yeats and Dante's influence on the other find a host of reciprocal insemination in Hyde's quatrain.[43]

The sepulchral aspects intrinsic to the composition of Stephen's "Vampire Poem" surface in the incoherent form of an interior monologue in the "Proteus" episode. These aspects are by far more relevant than the quatrain scribbled on the Strand, when it comes to appreciating Stephen's thematic and existential concerns on the Sandymount Strand.

> ...Across the sands of all the world, followed by the sun's flaming sword, to the west trekking to evening lands. She trudges, schlepps, trains, drags, trascines her load. A tide westering, moondrawn, in her wake. Tides, myriadislanded, within her, blood not mine, *oinopa ponton,* a winedark sea. Behold the handmaid of the moon. In sleep the wet sign calls her hour, bids her rise. Bridebed, childbed, bed of death, ghostcandled. *Omnis caro ad te veniet.* He comes, pale vampire, through storm his eyes, his bat sails bloodying the sea, mouth to her mouth's kiss.
>
> ...Mouth to her kiss. No. Must be two of em. Glue em well. Mouth to her mouth's kiss. (*U,* 3:393–400)

The vampirish imagery of this monologue has been almost unanimously associated with Bram Stoker's *Dracula* and its influence on Stephen.[44] Undeniably, in the quatrain we read of a vampire that "comes . . . on swift sail flaming / from storm and south," and in the meditation that triggers the poem's composition the same vampire "comes . . . through storm his eyes, his bat sails bloodying the sea, [his] mouth to her mouth's kiss" (*U,* 3:397–400). Adams Day points out that "though a vampire need not always be a bat, this one is"[45]—a predictable metamorphosis of the "batlike soul" that Stephen attributes to Emma, the inspiring muse of his villanelle,[46] into Yeats's Leanhaun Shee, the muse who feeds of the lives of young Gaelic poets,[47] the "malignant fairy" of Irish folklore whose power does not succumb to the power of death.[48] However, the dominant concern in the monologue relates to Stephen's desire to journey into the death of his own mother, as a means of unraveling the amalgam of natural drive ("womb"), cyclical curse ("moon"), and mortal condition ("tomb") that saturates his debt to her memory.

The sentence triggering Stephen's meditation on his poetic subject is evocative of the affinity between maternity and death: "Across the sands of all the world, followed by the sun's flaming sword, to the west trekking to evening lands. She trudges, schlepps, trains, drags, trascines her load" (*U,* 3:391–93). This imagery, derived from the biblical story of the Edenic Fall, shows a mortal Eve condemned to pain and labor, expelled from Eden by the swords of the Cherubim. The "moondrawn" journey toward aesthetic creation must lead Stephen across the perilous, "myriadislanded" sea of a maternal conception. He shall dive "within her," absorb vital fluids from a "blood not mine," sail the chancy, "winedark sea" of her menses, seek nocturnal nourishment when the "wet sign" of the moon brings her nipple to his lips,[49] share the "bed of death, ghostcandled"—a coffin carried away by ghosts— upon which his mother was lain in her agony, "ghostly light on her tortured face," "her hoarse loud breath rattling in horror" (*U,* 1:270–76).

Given the sordid practicalities weighing on Stephen's poetic vocation, one should not forget that Mary Goulding Dedalus, a devout and practicing Catholic, gave birth to "nine or ten" children before dying at a relatively young age (*P*, 241). If the liquid letters of speech of the Dantesque word-binder seem the ideal vehicle for the poet's journey across the sea of maternal conception, Stephen knows too well the repulsive perils of the "snotgreen" waters of this sea, contained in the stagnant "bowl of . . . green sluggish bile" at the bedside of the moribund (*U*, 1:78, 1:106–10, 3:3, 3:329–30). In his "figuration of maternity," Stephen associates his mother's "maternal body with waste"; the vomited bile, in particular, "is a graphic perversion of birth, a reversal of origination."[50] Together with this picture of self-depleting fecundity, predicated, as suggested earlier, on the convergence of deity and putrefaction, one must factor in the Church's rigid interdiction of contraception, which, complemented by the nationalistic discourse in favor of population growth,[51] exercised devastating effects on the existence and often the survival of a large portion of Irish women. How many fetuses did Mary Goulding Dedalus sacrifice to clandestine abortion in her lifetime? We will never know, nor does Stephen, who, disquieted by the implications of the word "Foetus" since his earliest teens (*P*, 89), is quick in "assum[ing] the presence of a misbirth" when he "thinks he sees a midwife's bag."[52] Stephen's phrase, "Bridebed, childbed, bed of death" resounds with too clear an echo from Blake's image of woman's destructive destiny—"Mother from the Womb, / Wife, Sister, Daughter, to the Tomb"—to go unnoticed.

An hour earlier, reflecting on the altruistic role played by the mother of his pupil, Cyril Sargent in her son's conception and early nurture, Stephen had equated maternal altruism with the gift of blood and vital fluids. "She had loved [Cyril's] weak watery blood drained from her own" (*U*, 2:142–43). And three hours earlier, sitting at the table of his mock-liturgical breakfast meal, Stephen had watched the milkwoman pour for him and his friends "rich white milk [that is] not hers," not drawn from her "old shrunken paps." The self-effacing spectacle of this odd wet-nurse made Stephen "listen . . . in scornful silence" to Buck and Haines, who treat the old woman in a patronizing manner. And his friends' haughtiness led him to contemplate the frail mortality of this "messenger," who was bringing them nourishment "from the secret morning" (*U*, 1:397–23).[53]

Even if the maternal gift of vital fluids may be experienced by the offspring as a violent theft (Buck and Haines's conversation with the milkwoman and compensation of her services enact symbolically such a theft), the altruistic reciprocity of maternal nurture makes it quite different from a Draculesque abuse. Although enslaved by the periodic laws of nature, in fact, Stephen's "handmaid of the moon" returns the vampirish bite that depletes her of her own vital fluids with a welcoming, unselfish, all-giving "kiss." It is not the proverbial kiss of the death-wishing maid from Stoker's gothic universe, but the secret miracle of the mother's kiss, which increases life by sacrificing her own life to the nurture of her offspring. Stephen may have learned from Yeats that the "life-draining effects" of procreation induce both a satiation comparable to sexual appeasement and a "vital antipathy," as Stubbings puts it, a merciless greed in the beneficiary of maternal nursing.[54]

From the perspective promoted by Stephen's monologue, Yeats's "love's bitter mystery," which made Stephen's mother cry "in her wretched bed," acquires the connotation of maternal self-effacement. This aspect of maternal altruism is intimately messianic, in the sense that, grafted on the life-giving commensality of self-sacrifice, it resonates with the tropic valence of crucifixion and Christic charity, as well as with that of the beneficiary's ingratitude.

It is noteworthy that a contiguity between maternal altruism and the messianic condition may be consistently found at the heart of Dante's Marian cult. It is underlined, for instance, in the third treatise of the *Convivio*, where Dante draws a heterodox analogy between Christ's incarnation and Mary's generous appearance on earth "in human semblance" (*in vostra similitudine venne a voi*);[55] immaculate conception in human flesh is the mark of both redemptive Mediatrix, as Bernard de Clairvaux calls her,[56] and redemptive Messiah. The contiguity between the Redeemer's kenosis and the Mediatrix's self-abnegation is especially stressed in the *Paradiso*, where Dante, encouraged by Bernard de Clairvaux, looks upon Mary's face three times in a row before he is enabled to see Christ (*Paradiso*, 32:86). As Thomas Altizer puts it, in his third vision of the Virgin Dante "sees the *face that most resembles Christ,* and only its radiance can grant Dante the power to look upon Christ."[57]

Jaroslav Pelikan observes in *Mary through the Centuries* that the resemblance underlined by St. Bernard de Clairvaux's words to Dante points to "a family resemblance"[58] that has been occasionally transferred to the painterly representation of the Madonna and Child.[59] This physiognomic motif cannot be overstressed. Family resemblance is a characteristic token of consanguinity, and the argument of mother-son consanguinity sustains, in the theology of the Marian cult, the doctrine of Christ's real incarnation in a human body, as opposed to the Gnostic doctrine of Christ's only apparent humanity and the various heresies pertinent to it—such as Arius, Valentinus, and Sabelllius's heresies, whose condemnation by the Trentine Council Stephen briefly considers in the "Telemachus" episode (*U,* 1:654–60). Mary's consanguinity with the Son of God bespeaks, in turn, the eschatological culmination in the punctuality of Jesus's body of the infinite rivulets that constitute the human species' bloodline. The "anastomosis of navelcords" is a "strandentwining cable of . . . flesh" (*U,* 14:300) running backward and forward in time; it regressively links all of the human species to its origin in the universal mother, "Heva, naked Eve" (*U,* 3:37–44), whose expulsion from the Garden of Eden and curse of inescapable sexual fertility Stephen envisions in his interior monologue on the Sandymount Strand; it progressively or teleologically links all of the human species to its destination in the womb of the new "Mother of all living."[60]

Stephen seems fully aware that the Kairotic instant around which hinges the revolution of Salvation History spans the diametrical events of incarnation and crucifixion, two events that, mediated by Mary's nurturance of the Son of God, join into the punctuality of an impossible phenomenon Jesus's birth and death, his origin and destination—his human, all-too-human existential enactment of the two impossible experiences of incipiency and termination of the conscious self, through his lapse into and exit from the mortal condition.

The Muse from the Crypt

The influence exercised on Stephen's interior monologue by Mallarmé's "Gift of the Poem" depends on the transmission of blood and vital fluids as a messianic trope of maternal conception and nurturance. This influence—the likelihood of whose impact on Stephen's imagination I have discussed in *Pruning the Genealogical Tree*—overshadows not only the escapist influence exercised by Stephen's recollection of *L'après-midi d'un faune,* but also the alleged influence of Stephen's Stoker-like fantasies. The lips of Mallarmé's poem are more voracious, more carnivorous, more vampirish than those of any Dracula ever imagined, as we shall see. (The literary critic should never forget the respective influence exercised by the symbolist and decadent movements of the late nineteenth century over the lurid fantasies of the gothic novel.)[61] The lips of Mallarmé's poem may be taken to prefigure the bloody monochromatism of his more mature and celebrated poetry, that of *Hérodiade* for instance, the history of whose composition begins even before Mallarmé wrote "Gift of the Poem."[62] Monic Robillard detects in the young Mallarmé's concerns with maternal fecundity the premises for his most sophisticated poetry, where he depicts the impossible, nonreferential image of a virginally menstruating mother, a wet nurse whose breast and vagina "exude" the liquid death of an inexhaustible vitality.[63]

Stephen's moon-womb-tomb amalgam, which we saw gradually exfoliate from the musaic and maternal metaphors of artistic creativity derived from Blake and Yeats, finds a plethora of punctual correspondences in Mallarmé's poem. The harp-strings-plucking muse invoked by both Dante and Yeats is here finally granted her proper instrument, her utterance resounding now as "soft . . . [as] a harpsichord." Her French rhymes march at the "two by two" pace of Stephen's own quatrain (*U,* 7:715). And her breast is freely offered to the "starved lips" of not just one but two distinct vampires, the first born of her fertile womb, the second born of the sterile womb of her husband's imagination, both voracious of the life—literal and allegoric in the case of her baby, phenomenally impossible and lacking referential verification in the case of her husband's poetic creature—that flows out of her body.

> I bring you the child of an Idumaean night!
> Black, and with bleeding wings, featherless and pale,
> Through the windows burnished with incense and gold,
> Through the rimed panes mournful, alas, from the cold,
> Dawn leaped upon the angelic lamp,
> Palms! and when she had offered this relic
> To this father trying out a hostile smile,
> The sterile and blue solitude shivered.
> O mother, cradling your daughter and in the innocence

Of your cold feet, welcome a horrible birth:
And your voice soft like a viol and a harpsichord,
Will you press your faded finger against your breast,
From which in sibylline whiteness woman flows
For starved lips by the air of the virginal azure."[64]

At the time of the composition of "Gift of the Poem," Marie and Stéphane Mallarmé lived at Tournon, where he taught English at the local *lycée*. On November 19, 1864, Marie gave birth to Geneviève. The strains of parental life caught Stéphane unprepared. "Geneviève, who eats up her mother, is as rosy as a flower, but my poor Marie, who is eaten up, is pale and endlessly fatigued. I survive like an old man. . . . "[65] Mallarmé was twenty-three years old when he wrote this letter to Henri Cazalis; Geneviève, his rosy vampire, was four months old. The verses of "Gift of the Poem" reveal that paternal responsibility and creative sterility are dramatically intertwined for the twenty-three-year-old poet. The maternal power to conceive and nurture life strikes him with both resentment and admiration. Is there a physiological or psychological limit, he wonders, to his beloved Marie's altruism and "faded" self-denial? Should he attempt to steal the inexhaustible secret of her maternal vitality and infuse it into his own tired verses? At what cost? He is certainly not going to squander his wife's altruistic self-effacement in order to "buy [the] bread"[66] of prosaic versification and mimetic reproduction. Nor is he going to sacrifice Marie's fast-fading vitality on the self-enamored altar of his poetic impasse. The context is the classical one of initiation and poetic rebirth. Stéphane dreams of a "pure Conception," as he writes to Henri Cazalis, a conception immaculately proportional to the life-draining effects of maternal nurturance.[67] "There is here," Roger Bellet remarks, "a Mallarmean dream of Immaculate Conception, of Immaculate Creation, which would take the place of the dream of religion."[68]

"Gift of the Poem" depicts an Annunciation scene.[69] The poet, a father, enters his bedroom shortly after dawn and contemplates his wife holding the vibrant life of their child in her arms. Standing on the room's threshold, he holds in his own arms a stack of scribbled pages, the lifeless product of the night he spent in the exclusive realm of his solitary talent. In turning his miserable poem into an offering to his wife's solicitude, the poet/father receives in return a miraculously salvaged poem. Line after line, his self-derogatory verses are gradually turned into an exceedingly good poem. The poet is redeemed from his misery by a virginal mother as pale as a vampire victim who, sucked dry by her voracious child, finds the strength to offer her breast to the "lips" of a sheaf of bad verses. The poetic "gift" or talent that the poet believes himself entitled to is redeemed by a maternal act of unconditional giving. The Augustinian reverberations are striking: in *De doctrina christiana,* not only does Augustine assimilate the infant at the breast with the condition of the initiate to the "first stages of interpretive activity," but he also refers metaphorically to him as a catechumen ready for the rebirth of baptism.[70]

At the heart of the poem we recognize the discordant similitude linking the poet's gift, or received poetic talent, at its lowest moment, that of self-doubt and self-recrimination, with a mother's gift, or selfless present of her own life, at its hardest moment, that of utter physical exhaustion. The two conditions are joined together by a nourishing kiss, predatory on the part of the poet, kenotic on the part of his wife. "I wish my lips were feminine!" Mallarmé will write a few months later to Henri Cazalis. "Or better not, because if they were they would bleed, wounded by the [poetic instrument] into which I blow with rage...."[71]

In this contradictory image of the bleeding lips one may unravel much of the crucial symbology to Mallarmé's imagery of feminine fecundity, as Monic Robillard remarks in his enlightening commentary to *Noce d'Hérodiade*. Mallarmé began his poetic treatment of the Salomé myth in 1864, at the age of twenty-two, and completed it thirty years later. He chose to assign to his heroine the name of the mother, Herodiade, "a sombre word, and as red as a cracked pomegranate."[72]

Having obtained Saint Jean's decapitation, the virginal Herodiade wants to exchange the "worst kiss" (*un pire baiser*) with his lifeless head—a kiss more repugnant to her than the contact exchanged by two lovers' oscular or genital intercourse. Herodiade symbolizes the poetic muse refusing authorial encryption, Robillard observes, and bestowing on herself two obscenely subversive lips, capable of chanting in plain words the poet's cryptic inspiration. The kiss envisaged by Herodiade will drown her vaginal lips in the blood pouring from Jean's decapitated head. Only such *pire baiser* may seal the nuptial knot between her first periodic menstruation and her murdered victim. The immaculate conception engendered by this chaste and impossible marriage is Mallarmé's poetry itself: the inertness and obscurity of his symbolistic encryption clamor to be brought to the life of significance by the "mothering reading" (*lecture maternante*) of his virginal muse.[73]

Dracula was published in 1897, about thirty years after Mallarmé's "Gift of the Poem"—too late for Mallarmé to be inspired by its gothic imagery, and too late as well, quite probably, considering the imaginative reach of Mallarmé's monochromatism of blood, for Stephen Dedalus to be influenced by Stoker's derivative and, after all, domesticated imagery of maidenly bleeding. Having endowed the black light of dawn with "bleeding wings, featherless and pale"—a germane image of Stephen's "bat sails bloodying the sea"—Mallarmé invites the nursing mother from the second half of "Gift of the Poem" to set aside her newborn daughter and feed the milk of her breast to the "starved lips" of his aborted poem. The breast of the nursing mother is wet with milk and she nurses at dawn—another germane image of the "handmaid of the moon" from Stephen's meditation in "Proteus," who wakes up at the call of "the wet sign." Both the mother and the "handmaid" seem eager for a demonic kiss. In turn, the incorporeal lips of Mallarmé's "funereal abortion" (*rejeton funèbre*, as he calls it in his private correspondence)[74] are eager for the woman's nipple; analogously, Stephen's pale vampire glues "[his] mouth to her mouth's kiss," and Stephen's own "lips lipped and mouthed fleshless lips of air...."

At dawn the poet shows the creature of his imagination to his wife. This creature is barely alive: a "horrible birth." It is also a "relic" from a mystical night spent in the land of poetic exaltation, Idumaea, where kings and poets "... reproduce themselves without sex and without women."[75] This is also the aesthetic territory of artistic parthenogenesis probed by Stephen in "Scylla and Charybdis"—a germane image of the heaven of poetic transfiguration "foretold by Hamlet, [where] there are no more marriages, glorified man, an androgynous angel, being a wife unto himself" (*U,* 9:1051–52). From the secrecy of this gender-exclusive realm of uncontaminated creativity—delusionally immune from the decay and finitude of female procreation—the poet has brought back his lifeless "gift," a creature badly in need of fresh nourishment. Ominously black, "dawn leaps upon the [poet's] angelic lamp" and unveils this strange baby: it is a poem, a sheaf of scribbled pages, a dying "relic" with hungry lips. Lifeless and sickly as it is, this reliquial creature is a mystic present, however, a "gift . . . burnished with incense and gold," as if for a representation of the Nativity. It is delivered to the nursing mother upon a bed of palm leaves (*Palmes!*)—a germane image of "the branches from the trees" that on Palm Sunday the people of Jerusalem "spread on the road" in front of the Messiah (Matthew 21:8). But this reliquial creature is also a "horrible birth": only the "sibylline white" of the maternal milk, "flow[ing] for [its] starved lips" in the "virginal azure" light of the morning, may infuse it with life.

White and blue are the emblematic colors of the Virgin Mary,[76] the doctrinal descendant of Stephen's Edenic "handmaid of the moon." Less primitive and less telluric than Eve, Mary is at one and the same time submissive to the laws of nature and capable of virginal fecundity. The "white" of the Sibyl alludes also to Virgil's Sibyl of Cumae, who wrote her oracles on fluttering leaves,[77] as laconic as Stephen's weary attempts to add a few new lines and a new rhyming pair to his quatrain, as elusive as the "empty sheet[s] defended by whiteness" that cluttered Mallarmé's desk in Tournon when he worked on "Gift of the Poem."[78] This "sibylline whiteness" emblematizes the cryptic poetics—the laconic *page blanche*[79]—of the silence-in-progress.[80]

In order to emulate maternal altruism, Mallarmé must engage himself in maternal self-effacement. In order to infuse life into his own skeptical verses, he must deplete himself of artistic self-sufficiency. His poetic lips must become "feminine," bleeding from the wounds provoked by his poetic instrument.[81] We are clearly on the familiar turf of Sam Slote's "disempowered poet" who "inachieves writing" by effacing himself in the artwork.[82]

Derrida has suggested that "Gift of the Poem" is not written like a poem but performed like the enactment of a gift, "which gives itself by giving nothing other than the gift in question. . . ."[83] The gift is not the topic of the poem then—the poem itself is a gift. The giving is not related to a poem being given to an audience but to the poem being given to the author himself—the talent of his artistic gift being confirmed or given back to him once again, at the moment when his moribund composition begins sucking away at the maternal breast and is transmogrified into an excellent poem. "Gift of the Poem" presents itself as a gift, turns itself into a present, at the same time that it gives itself away as the insignificant artifact of a misused talent. The poem is ultimately an instantiation of the messianic logic of life-giving altruism. To paraphrase Blanchot's *"La littérature et le droit à la mort,"* one might say that this poem by Mallarmé must die as a poem in order to live as a gift of love, however bitter the deliverance of such a gift.[84] However, even in a regime of self-abnegation the virgin-mother muse remains inherently fruitful. The poet must unburden him/herself of the poetic gift by submitting, as Diane Stubbings puts it, to the mother-like "burden of creative labour."[85] As Mallarmé's enacted performance in "Gift of the Poem" confirms, the poet cannot keep the gift of poetic inspiration bottled within, unless s/he gives up writing.[86] The silence-in-progress of poetic apophasis does not exonerate from the labors of poetic utterance. Stephen Dedalus's poetry of the afterlife, however, does.

The Extirpation of Poetry

It is noteworthy that in the canto from the *Paradiso* preceding his apostrophe to the Virgin Mary, St. Bernard foreshadows the Edenic inauguration and the eschatological termination of the human bloodline by means of a metaphor of menstrual discharge.

> *La piaga che Maria richiuse e unse,*
> *quella ch'è tanto bella da' suoi piedi*
> *è colei che l'aperse e che la punse*
> [The wound that Mary sealed and anointed
> Is that wound which Eve, who sits so lovely
> At her feet, opened and pierced.]
>
> (*Paradiso,* 32:4–6, my translation)

In his drunken stupor at the National Maternity Hospital, Stephen Dedalus declares, "In woman's womb word is made flesh." Given the mock-serious, theological and gynecological thrust of the ongoing discussion on female fertility between Stephen and his fellow loafers, Stephen's proposition is meant to apply not so much to any and all women, as to the two eminent figures of motherhood in the Bible, that is, Eve, who was granted, in the beginning of time, the burdensome privilege to populate the earth, and the Virgin Mary, who, in the neo-Testamentary recurrence of John's "beginning," gave birth to the Incarnated Word. After this short-lived homage to woman's carnal creativity, however, Stephen retracts with the words, "But in the spirit of the maker [i.e., the Holy Spirit] all flesh that passes becomes the word that shall not pass away. This is the postcreation. *Omnis caro ad te veniet"* (*U,* 14:292–94).

The Latin citation of Psalm 64:2 from the Vulgate—"All flesh shall come to thee"— is a part of the *Introit,* or the entrance chant of the Requiem Mass. In the "Proteus" episode of *Ulysses,* Stephen had recourse to the same citation in the course of his mournful reflection on the unhappy destiny of his own mother: "Bridebed, childbed, bed of death, ghostcandled. *Omnis caro ad te veniet"* (*U,* 3:396–97). Stephen's disclaimer of his own praise of maternal fecundity refers to the extirpation of procreation that accompanies the apocalypse, the "time of the end," described in the Book of Daniel, which coincides with the "dominion [of the Word] that shall not pass away."[87] At the end of time the "anastomosis of navelcords" (*U*, 14:300) will have been abruptly broken, and with this rupture the biblical prescription of human proliferation will have been reversed. The lapsarian condition, symbolized by "the [navel] cords of all link[ing] back, strandentwining cable of all flesh"—the cumulative tangle of all umbilical cords linking back, that is, to the universal mother, "Heva, naked Eve" (*U*, 3:37–44)—will have been reversed in the expurgation of the Edenic fall and the extinction of Eve's "womb of sin" (*U*, 3:44). Eve, as the primal source of human life, will have been substituted by Mary, "the second Eve" (*U*, 14:298), who figures as the terminal point of human life and, at once, the exemplar model for the prelapsarian creature (*U*, 3:42).

One might say that Stephen imagines divine Creation in the guise of a gynecoid sandglass with not one but two necks, a neck of entrance or origination and a neck of exit or extinction, the former corresponding to the beginning of historical time, the latter to its closure. The first neck runs metaphorically through the cervix of Eve, who represents the universal mother, the fulcrum of human procreation and "anastomosis of navelcords," the gate of *creatio ex nihilo*: "Aleph, alpha: nought, nought, one" (*U*, 3:39–40). The second neck runs metaphorically through the virgin cervix of Mary, who represents the universal daughter—*figlia di [suo] figlio* (*U*, 14:303)[88]—the fulcrum of postcreation, the gate of extinction whereby the immense tangle of the "cable of all flesh" (the multitude of generated humanity) runs back to the Maker and coalesces apocalyptically into the unity of the Word (*U*, 14:294, 3:37). "Eve. Naked wheatbellied sin. A snake coils her, fang in's kiss" (*U*, 9:541). These three truncated periods from Stephen's interior monologue in "Scylla and Charybdis" effectively allude to the transition from creation to postcreation.

Stage one: in Eve's surrender to the seductions of the serpent, her "naked wheatbellied sin" (*U*, 9:541) coincides with the inauguration of the biblical curse of female fertility (Genesis 3:16).

Stage two: in the joyous celebration of Eros by the Shulamite virgin of the Song of Songs, the "whiteheaped corn" of her virginal belly (*U*, 3:43; Song of Songs 7:3) represents the apotheosis of human procreation.

Stage three: in the erotic reticence of the "handmaid of the Lord," iconically represented as she crushes the serpent at her feet, the virgin's surrender to the Word announces the apocalyptic extirpation of female fertility.

In "Oxen of the Sun" Stephen draws an analogy between the reproductive potency of Dante's "wind of seeds of brightness," which stands for purgatory's prolific wind, capable of making the plants on earth fructify without recourse to any seed (*seme palese* [*Purgatorio*, 28:103–17]), and the "potency of vampires mouth to mouth" (*U*, 14:242–44).[89] This analogy is not as arbitrary as it may at first appear, because both potencies—the chaste pollination by an incorporeal, intangible seed of light, and the unchaste one by a daemonic agent of periodic ovulation—share the same gynecoid generative power, the miraculous (prelapsarian, as it were) fecundity of a "pregnancy without joy, . . . a birth without pangs, a body without blemish, a belly without bigness" (*U,* 14:309–11): a fecundity that bespeaks, in Stephen's vision of postcreation, the extinction of procreation and the eclipse of Eros.

In Stephen's view, postcreation consists of a fulminant condensation of the three fundamental types attributed to womanhood by Western Christianity: the carnal mother, the erotic lover, the fertile virgin. As we have seen, postcreation corresponds to the reverse-event of cosmic procreation, whereby the entire human race and its tangle of umbilical cords come to be absorbed back into the virgin womb that will have returned the Word of God to its originary, prelapsarian absoluteness. In the God of postcreation, the virgin womb *mothers* a nihilistic divinity uncontaminated by the accidents, lapses, and contingencies of the history of Creation; immense human multitudes leave the necropolis and cross the neck of the virgin womb backwards, to coalesce, contracting to a dimensionless dot, into the ground-zero of this atemporal, aspatial, silent Word.

Stephen's poetic muteness is the faithful mimesis of such an instantaneous punctuality, of such an absolute *Punkt,* point, period, or full stop—a muteness expressive of the absolute contraction of the apocalyptic cosmos into a Word that refuses itself to human speech. One could say that the oppressive burden of his historical and domestic responsibilities has ultimately prevailed over Stephen's best intentions. It has kept him from acknowledging that this hypercontracted cosmos of postcreation owes its own germination to human history, more specifically, to the history of the Word's contamination with and involvement in the accidents and contingencies of Creation. Figuring the Word's coming into its most authentic own in total silence at the end of human history, Stephen's notion of postcreation is the virtual countertype to all Scriptural types, inclusive of Incarnation and Crucifixion. That such an apocalyptic notion hinges on the human faculty of discursive construct is not a lost lesson on the Joyce of *Finnegans Wake,* as we shall see in chapter 8.

LEOPOLD BLOOM'S
BURIAL MEAL

There was a right royal old nigger,
Who ate or something the somethings of the Reverend Mr MacTrigger.
His five hundred wives had the time of their lives.
It grew bigger and bigger and bigger.

Ulysses, *8:748–49, 778–79, 783*

Incorporation by Death

In the present chapter I discuss the function of food, corpses, and excreta in the adventures of Leopold Bloom in *Ulysses*. It is well known that burial and nutrition play a pivotal role in these adventures, but it has never been sufficiently stressed how intimately related these two functions are to each other. Bloom partakes of food several times in the course of the day, starting with his tref breakfast meal shortly before the funeral of his Catholic friend, Patrick Dignam. Bloom's culinary feats bestride the analogy between the ordinary food necessary to the process of vital functions and the sacred food under whose aegis a corpse is ceremonially dispatched to the afterlife—ordinary and sacred food resulting analogous with each other in this simple consideration, that to Bloom they are both imminently prelusive of excretion and decomposition. Dignam's corpse is emblematic of this analogy. First, it is consecrated through a Requiem Mass (*U*, 6:601–3)—a liturgy that is a remote offshoot of the theophagous rites into which primitive religious cults transposed the archaic funeral practice of cannibalistic incorporation. Then it is rapidly reduced to the most profane of foods, a decomposing waste product feasted upon by rats.

Leopold Bloom begins his day with a breakfast of pork kidney fried in butter, a profanation of the Kosher interdiction, shortly followed by a long interval of defecation. Then he fills the time before Patrick Dignam's funeral with the retrieval of a letter from his secret epistolary correspondent, a resting meditation in a church during a service attended by the members of a sodality, and an ablution at the Leinster Street Turkish and Warm Baths. After the funeral, during which he indulges in sepulchral and sobering thoughts, he takes care of business matters for an hour or so. Then comes the time to eat. Around 1:30 P.M. Leopold enjoys a snack at Davy Byrne's pub (a gorgonzola sandwich and a glass of Burgundy) (*U,* 8:758–64). And later in the afternoon, around 4:30 P.M. he shares a meal with Richard Goulding at the restaurant of the Ormond Hotel (liver and bacon for Leopold, who drinks a bottle of cider; steak and kidney for Richard, who drinks a glass of Irish whiskey) (*U,* 11:447, 499).

The extemporaneous limerick composed by Bloom during his snack at Davy Byrne's, and cited as the epigraph to this chapter, is the centerpiece of Bloom's culinary feats. The limerick is a poetic form composed of two lines made up of three feet each, followed by two lines (often collapsed into one line, in conformance with the examples found for instance in Edward Lear's *A Book of Nonsense*) of two feet each, followed by a last line of three feet. The feet are triple measures, that is, made up of three syllables.[1] Bloom's limerick is hybrid rather than regular in metric structure, yet scrupulously modeled on the typical form, integrating the third and fourth rhyme (wives-lives) in one line, in conformance with Lear's models.[2] Bloom's comic poem gives creative form to his two previous moments of meditation, namely, the reflective pause during the church service and the long interior lucubrations in the course of Dignam's funeral; moreover, it amalgamates these meditations with the considerations that seasoned his midday meal at Davy Byrne's, regarding the deep logic of human nutrition.

This limerick is evidently a comic poem about primordial sacrifice. It deals with five distinct aspects of primordial sacrifice, namely: cannibalism and burial: a tribal chief ("a right royal old nigger") disposes of the corpse of a missionary priest, "Reverend Mr Mac Trigger," by devouring it; the hierarchical food-sharing procedure inherent in the communal burial rite:[3] as the choicest bite, Father MacTrigger's genitals are eaten by the chief; the apotropaic incorporation of the corpse's superior attributes by the participants in the burial feast / rite:[4] the chief undergoes a metonymic magnification of his own sexual powers, which grow "bigger and bigger and bigger"; the participants' immunization from the corpse's inimical attributes: as *longa manus* of colonial rule, the Christian minister is both deposed and disposed of, while the tribe's chief is greatly empowered; the prolificacy to be derived from burial commensality: the chief's five hundred wives have "the time of their lives" at the comic sight of the improbable arousal of their master inseminator—who is, after all, an "old" chief.[5]

After his brief visit to the Burton restaurant at lunch time, and in unpremeditated anticipation of the composition of his limerick, Bloom devoted a brief, interior consideration to the apotropaic transposition of burial commensality to folkloric medicine.

> Hot fresh blood they prescribe for decline. Blood always needed. Insidious. Lick
> it up smokinghot, thick sugary. Famished ghosts. (*U,* 8:729–30)

In Bloom's days, a drink of the "fresh blood" taken from butchered animals was the folkloric prescription for patients affected by wasting diseases. This kind of prescription reduces burial commensality to its purest essence, the assimilation of alien blood. There are noteworthy Homeric overtones to Bloom's imagery of "smoking-hot" blood for "famished ghosts," of course. This imagery is an evident allusion to the scene in book 11 of the *Odyssey*, where Odysseus is shown brandishing his sword to keep the specters of the dead from drinking the sacrificial blood poured for the benefit of the soul of the prophet Tiresias. This literary analogy suggests, in turn, that Irish folkloric medicine at the beginning of the twentieth century was not above being sidetracked by the reciprocity between the physiology of nutrition and the archaic or transcendental psychology of death.

Let us take a closer look at this archaic psychology of death and its relationship with the physiology of human nutrition. The group of Parisian anthropologists composed by Émile Durkheim, Robert Hertz, and Marcel Mauss was actively discussing matters pertaining to this issue at the time of Joyce's composition of *Ulysses*. Primitive men and women enter the scene of prehistory as predatory individuals, primarily focused on their own brutal nutrition and survival. Only gradually do they graduate from predation to the bartering stage of fair and equivalent exchange. A fundamental threshold in the history of human culture was crossed when primitive human beings began envisioning the advantages of the reciprocity attained in a meal shared with the community vis-à-vis the predatory selfishness of one's own personal nutrition. It may be argued that special mental faculties needed to be developed in order to sustain the transition from the privacy of individual nutrition to the reciprocity of the communal meal.[6] These mental faculties prelude to the introduction of the responsible regime of interpersonal exchange; they bring humankind one step closer to history and civilization. As suggested by Émile Durkheim, this transition from privacy to reciprocity could not have occurred without the institution of the liturgy of primordial sacrifice, which was based on the act of renunciation whereby relevant parts of the victim were gratuitously distributed to the weak members of the community, incapable by definition to reciprocate. The ritual commensality in the presence of the invisible god hinges thereby on the abstraction from all equivalent, reciprocative obligations.[7] The weak member of the community accepts the sacrifice in behalf of the invisible god, but does not offer any explicit promise of an equivalent compensation in return for it; when and if the god's retribution will come, it will be delivered in surprising and disproportionate amounts, in the form, for instance, of a bountiful harvest or a providential rain or the generous delivery of male descendants. Only after the model of this gratuitous gift is firmly established in the cultic logic of collective imagination, can the paradigm of proportional exchange gain social currency, together with its corollary sense of communal responsibility.[8]

This is why it may be argued that the mental faculties needed in order to sustain the transition from the privacy of self-sustenance to the reciprocity of social exchange stem from a transcendental psychology of death. Before engaging in barter-based exchange and ordering thereby their communal life around the criterion of equivalent transaction, primitive human beings needed to develop the mental capacity to conceive of a sacred meal shared with a virtual presence, a god, who, present at the consummation of the meal only in absentia, had been actually present at some previous meal, long before the actual rite will have taken place. The mental ability to conceive of an interactive commensality in the company of an invisible presence portends the interiorization of a transcendental notion of life and personhood; just like the absent god, who is present only in absentia at the sacred meal, and vicariously in the persons of its cultic proxies or avatars, the individual human being learns to envisage his (her?) own virtual presence in the process of events that may at one and the same time concern his individual interests and occur in his actual absence. Ultimately this individual learns to envisage the occurrence of events wherein his views, interests, and concerns are factored in and balanced with those of the event's actual actors; the actors' duty or debt to his personal rights stems from his virtual presence in their remembrance of him. Like the god, this individual will be entitled to claim his share in the communal meal even after his own death, participating occasionally in the vicarious person of a stranger, a pilgrim, or a beggar.

Just as commensality in the company of the god is a symbolic substitute for the devouring of the god itself, as made explicitly evident in the sacrament of the Eucharist, so commensality at burial, in the company of a corpse, stands symbolically for the archaic practice of burial via cannibalistic incorporation of the ancestor's virtues and power. In unpremeditated anticipation of the composition of his limerick, Bloom's resting meditation at the Church of St. Andrew in the "Lotus Eaters" episode devotes a brief consideration to this analogy. While observing the Catholic Mass service, Leopold reflects on the paradoxical affinity between cannibalism and burial commensality, and on this affinity's apostolic efficacy.

> The priest . . . took out a communion . . . and put it neatly into her mouth, murmuring all the time. . . . What? *Corpus:* body. Corpse. . . . They don't seem to chew it: only swallow it down. Rum idea: eating bits of a corpse. Why the cannibals cotton to it. . . . Yes, bread of angels it's called. (*U,* 5:344–60)

Later, during Dignam's funeral service at Prospect cemetery, Leopold reflects on the profane implications of burial commensality, observing how the local celebrant of the Requiem Mass is caught in the interplay between the physiology of nutrition and the liturgy of death.

> Father Coffey . . . name . . . like a coffin. . . . Want to feed well, sitting in there all morning in the gloom kicking his heels waiting for the next please. . . . What swells him up that way? . . . Air of the place maybe. Looks full of bad gas. . . . Butchers, for instance: they get like raw beefsteaks. (*U,* 6:595–630)

Of the abovementioned group of French anthropologists, active at the time of Joyce's composition of *Ulysses* in Paris, one must look especially at Robert Hertz for the discussion of funerary cannibalism and necrophagy. According to Hertz, the eating of parts from the decomposing corpse was one of the typical moments in the burial rites of the aboriginal Australian tribes, which were his primary object of study.[9] The burial meal, which in Joyce's Dublin goes especially under the name of the wake, but in the "Hades" episode of *Ulysses* is identified in the more orthodox celebration of the Requiem Mass, is a specialized version of ritual commensality; being shared with a corpse, it hinges on the denial of the ineluctable waste of the persona whose life had previously vivified the dead body. No less than in the case of sacrificial commensality, a concept of the afterlife is the crucial mental prerequisite required of the specific transition from profane to burial commensality. Just as primitive imagination tends to attribute human agency to natural phenomena by personalizing their concrete manifestations, as in the classically Viconian examples of the divinization of thunder or of the grumbling mountain,[10] so commensality in the company of a corpse tends to attribute supernatural or transcendental agency to the corpse itself by selecting, abstracting, spiritualizing, and appropriating its original capacities—exactly as we have read in Bloom's limerick.

The assimilation of the corpse's superior attributes through manducation and the disposal of the corpse's inimical attributes through entombment are two of the essential factors in Freud's scheme of theanthropic sacrifice. In *Totem and Taboo* Freud describes the ceremony whereby the scapegoat, as an animal substitute for the deposed ancestor-king, is killed and devoured by the king's descendant, who, as chief and/or priest, stands for the ancestor restored as deity.[11] The deposition/expulsion of the old ancestor is symbolically sanctioned in theanthropic sacrifice when chosen parts of the butchered scapegoat are offered as a meal to the absent ancestor himself; abandoned to decomposition, this flesh and innards stand for the communal liberation, or purgation, or catharsis from the inimical attributes of the deposed ancestor. This latter, disquieting side of entombment is alluded to in Bloom's pause of reflection at the conclusion of Dignam's funeral, just before leaving Prospect cemetery, when he confronts the sobering idea that the burial ceremony has turned his friend Patrick into a recyclable waste product.

> An obese gray rat toddled along the side of the crypt . . . crushed itself in under the plinth. . . . One of those chaps would make short work of a fellow. Pick the bones clean no matter who it was. Ordinary meat for them. A corpse is meat gone bad. . . . Regular square feed for them. (*U,* 6:973–92)

The restoration of the superior attributes of the ancestor is symbolically sanctioned when chosen parts of the butchered scapegoat, eaten by the successor to the ancestor, are revitalized via digestive assimilation. It goes without saying that Freud's theory of theanthropic sacrifice virtually identifies the sacrificial and the burial meal, suggesting therefore that the divinized ancestors are the originary object of religious worship.

In conclusion to this excursus into the archaic psychology of death and its relationship with the physiology of human nutrition, it should be emphasized that the participants to the burial meal experience both the assimilation of superior attributes and the expulsion of inimical attributes as the communal activation of an essential bodily function, one which restores the integrity of the social corpus, or body

politic: ingestion in the case of superior attributes, excretion in the case of inimical attributes. The psychology of death plunges its roots deep into the physiology
of nutrition. As a life-promoting apparatus, the digestive system selectively incorporates vital nutrients and expels superfluous and indigestible materials. So does the
liturgy of burial.

Bloom's limerick copes allusively with this interplay. It is not simply relevant to
our discussion that the psychology of death derives its archaic cultural background
from the physiology of nutrition, or that this derivation treats the natural processes
of excretion and decomposition in the guise of servomechanisms functional not only
to the perpetuation of individual life but especially to the proliferation of communal life; it is especially relevant, in the apprehension of this interplay, that the psychology of death transfigures physiology into transcendence, and bodily putrefaction
into the teleological promise of an afterlife.

How does Bloom position himself vis-à-vis the complex scenario suggested by
his own limerick? We know of Bloom that he is a radical skeptic when it comes
to the transcendence of the afterlife. He makes his simplistic philosophy of mortality rather explicit in the "Hades" episode: "The resurrection and the life. Once you
are dead you are dead" (U, 6:677). To Bloom the afterlife is "Corpus Paradisum":
a heaven full of rotting corpses and decomposing matter (U, 11:805). Karen Lawrence has aptly observed that "corpus and corpse continually collapse in his thoughts
about food."[12] When it comes to an affection and a state of mourning closer to
home, though, Leopold's attitudes toward death manifest subtler modulations. His
voluntary and involuntary memories of his son's death are pervaded by a cathartic
feeling of personal purgation, not too dissimilar from the "Aristotelian purgation"
or catharsis that Martha Nussbaum attributes to the Joycean philosophy of life.[13]
Triggered by the remembrance of Rudy's burial, Bloom's mournful despair sets the
nihilism of decomposition and the child's invisible and enduring presence by his
side in an intriguing sort of reciprocal interplay.[14] The next section of the present
chapter is devoted to the catharsis or purgation that Rudy's death affords his father.
Before embarking on this discussion, however, it is important to devote closer attention to the relation between catharsis on the one hand, and the interplay between
the psychology of death and the physiology of nutrition on the other.

As mentioned earlier, the logic of purgation plays a central role in Freud's scheme
of theanthropic sacrifice; it is an essential factor in the dynamic process whereby an
ancestor's merely anthropomorphic attributes and behavior come to be deified. A
similar logic has informed most discussions of the Aristotelian catharsis intrinsic to
the tradition of Greek tragedy. As Nietzsche points out in The Birth of Tragedy, theatrical catharsis has been constantly misapprehended as a "pathological discharge"
of emotions. Having discharged the emotional frenzy experienced at the theater,
this frenzy being the manifestation of the illogic and instinctual drives buried within
the audience's genetic constitution, the Greek spectators obtained a state of mental
sobriety; this sobriety allowed them, in turn, to achieve unanimous agreement regarding the divinely-sanctioned judgments of value dictated by the polis's legal statutes.

In this conventional interpretation, the logic lawfulness of communal life required the institution of exceptional pauses of collective madness. Nietzsche suggests that the logic-versus-emotion dualism plays only a collateral role in tragic catharsis.[15] To him the catharsis obtained on the Greek stage is not primarily an illogical discharge of emotion and an affirmation of transcendental logic, but rather a dramatization of the physical purgation or expulsion of the scapegoat from the polis.

A close affinity relates the Greek tradition of sacrificial rite to tragic catharsis. As a matter of fact, not a few among the classical Greek tragedies consist of mythical representations of scapegoating, wherein it is not the lowly scapegoat who is expelled from the polis, but the king himself. As Daniel Ogden points out, "a link [of the lowly scapegoat] with the opposite status [of the tragic hero] can be made"; in some tragic representations the king is expelled "dressed as a slave," while some historically attested episodes of scapegoating described "the lowly real life scapegoat [being] fed like a king . . . before his expulsion." It is agreed, Ogden writes, "that kings and the assorted lowly individuals actually attested as [scapegoats] have in common an exteriorness or marginality to society."[16] What turns an individual into a scapegoat is not his inferior social status but rather his exceptional, extraordinary condition; he is either a beggar, preferably repulsive, disabled by some physical deformity, or a god-like king.

The figure of King Oedipus is the emblematic example of a mythical representation of the scapegoat, the "lonely marginal at the top"[17] who must be expelled to bring the pollution away from the city. The communal healing and the restoration of social cohesion brought about by Oedipus's self-mutilation and expulsion from the city constitute the transposition to the stage of a ritualistic effect. Furthermore, as attested by Sophocles's version of his story, the fate of Oedipus undergoes an astounding mutation in time, from guilt-ridden scapegoat in *Oedipus the King* to consecrated victim in *Oedipus at Colonus*. It is this sort of mutation that enables Walter Burkert to detect a relevant affinity between the Greek scapegoat and the victim of Crucifixion. With reference to Deutero-Isaiah's prophecies of the Suffering Servant's atoning death, Burkert points out that the scapegoat "may be marked by a touching ambivalence, despised and worshiped at the same time. This has been elaborated, most of all, in the Christian tradition."[18]

The above considerations leave us with three crucial connotations of the cathartic experience, namely: catharsis as socially indispensable to communal solidarity; catharsis as primarily a physical rite of expulsion and only secondarily an individual experience of emotional purgation; catharsis as an intermediary stage toward the sanctification of the scapegoat.

Purgation by Death

The physiology of nutrition and the psychology of death are patterned according to intersecting paths within Bloom's consciousness, each distinct path winding along the uneven boundary separating "putative fact from marginalized . . . folklore."[19] Bloom's ambivalence toward the objective rigor of physiological facts and the subjective prejudice of curative folklore, suggested by his consideration—sarcastic, undoubtedly—on the effectiveness of the prescription of "fresh blood" to fight wasting diseases, is reflected in the "two systems of medical professing" prevalent in Dublin at the beginning of the twentieth century. Cheryl Herr has shown that these two systems competed with each other in offering assistance to pregnant women. Midwives stand on one side of the spectrum, professional obstetricians on the other. Because midwives' traditional procedures granted "[personal] control over the birth process" to women, especially by performing clandestine abortion (not rarely with mortal consequences for mother, child, or both) or secret delivery, midwives were "anathema" and unfair competition in the eyes of the medical profession. The medical containment of natality and mortality intersects here with the physiology of maternal conception.

We will see that Bloom's concerns with the physiology of nutrition and the psychology of death serve as hosts to collateral concerns relating to the physiology of maternal conception. More precisely, we shall now discuss two coordinated issues: first, the crossroads where the intersection of death and nutrition manifests its "gendered distinctions" in the physiology of maternal inception, conception, gestation, delivery, and nurturance; and second, the impact that this crossroads exercises on Bloom's personal experience of procreation.[20]

Bloom's ambivalent attitude toward death, procreation, and nutrition is displayed in the "Oxen of the Sun" episode. While he soberly partakes of the medical students' ribald banquet at the National Maternity Hospital, such controversial issues are debated as "whether the mother or child should die during childbirth in cases where such a choice needed to be made, virgin birth, Immaculate Conception, condoms, causes of sterility, . . . monstrous births, . . . and infant mortality."[21] While the congregated youth debate wildly under the influence of alcohol, Mrs Mina Purefoy is enduring her third day of birth pangs. Mrs Purefoy's life-threatening delivery, in the hands of the official medical establishment, calls insistently to Bloom's mind the birth and death of his son Rudy, which were presided over by a midwife, Mrs Thornton (U, 4:416–20). Symptomatically enough, the medical students' banquet during Mrs Purefoy's delivery reminds one of a wake for the dead.

It is precisely gender distinction that keeps the intersecting paths within Bloom's consciousness from overlapping. Bloom's view regarding this distinction emerges with special clarity during the funeral procession in "Hades," when, in agreement with anthropological opinions elaborated by Marcel Mauss in the first two decades of the century,[22] he envisions burial as the exclusive task of women; a task, as he envisions it, dutifully performed in silent discretion, not to disturb the resting male body.

Glad to see us go we give them such trouble coming. Job seems to suit them. . . . Slop about in slipperslappers *for fear he'd wake.* Then getting it ready. Laying it out. Molly and Mrs. Fleming making the bed. Pull it more to your side. (U, 6:14–18, my emphasis)[23]

The women's fear that the corpse could "wake"—while of course participation to the wake is reserved for the living—foreshadows the punning stylemes of *Finnegans Wake*. This passage conflates Bloom's remembrance of Molly's laying out of their eleven-day-old son, Rudy, with his morbid anticipation of Molly's laying out of his own corpse with the help of Mrs. Fleming, their part-time domestic. The allusion to the wake is implicitly assigning to the male side of the bereaved not only the privilege of being given burial, as though this crucial event were not expected to figure in the personal biography of Irish women, but also the privilege of presiding over the proper wake or banquet for the dead. Once the women have completed all necessary prearrangements, Leopold seems to believe, the work of memory must be perpetuated principally by men.

Rudy Bloom died almost eleven years before, but his father has never ceased to mourn his memory. "Rudy is always just at the fringe of his consciousness," argues John Bennett, and this is true especially in "Hades," the funeral episode, where Bloom feels envy toward Simon Dedalus's being "full of his son" (*U,* 6:74), and in "Oxen of the Sun," the maternity episode, where Bloom grieves for his "only manchild" (*U,* 14:266–67, 272).[24] But it is the "Lestrygonians" episode of cannibalism in the Burton restaurant, celebrated in Leopold's limerick, which brings memories of Rudy—halfway between mournful and nihilistic memories—to the surface of Bloom's consciousness. In hurriedly leaving the Burton he equates Homer's "famished ghosts" drinking "smokinghot" blood with the voracious "men, men, men . . . wolfing gobfuls of sloppy food," made as vociferous as the Homeric shades were made by the drinking of blood (*U,* 8:653–56, 8:729–30). It is in "Lestrygonians" that the superstitious prescriptions of curative folklore, discussed earlier, display all their contradictory, thaumaturgic potency; at first their effects menace to reduce burial commensality at the wake to its purest essence, that is, the assimilation of alien blood, but then they reveal a tenacious, redemptive capacity for sacramental anamnesis. These Homeric corpse-eaters, all male, participant in an instinctive form of ritual cannibalism,[25] were preceded in "Hades" by the gentler Homeric shades of mortuary statues, the majority of them most likely virginal and feminine, that escort Dignam's funeral procession through Dublin.[26]

> Crowded on the spit of land silent shapes appeared, white, sorrowful, holding out calm hands, knelt in grief, pointing. Fragments of shapes, hewn. In white silence: appealing . . . rare white forms. Forms more frequent, white shapes thronged amid the trees, white forms and fragments streaming by mutely, sustaining vain gestures on the air. (*U,* 6:459–62, 486–89)

In her discussion of the sacramental overtones of the "Lestrygonians" episode, Karen Lawrence maintains that the imagery of corpse-eating induces Bloom to the degrading identification of "Rudy as dead matter [with] the host [of Holy Communion] as dead meat." Even as he hurries out of the Burton, she remarks, Bloom has come face to face with "[Rudy's] unredeemed and unredeemable corpse, a vision exacerbated by his recent experience in the cemetery."[27]

The mortuary statues escorting the funeral procession in "Hades" stand for Homer's unsubstantial shades, their gestures streaming in the void, as though in remembrance of Odysseus's "futile embrace of the maternal specter." But they are only subliminal and ethereal signifiers of the funereal absence they "purport . . . to memorialize," as Kimberly Devlin has aptly observed.[28] These mortuary simulacra can only monumentalize Rudy Bloom's real dissolution of presence in death. Bloom's most direct experience of Rudy's extinguishment in death—his most direct experience of the real dissolution of presence that mortuary simulacra can only monumentalize—is conveyed by the putrefying "corpsemanure" that fertilizes the graveyard. A "tallowy kind of a cheesy [matter . . .] swirling [with] a devil of a lot of maggots" (U, 6:776–84), it can neither be intended as the literal referent of Rudy's absence from life, since it is literally saturated with life instead of death, nor as its proper signifier, since its repugnant substance can only signify the diametrical opposite of signification, namely, that total voiding of experience that Bloom, as Julia Kristeva puts it in a different context, must "permanently thrust aside in order to live."[29] The signifying persistence of human life is conceptually inconceivable in a regime of decomposition. Faced with the evidence of the reciprocal compenetration of the food chain, human mortality, and organic putrefaction, Bloom is bound to lose faith in the logical meaning and orderly signification that in ordinary circumstances would be spontaneously assigned to his existential predicaments.

In discussing Stephen Dedalus's relation to his mother's memory, I argued in chapter 1 that short of his own death, Mary Goulding Dedalus's death constitutes Stephen's most vivid experience of radical finitude. A similar observation holds in Bloom's case. The "corpsemanure" at the graveyard constitutes Bloom's most vivid experience of that impossibility of personal experience that is one's own death. This may explain why, two hours after the funeral, Bloom will anticipate the feeling of having been "eaten and spewed" himself even before having entered the Burton (U, 8:494–95). The distinction between Rudy in terms of unredeemable corpse, ritual manducation in terms of brutal cannibalism undiluted by the "idealization of mourning,"[30] and Bloom's desolate fate at home in terms of sexual deprivation all but collapse at his entrance into the Burton restaurant in search of food. Bloom enters the Burton restaurant to escape the oppression of the "warm human plumpness settled . . . on his brain" (U, 8:637), which torments him with his constant awareness of Molly's and Boylan's adulterous assignation. In the restaurant he is afforded an infernal vision of "the gospel according to Bloom," as Patrick McGee phrases it, where "death is death,"[31] corpses are waste and refuse, and eating is voracious consumption of dead life forms. He rushes out at once.

I referred earlier to Bloom's simplistic philosophy of death, made explicit when he declares in the "Hades" episode that "once you are dead you are dead" (U, 6:677). And yet, not even Bloom's skepticism can tolerate the prospect of the terrifying food chain he envisages for a few instants at the Burton restaurant, which appears to reduce human existence to a sequence of eating and copulating, productive and reproductive acts. "Nothing to feed on [they] feed on themselves"—the fate he assigned to the cadavers buried at the Prospect cemetery applies as well to the customers at the Burton restaurant (*U,* 6:781–82). But in his love of the absent Rudy and the unfaithful Molly, Bloom is not as resourceless as it may appear. In the course of the snack he eats at Davy Byrne's pub (*U,* 8:758–64), he is inspired to dramatically reconceive the intersection, patterned in his consciousness, between the physiology of nutrition, the psychology of death, and the experience of pro-creation.

> O wonder! Coolsoft with ointments her hand touched me, caressed: her eyes upon me did not turn away. Ravished over her I lay, full lips full open, kissed her mouth. Yum. Softly she gave me in my mouth the seedcake warm and chewed. Mawkish pulp her mouth had mumbled sweetsour of her spittle. Joy: I ate it: joy. Young life, her lips that gave me pouting. (*U,* 8:904–8)

This memory goes back to Bloom's youthful courtship of Molly on Howth Head, on September 10, 1888 (*U,* 17:2275–77). As discussed in the prologue, Leopold and Molly are engaged in heavy petting among the rhododendrons. Molly is chewing a seed cake, which she forces into Leopold's mouth when they kiss. This mouth-to-mouth, semifluid nutrition flowing from her to him is almost immediately followed by the seminal counterflow whereby he impregnates her with their daughter Milly, who will be born nine months later, on June 15, 1889 (*U,* 17:865).

A distinctly classical allusion is immediately called to mind by this closed-loop interaction. The flow and counterflow of seminal and nutritional secretion linking Molly's to Leopold's respective orifices suggests a creative variant of the myth of spherical human beings described by Aristophanes in Plato's *Symposium:* "[In the ancient past] each [of these creatures] had four arms, and legs equal in number to his arms, and two faces . . . and four ears, and two sets of genitals, and all the rest that one might conjecture from this."[32] After Zeus made these creatures properly human by cutting them into two distinct and reciprocally attractive halves, they took to reuniting eagerly with each other.

> Throwing their arms around one another and entangling themselves with one another in their desire to grow together, they began to die off due to hunger and the rest of their inactivity, because they were unwilling to do anything apart from one another.[33]

Leopold and Molly nurture (as do most pairs of young passionate lovers, after all) the velleity of a private, spherical universe informed by a regime of androgynous and immortal self-sufficiency. Like Aristophanes's creatures, they both fantasize of blending into each other and becoming a double-sexed creature who can manage to subsist in a regime of complete autarky from the surrounding environment—a beast feeding of its own excretions.

Molly is simultaneously chewing a seed cake, whispering endearing words, kissing Leopold, transferring a mouthful of chewed cake into his mouth, and figuratively impregnating his mouth, while he literally impregnates her womb. All of her side of this complex equation is expressed by the image of her "mumbl[ing]" sweet-and-sour "pulp" into Leopold's eager mouth. In this passage the verb mumble is pregnant, if you'll forgive the pun, with a spreading condensation of meanings, consisting of the simultaneous acts of chewing, whispering, kissing, and forcing the "pulp" through Leopold's lips. This reach of polysemantic condensation is inversely proportional to the limitation of the verb's punctual metaphor (i.e., Molly's mandibular act of chewing being figured as the subdued emission of sound from her vocal chords) and to the limitation of the verb's punctual literal sense as well (i.e., Molly's actual mumbling, hindered by the food in her mouth, consisting of the expression of endearing words). The two lovers' shared fantasy of reciprocal incorporation undermines in sum both the literal and metaphorical implications of the language describing their embrace. Literal and metaphoric meaning are displaced because one can hear resonate in the language of this scene the more primordial, prelinguistic vestiges of curative, procreative, and sacramental folklore.

We are back on the domain of our initial discussion. Leopold and Molly's kiss enables us to establish the direct connection linking Leopold's extemporaneous limerick, composed during his snack at Davy Byrne's pub, shortly before he recalls Molly's kiss, with the hosts of archaic concerns that crowd his conscious and semiconscious thoughts in the course of the entire day, ranging from the psychology of death and the physiology of nutrition to the physiology of maternal conception. "Fermented drink must have had a sexual origin. . . . In a woman's mouth, probably," Joyce had told Frank Budgen at the time of his composition of the "Lestrygonians" episode. And he added: "I have made Bloom eat Molly's chewed seed cake."[34]

Bloom's recollection of the amorous episode on Howth Head signals the most Proustian passage in *Ulysses;* it assigns a previously unsuspected role to remembrance in Bloom's self-representation of his existential predicament. Marcel Proust is the master and unchallenged model when it comes to assessing the pervasive influence exercised by one's voluntary and involuntary recollection of one's own past on the construction of one's present biography. Proust was keenly aware of the vital efficacy of mnemonic mediation; the incorporation and virtual repetition of one's past at several mnemonic removes from the immediacy of one's original experience was at the heart of his existential and artistic vocation.[35] Joyce was an attentive reader of Proust's work, as revealed by several playful allusions to the *Recherche* found in *Finnegans Wake.* Being less vehemently secular than Proust, however, Joyce was acutely aware that the fundamental human experience regarding the repetition of the past stemmed from the tradition of sacrificial or liturgical ceremonies. The meal in the company of the god is never original; it is always the repetition of a previous, irretrievable meal, where the god had been not only the virtual guest but also the consummated food. In the "Lestrygonians" episode of *Ulysses* Bloom shuffles together the gist of Proust's strategy and of Joyce's liturgical concern with repetition. His incorporation of Molly's chewed seedcake episode on Howth Head hinges especially on the mnemonic core of liturgical repetition.

Critical discussions of the kiss on Howth Head between Leopold and Molly tend to stress the framing device of the two copulating flies stuck to each other on the windowpane, which Bloom watches at the beginning and end of his recollection. Bloom's Proustian mood begins with the words: "Stuck on the pane two flies buzzed, stuck," and ends twenty-two lines later with the words: "Stuck, the flies buzzed." This device has been unanimously understood as depressive and counterclimactic. Karen Lawrence has defined the image of the two flies as "the antithesis of the erotic moment he has just remembered."[36] Understood as such a deflating factor, this device discourages the critic from devoting proper attention to the sacramental resonance of the remembrance itself.

It should be pointed out, first of all, that the twice-repeated image of the flies stuck together in copulation is in turn a mnemonic device, compounding Leopold's recollection of Milly's conception with his recollection of the day when he and Molly conceived their second child, Rudy. This episode occurred in the spring of 1893, when they lived in Raymond Terrace. Molly "was at the window watching ... two dogs at it by the wall of [the prison nicknamed] cease to do evil" (*U*, 6:78–79). The scene of copulating dogs, in their notorious position of enervating immobility, suggestive of a "stuck" condition (the male "up in [the bitch's] behind in the middle of the naked street," as Molly puts it in her monologue [*U*, 18:1446–47]), was rather ordinary in the streets of European cities at the beginning of the twentieth century. It is while she observes the two dogs that Molly invites Leopold to "give [her] a touch." She is "dying for it," as she puts it. And that's "how life begins," as Bloom himself will put it, when he remembers the event in the "Hades" episode (*U*, 6:80–81). The diction and the description of the scene suggest that Leopold gives Molly her "touch" from behind, while she keeps standing at the window and they both look at two dogs in their similar position and predicament (which interpretation explains, incidentally, why Bloom knows that the prison sergeant was "grinning up") (*U*, 6:79).

Karen Lawrence has aptly pointed out the correspondence between Bloom's memory of the kiss on Howth Head and his choice of food at Davy Byrne's. Both gorgonzola cheese and Burgundy wine are severely fermented aliments, all-digestive ("Cheese digest all but itself" *U*, 8:755). In eating this fermented food Bloom's interior monologue not only celebrates, but even emulates Molly's mumbling of a "mawkish pulp" (*U*, 8:907–8) in the Howth Head episode: "Wine soaked and softened rolled pith of bread mustard a moment mawkish cheese" (*U*, 8:850–51). Lawrence seems to have distilled the subtlest essence of literary motif when she explains that here "parts of [Bloom's] speech liquefy in imitation of the process of transcorporeality occurring in [his] mouth, as he tongues the soft pulpy mixture."[37]

But there is more. This manducatory transcorporeality does not pertain only to Bloom's digestive system, as Lawrence suggests in pointing out the "gentler form of organic breakdown [that] liquefies the bodies of food [through] enzymatic transformation."[38] Bloom's mastication may be seen as sacramental; its mouth-watering liquefaction amounts to a ritualistic repetition of his and Molly's symbiotic kiss on

Howth Head. And this anamnetic or mnemonic celebration of the closed-loop interaction between his seminal and Molly's nutritional secretions bespeaks a profane sacrament of *transcorporealization*. Leopold and Molly lay down the future foundation for their shared solidarity in front of illness, death, life, and procreation. It is on Howth Head that their genuine marriage is celebrated in their reciprocal attribution of existential significance. This seminal and nutritional exchange figures as the analogue to Stephen's horrid kiss of the maternal menses,[39] while its transcorporeal liturgy may be taken to figure as the precursor to Shem's personal *transaccidentation* onto the Word of God, which is discussed in the next chapter.

It is true, as argued by Lawrence, that Bloom feels induced to perform his voluntary recollection of the embrace on Howth Head only after that "this image of ingestion links fermentation with the very action of memory."[40] The enzymatic transformation enhanced by the gorgonzola cheese triggers Bloom's semiconscious awareness of the analogy between the conservative transformation—a ruminative form of creative repetition[41]—intrinsic to both the digestive and the mnemonic apparatus. "Seems to a secret touch telling me memory," he considers (*U,* 8:898–99). Yet, it is evident that this amorous remembrance has been present to Bloom's consciousness all along in the guise of an involuntary memory; I maintain that his second child's cathartic death has contributed, in the course of the last eleven years, to the permanent incorporation in Bloom's most vital instincts of a creatively enriched memory of the day when he and Molly conceived their first child.

His transcorporeal communion with Molly on Howth Head was, like most passionate lovemaking, truly irresponsible. Unlike most ordinary experiences of lovemaking, it was inordinately uncompromising with the rest of the universe; these two youth embrace as though for them there were no tomorrow—an autarkic, self-sufficient, and even androgynous embrace, as we have seen. But here our omnipotent author intervenes as a benevolent god, blessing their irresponsible and ultimately arrogant lovemaking with the conception first of Milly, and then of Rudy. Rudy's birth will turn into a sudden tragedy, as we know, and yet, this premature death, however devastating, is destined to function as the miraculous, cathartic factor of permanent cohesion in the pact of reciprocal solidarity they sealed on Howth Head.

In this perspective Rudy figures as a close relative of Mallarmé's *rejeton funèbre,* from which we saw Stephen Dedalus seek poetic guidance. Rudy's constant remembrance cannot be exorcised; it turns the festive memory of his parents' reciprocal incorporation into a burial meal. Ultimately, it is Leopold and Molly's symbiotic kiss, exchanged sixteen years before and turned into a burial meal in Rudy's memory by their shared experience of life and death, that determines all of Bloom's culinary feats and decisions on June 16, 1904. These feats begin with his irreverent "burnt offering" at breakfast time (*U,* 17:2044); are interrupted by his refusal to mingle with the bestial customers at the Burton restaurant; climax with the "rite of Melchisedek" at Davy Byrne's, during which his ritual incorporation of Molly's seedcake is sacramentally celebrated; and end with the hot cocoa cup shared with Stephen Dedalus at Eccles Street (*U,* 17:354–70).

To Leopold Bloom nutrition is sacramental. Each single meal renews the inspired anamnesis of his incorporation of Molly's fecundity, as well as the catharsis of his unconsoled mourning in the wake of their son's death. In this perspective, with each single meal Bloom celebrates in advance the apotropaic purgation of any betrayal, sordidness, or meanness that he and Molly will have ever inflicted on each other.

SHEM'S SCRIPTURE

Sacramental Immolation

In his brilliant study of Joyce's use of the Eucharistic image, Robert Boyle shows that Joyce's reenactments of the Eucharistic liturgy are disseminated in innumerable variants throughout the entirety of his oeuvre—from Stephen Dedalus's transmutation of "the daily bread of experience into the radiant body of everliving life" (*P,* 221) to Leopold Bloom's imaginary immersion in a bathtub "holding his body consecrated by nature to life" ("This is my body" [*U,* 5:566]), from Molly Bloom's confection of a Eucharist in menstrual blood,[1] to, again, Stephen's pouring of the (poetic and bodily) secretions of his infatuation for Emma into a "chalice flowing to the brim" (*P,* 221, 223).[2]

It is by means of these sacramental reenactments that Joyce, in Boyle's view, "comes face to face with the ultimate mystery of human existence."[3] This procession of liturgies reaches a culmination in *Finnegans Wake,* in the episode where Shem, in his impersonation of the *altus prosator* (i.e., the exalted procreator but also—from a simple pun on the Latin noun *prosa* and the English "prose"—the August writer of Holy Writ) offers his "transaccidentated" body to a most "unheavenly" (*FW,* 186:4, 185:29) form of worship. After preparing, *in vas honorabile tristitiae* ("in a honorable vessel of sadness"), *encaustum indelebile* ("an indelible ink"), made out of his own body wastes (*FW,* 185:19–20, 25–26), Shem proceeds to write "universal history" on his own skin.[4]

> *Primum opifex, altus prosator, ad terram viviparam et cunctipotentem sine ullo pudore nec venia, suscepto pluviali atque discintis perizomatis, natibus nudis uti nati fuissent, sese adpropinquans, flens et gemens, in manum suam evacuavit* (highly prosy, crap in his hand, sorry!), *postea, animale nigro exoneratus, classicum pulsans, stercus proprium, quod appellavit deiectiones suas, in vas olim honorabile tristitiae posuit, eodem sub invocatione fratrorum geminorum Medardi et Godardi laete ac melliflue minxit, psalmum qui incipit: Lingua mea calamus scribae velociter scribentis: magna voce cantitans* (did a piss, says he was dejected, asks to be exonerated), *demum ex stercore turpi cum divi Orionis iucunditate mixto, cocto, frigorique expositio, encaustum sibi fecit indelebile* (faked O'Ryan's, the indelible ink). (*FW,* 185:14–26)

The translation of this Latin passage from *Finnegans Wake* was published by Robert Boyle in a 1966 issue of the *James Joyce Quarterly* (my modifications are added in brackets):

> First of all, the artificer, the old father [August prosator], without any shame and without permission, when he had donned a cope and undone the girdles, with rump as bare as on the day of birth, squatting on the viviparous and all-powerful earth, weeping and groaning the while, defecated into his hand: and secondly, having unburdened himself of black air, while he beat out the battle-signal, he placed his own faeces, which he entitled his "purge" [or "dejection," as Joyce himself suggests in a parenthetical remark], in a once honorable vessel of sadness, and into the same, under the invocation of the twin brothers, Medardus and Godardus, he pissed happily and melodiously, continuously singing with a loud voice the psalm which begins, "My tongue is the reed of a scribe swiftly writing." Finally, from vile crap mixed with the pleasantness of the divine Orion, after the mixture had been cooked and exposed to the cold, he made for himself imperishable [indelible] ink.[5]

In Aquinas's doctrine of transubstantiation Jesus results both substantially and accidentally unaffected by the change of substance of bread and wine, the accidents of the latter species remaining in being despite the dissolution of their respective substances. Conversely, in the case of Shem's immolation of both his own authorial persona, as *altus prosator,* and his physical body (as an immolation to "a dividual [as opposed to individual] chaos, perilous, potent, common to all flesh, human only, mortal" [*FW,* 186:4–6]), there occurs a total and unconditional surrender of the "author" (*prosator*) as sacrificial victim. Having relinquished his identity, individuality, and self, Shem is "transaccidentated" (*FW,* 186:3–4) into a text, or Scripture, made of human parchment (his own skin) and of human waste (feces and urine, his own as well). Shem has become these accidents of brute matter whereby and wherein the "cyclewheeling history" of the human race is typologically turned, as Boyle puts it, into "Shem's Eucharist."[6]

This is an exquisitely liturgical moment in *Finnegans Wake,* a moment whose sacramental character can be better grasped when proper attention is paid to Joyce's citation from Psalm 44 of the Vulgate Version. This citation leads the reader to infer that, by some wonder of "transaccidentation," Shem is going to write on his own body by means of his own tongue. *Lingua mea calamus scribae velociter scribendi* (*FW,* 185:22)[7] is translated by Boyle with the words, "My tongue is the reed of a scribe swiftly writing."[8] A change of accidental nature—both unnatural and "unheavenly" —occurs in this living and embodied Scripture, whose graphemes—a "continuous present tense integumentum," susceptible, as the term "integumentum" indicates, to anagogical interpretation[9]—are *orally* produced, their inscription being effected with a tongue, paradoxically, instead than with a stylo. One might suppose that we are facing, in this episode, a literal enactment of the transmission "via the voice of the scribe," *per scribentis vocem,* through which, according to Gregorius Magnus, the

Holy Spirit *scribenda dictavit [et] transmisit* ("dictated and transmitted that which was to be written").[10] The graphemes that cover Shem's body consist, in sum, of a literal *incarnation* of that divine dictation (oral, spiritual, or "pneumatic") in which the Patristic and Scholastic tradition identified the source and original intention of Scriptural inspiration.[11] More importantly, for this change of Scripture's accidental nature to occur (Scripture coinciding here with the incarnated Word, the Eucharistic Host, the sacrificial victim Himself), Shem, a most unholy communicant, must partake of the matter of his own bodily wastes. He must dip his tongue/reed into the species of an ink whose brute substance could hardly be accommodated by the transcendental paradigms of the orthodox doctrine of transubstantiation.

Boyle neglects to stress the profound implications of this Joycean reenactment of the Eucharistic liturgy with regard to that *anamnesis* of Crucifixion that is the most vital element of the sacrament. In my previous discussion of catharsis (see chapter 7), I argued that Greek sacrificial customs may be best understood when a relation of affinity is established between holy rites and the sacrificial murder represented on the stage (or, more precisely, evoked behind the scenes) of Attic tragedy. Such an affinity justifies Burkert's qualified identification of sacred and profane victim: "The pattern [of] the victim ... marked by a touching ambivalence, despised and worshipped at the same time, ... has been elaborated, most of all, in the Christian tradition."[12] The sacred victim of ritual sacrifice is holy and must be ingested for an expiation to occur; the profane victim of tragic catharsis is unholy and must be expelled for an expurgation to occur. In turn, the unholy scapegoat of Attic tragedy undergoes more often than not a metamorphosis into the condition of sanctified victim and redeemer. Furthermore, both the manducation of the holy victim and the expulsion of the profane victim are experienced by the respective participants to the rite and to the spectacle as the collective activation of an essential bodily function, one that restores the integrity of the social corpus, or body politic—ingestion in the case of the holy victim, secretion in the case of the profane victim.

Calvary constitutes the historical locus where the archaic identification of sacred and profane victim comes to a typological resolution in the immolation of a *sacred scapegoat*. And the Eucharistic meal provides the liturgical setting for this immolation, the immolation of a sacrificial victim who, as "a curse for us,"[13] must be secreted, but, as the bread and blood of the "new covenant,"[14] must be ingested too. This historical and typological resolution of the tradition of archaic sacrifice is diluted into a wander of speculative ontology in Aquinas's doctrine of transubstantiation; centered on an empty form of ritualized commensality, the latter domesticates the liturgical meal, depriving it of the essential moment of experiential or existential reenactment. The concept of Eucharistic substance grounds the doctrine of transubstantiation whereby Aquinas explains the process that brings Jesus's body to presence in the Eucharist. It all comes down to a matter of ontological presence *by concomitance:* "Neither the divinity nor the *anima* of Christ is in this sacrament as a result of the strength of the sacrament; they are there by a natural *concomitance*. Since divinity never renounced the body it assumed, wherever the body of Christ is, there you must have also his divinity."[15] Since Jesus's substance inheres in Jesus's mortal body, the result of Aquinas's doctrine of transubstantiation *ex reali concomitantia*[16] is that Jesus's body would be verily present in the consecrated species of the Eucharist. Moreover, by the elusive game of the "natural concomitance" linking Jesus's body to the substance of his divinity and *anima,* this corollary applies, that Jesus's *anima* and divinity would also be ontologically present in the sacrament. This divine presence is, however, a presence by subtraction, a presence by omission, based on the presumption that Calvary is unrepeatable, that the passion and death of the Word of God[17] is a once-and-for-all event. Jesus does not die—does not even change, existentially and metaphysically speaking—in transubstantiation. "Having risen from the dead, Christ will never die again."[18] Jesus, the victim of the original sacrifice that inaugurates Christianity, becomes, through Crucifixion, sovereign and immutable —*gloriosum et impassibile.* It is the substance of the Eucharistic species, bread and wine, that changes, that passes "into the potency of matter and disappear(s) altogether,"[19] to be substituted, in the ontological function of holding-in-being the accidents of bread and wine, by the divine substance that contributes to the miracle of transubstantiation without being directly and immediately affected by it. Aquinas's Eucharist is reduced essentially to the celebration of a table rite, a rite of manducation grounded on a paradigm of ontological presence by concomitance that eludes the experiential or existential immediacy of the archaic sacrifice

By contrast, Shem's reenactment of the Eucharistic liturgy has the visionary peculiarity of bringing felicitously together, in the liturgical meal, the ingestion and the secretion of the sacred scapegoat. The scene of Shem's partaking of his own bodily wastes goes further than the depiction of a horridly unholy communion; it goes even further than the doctrinal entertainment of a hypothetical "transaccidentation" of substance, obtainable for instance via the "vicus of recirculation" (*FW,* 3:2) of excreta foregrounded, as we saw, in Leopold and Molly Bloom's transcorporeal kiss on Howth Head (see chapter 7). A veritable and intense liturgical vision emanates from this episode of *Finnegans Wake.*

Shem partakes of the *deiectiones suas* (his "purge," as Boyle translates, or his "dejection," as Joyce suggests [*FW,* 185:19]), which he poured into the *vas olim honorabile tristitiae* (the "vessel of sadness" that was once, as indicated by the implicit reference to the litany of the Virgin Mary, the "honorable" womb of Christ's gestation [*FW,* 185:19–20]). In doing so, Shem comes to personify, at once, the sacrificial, messianic victim to be ex-purgated and the celebrant of the liturgy who, needing expiation, ingests the victim. This sacramental ubiquity is congruent with the Church Fathers' early debates about Christ's ubiquitous role in the Eucharist. For example, St. Augustine writes in *De civitate dei: In hac [forma servi] oblatus est . . . In hac sacerdos, in hac sacrificium est.* (In the shape of a servant he is offered, in this same shape he is priest and sacrifice.) And also: *Et sacerdos est, ipse offerens, ipse et oblatio* (He is both the priest, since he celebrates the offering, and the offering itself).[20] Sacramental ubiquity makes of Shem the origin and destination, at once, of the reenactment of primordial sacrifice.

If Altizer is correct in postulating that "the worshiper and the god pass into each other" in the event of the primordial sacrifice,[21] one might say that Joyce has here displayed this theological principle of sacramental osmosis in its most consistent liturgical implementation, an implementation in radical opposition with Aquinas's doctrine of transubstantiation.

Even if the emergence of this sacred and horrific catharsis brings to full typological resolution the abundant procession of Eucharistic reenactments and profane liturgies disseminated in Joyce's works, and especially in *Finnegans Wake,* an extraordinary element of equivocation with respect to the identity of the sacred scapegoat is determined by the consideration, just discussed, that Shem, the partaker of his own species as feces, is both the subject and the object of this celebration. Furthermore, as is well known to the readers of the *Wake,* Shem is often identified with Old Nick, the folkloric incarnation of Lucifer. This bivalve equivocation, a deliberate one, I venture, on Joyce's part, seriously impacts the thrust and resonance of the above interpretation.

Equivocations of comparable magnitude occur elsewhere in Joyce, and also in Dante. In his description of the mystic procession of *Purgatorio,* for instance, Dante's heretic imagination does not hesitate from submitting the sacred scapegoat of the Eucharist to a most literal and lyrical transformation into his beloved Beatrice (*Purgatorio,* 30). In turn, it is already in *Ulysses,* as early as at the close of the first part of the book, conventionally identified as the *Telemachiad,* that Joyce, in typically Blakean fashion, brings Christ and Lucifer to a *coincidentia oppositorum* by having Stephen take on both roles.[22]

> . . . I thirst. Clouding over. No black clouds anywhere, are there? Thunderstorm. Allbright he falls, proud lightning of the intellect, *Lucifer, dico, qui nescit occasum.* (*U,* 3:485–87)

Incidentally, *coincidentia oppositorum* may also apply here, ironically, to Stephen's parody of the thirsty Christ on the Cross. The consideration that Stephen may have been made thirsty by the sight of a porter bottle "in the cakey sand dough" of the beach ("A sentinel: isle of dreadful thirst" [*U,* 3:152–54]) suggests an ironic typological variation, perhaps not quite Blakean yet, with respect to the episode of the crucified Christ's drink of vinegar—which occurs in typological sequence, after Christ refused to drink wine "mingled with gall" on the way to Golgotha and, the day before in Gethsemane, asked his Father to "let this cup pass from [Him]" (Matthew 27:48, 27:34, 26:39). As regards the more properly Blakean coincidence of Christ and Satan in the above citation from *Ulysses,* Altizer provides an incisive comment in *Genesis and Apocalypse:*

> *Ulysses* does initiate us into that Christ who is Satan. . . . Christ here and now becomes indistinguishable from that Lucifer who falls and yet knows no fall.
> . . . Joyce's Latin phrase [*Lucifer, dico, qui nescit occasum*] is borrowed from a phrase in the Roman Catholic liturgy for Holy Saturday, [which indicates that] Joyce

wholly knows the fall as a fortunate fall, a fortunate fall that is the very plot or action of both *Ulysses* and *Finnegans Wake.* (170–71)

Revision of the Christ Type

After Shem's transaccidentation has taken place, it is explained in the *Wake* that at each new word added to the writ he inscribes on the parchment of his own body —at each further step, I venture, taken by Shem in the kenotic relinquishment of identity and individuality that will turn him into the Augustinian "word that would not pass away"—corresponds the recurrent phenomenon of Shem's own self "wan-[ing] chagreenold and doriangrayer" (*FW*, 186:6–9). Robert Boyle glosses this phrase with the subtle observation that "Shem's ink goes through the shades of the Irish flag ('chagreenold [green and gold] and doriangrayer [*or* {French for gold} and off-white]')."[23]

To complement the patriotic with the theological interpretation, one ought to remark that the suffixes "-old" in "chagreenold" and "-grayer" (more gray) in "doriangrayer" also suggest that Shem's waning is related to an accelerated process of physical deterioration. In turn, the prefixes "chagreen-," which alludes to the title and subject of Balzac's *La peau de chagrin,* and "doriangray-," which alludes to the protagonist of Wilde's *The Picture of Dorian Gray,* suggest, as we will see presently, that this accelerated deterioration has everything to do with Shem's transaccidentation not being "true to type" from a doctrinal standpoint (*FW*, 172:17–18).[24]

From the Thomist perspective, true to type are only those characters and events from Scripture that conform to the "type of types" that will have come about with Christ's incarnation. The teleology established by Aquinas in the evolution of vetero-Testamental types points toward Crucifixion as its final destination. When a previous manifestation of type does not coincide with the teleological "type of types," then this type may be relegated to the status of a poetic and didactic expedient devoid of spiritual meaning. All other types must be Thomistally intended as analogical and etiological manifestations of Christ's Incarnation and Crucifixion. To Aquinas Jesus Christ is the paradigm or ultimate noetic object anchoring all quests for interpretive understanding undertaken by the biblical exegete.

> The Old Testament was a figure of the New Testament: both the Old and New Testament are figures of celestial things, hence spiritual sense can be grounded on figural sense in the manner whereby the Old Testament prefigures the New Testament: such is the allegorical or *typical* sense, according to which those things that occurred in the Old Testament were being told about Christ and the Church.[25]

Balzac's *La peau de chagrin* had a profound influence on Wilde's *The Picture of Dorian Gray,* deeper probably than acknowledged in Richard Ellmann's biography of Oscar

Wilde.[26] In the case of both novels, the central plot concerns a young man trading the youthful grace and innocence of either his body (Balzac's Raphael) or his soul (Wilde's Dorian) in return for unbounded pleasure and satisfaction. Balzac's Raphael and Wilde's Dorian experience lives of accelerated intensity and unrestrained fulfillment, and this leads to their premature demise. The emblem of Raphael's corruption is a piece of leather, made from the hide of an onager,[27] endowed with the power to grant all of Raphael's desires, but fated to shrink further and further every time Raphael expresses a new wish. Ownership of this magic amulet comes with a curse: its owner's allotted lifetime is bound to shrink together with the shrinking of the leather. In turn, the emblem of Dorian's corruption is a portrait that incorporates the growing moral ugliness of Dorian's soul, leaving Dorian's own external appearance intact and forever young. In both cases, the individual protagonist rapidly dissolves into a type or simulacrum of his own physical and/or spiritual deterioration.

Balzac's amulet represents the fateful wearing out to which human will power is bound to succumb:[28] as Raphael runs through all the resources, whims, and fantasies of his capricious volition, his physical constitution withers—shrinks literally away—into a bodily concretization of the human type embodied in his lifestyle. Wilde's portrait is the ironic allegory of the power of mimesis to duplicate every human self-expression, even the decay of a singular, unique, virtually unduplicatable and irreproducible soul: soon in the story Dorian's depraved soul abdicates its spiritual individuality to turn itself—to literally materialize itself—into a mimetic reproduction (made up of canvas and artificial colors) of the corruption it represents. In both cases, the individual protagonist loses gradually his individuality to become transfixed into a type of the ineluctable human condition of being-toward-death; at the same time, the emblem of this human condition, the objective type, or simulacrum, be it a painting or a piece of leather, turns out to be malleable and transitory, a faithful and changing duplicate of those individual destinies that, typologically speaking, would normally be perceived as the type's, the emblem's, or the simulacrum's merely circumstantial duplications, or phenomenological incarnations, in time. In sum, as the protagonist is typified, the type is personified.

Alternative readings of La peau de chagrin and The Picture of Dorian Gray are possible, but the present one is specifically suggested by the inclusion of these literary allusions to Balzac and Wilde in the description of Shem's transaccidentation. Not being "true to type," when type is Thomistally intended as teleological, Shem sacrifices his self, his identity, and his very body to the Word of God by becoming a latter-day type of the Messiah. Through this self-abnegation he grows as prematurely old as Raphael in La peau de chagrin ("chagreenold") and as prematurely gray-haired (symbolically or pictorially speaking) as Dorian in The Picture of Dorian Gray ("doriangrayer"). He sets therefore his messianic incarnation in a rapport of creative interplay with these two modern literary types, incorporating them in a "cycle-wheeling" process of recursive (prospective and retrospective) reconfiguration of the type itself of the Son of God.[29]

Corpus of Scriptural Poetics

Having celebrated this ritual of scriptural *and* literary transaccidentation upon his own body, Shem has incarnated himself into the stercoraceous and desecrated species of Scripture; his body has been minutely tattooed, "transaccidentated" (*FW,* 186:4) into the textual "integument" (*FW,* 186:1) of the salvific immolation at the core of the messianic vision; his tongue has partaken of the Eucharistic matter of his own body wastes (*FW,* 185:22). Step by step, Shem relinquishes his own self ("squid-self"), the perishable integumentum of his "squirtscreened" individuality, and, through the accelerated physical deterioration typified in the allusions to the characters of Balzac and Wilde, becomes a posthumous scriptural incarnation of the crucified Messiah. Or should I say, considering the integumental nature of his dead skin ("dudhud," or Danish *dødhud,* for "dead skin"), that he becomes, on top of incarnation, a dead im-parchment, a belated, twentieth-century anachronistic transcription of the archaic scrolls of divine revelation (*FW,* 186:6–8).

Shem's tattooed skin—aptly related by Robert Boyle to the literary type of Balzac's *peau*—functions as the papyrus of this de-individualized or, in the local diction of this passage, "dividual" type (*FW,* 186:4).[30] It is not, as Robert Boyle would have it, a shield ("hud" being akin to the verb "hide") protecting Shem from Milton's "rational crystal universe hanging in chaos."[31] It is rather, I wish to suggest, the opaque, inert matter of *anamnesis* that bestows permanent participation in Dante's "crystalline world" on this automotive corpus of Scripture (*FW,* 186:8). The passage under consideration presents several densely doctrinal implications relating to Jesus's hypostatic nature. It is in the light of these implications that I venture to move the focus of interpretation away from the Miltonic contiguity of crystal and chaos suggested by Boyle, and toward the crystalline essence of Dante's *Cielo empireo.*[32]

Joyce's reference to the "crystalline world" (wherein Shem's "transaccidentation" has occurred) alludes to Dante's visualization of the universe as a crystal filled with the light of God.[33] Dante's *cristallino,* an epithet specifically attributed to his Empyrean *Primum Mobile,* is conventionally understood as "a term of comparison for the entire cosmos."[34] In Dante's anagogical sublation of the universal history of Creation under the event of Incarnation, *cristallo* signifies the polysemic convergence of *Cristo-stallo,*[35] that is, the total, cosmic, all-pervasive grace-infusion determined by Christ's condition of *stallo,* or stasis (hypostasis, precisely), that "final and complete integration of Christ's *utranque naturam*"[36] that brings to reciprocal coalescence, in the ultimate harmony of his Passion, his carnal and divine essence. Yet, just as the spiritual nature of Shem, who is turned by transaccidentation into a latter-day "type of types," entitles him to participation in the crystal glory of the *Primum Mobile,* so his carnal nature sentences him to participation in the "dividual chaos . . . common to all flesh, human only, mortal" (*FW,* 186:4–5). The miracle of the Eucharist, revisited and revisioned in the liturgy of Shem's "transaccidentation," consists, doctrinally speaking, of the ultimate coincidence of these two destinations.

Shem has then turned his body into the Augustinian species, however stercoraceous and desecrated, of "each word that would not pass away"—that is, Holy Writ

(*FW,* 186:6; *Confessiones,* Liber IV, cap. 11). In doing so, he has offered himself to a *kenosis* in reverse, a most secular liturgy enacting the end of Christian eschatology and the affirmation of base, scatological, perennial human reproduction. His scriptural body has been turned into the ultimate rhetorical mode of messianic discourse —a mode dependent on a paradoxically oral textuality, an oral inscription (and, one might add, encryption) that brings the Word of God to resonate in the flesh and tongue of (the) man (of letters), that brings the sacred immortal Word to resonate perennially—to the point of self-extinction—in the profane, the secular, the mortal, the utterly corporeal, bound to end in putrefaction.

Now Shem is the word–made–flesh that shall not pass away. "As we . . . weave and unweave our bodies . . . from day to day, their molecules shuttled to and fro, so does the artist weave and unweave his image" (*U,* 9:376–78): the analogy that Stephen Dedalus draws in *Ulysses* between the body's molecular transformation and the self's tropic transfiguration or self-begetting, an analogy derived from Walter Pater,[37] has now blossomed into a paradox: the biographical enactment of a liturgical trans-figuration. The figural trope or synecdoche of a writer being "read" is inaugurated by Ovid's prophecy at the end of the *Metamorphoses,* where he predicts that *ore legar populi . . . [et] uiuam* ("I will be *read* by the tongue of the people . . . [hence] I'll live").[38] The same trope is then given a sinister twist in Dante's *Inferno,* where Brunetto Latini derives consolation for his eternal damnation from securing himself a prospect of perpetual writerly fame on earth (15:120). This trope finds now a most literal validation in the messianic poetics of *Finnegans Wake:* in reading the corpus of the text, we read the body or corpus; in reading the word, we read the story of Shem's transaccidentated flesh. Negative poetics, negative hermeneutics, and negative biography are here one and the same.

With regard to Shem's transaccidentation, we still have to properly consider the phenomenon of reverse filiation whereby the Incarnate Word, whose messianic coming is typologically announced in Scripture, undertakes to beget—under the guise of a character from *Finnegans Wake*—a novel inscription of the divine *Verbum,* ultimately a novel origination of the original act of Creation itself. A reverse filiation of Scripture: but how does filiation reverse itself into an original generation of its own origin? The answer found in Shem's transaccidentation is that such a reverse filiation occurs via an act of revisionary writing that reconceives and restipulates the entirety of Scripture, down to the materiality itself of its inscription—a novel inscription of the divine *Verbum,* in other words, as though upon a virtually inverted Veronica, or *vera icona,* as though upon the decomposing skin ("human only, mortal" [*FW,* 186:4–6]) of the divine *Verbum*'s own sacrificial corpse.

As we saw, in the middle of the preparation of his *encaustum indelebile* (indelible ink), Shem sings in a loud voice a line from Psalm 44 of the Vulgate Version of the Bible: *Lingua mea calamus scribae velociter scribentis* (My tongue is the reed of a scribe swiftly writing). Robert Boyle writes that *"Calamus,* a reed, is not without some tonality of the pointing ash-plant that Stephen [Dedalus] used, and surely close to the life-wand that Shem lifts at the end of this chapter [in order to return, in Christ-like fashion, the gift of speech to the dumb]."[39] Boyle could have also underlined the triangular intertextuality that hides behind Shem's choice for a biblical verse to sing. In this passage, Joyce's depiction of Shem's scriptural inspiration is either strikingly felicitous or ingeniously purposeful, because Psalm 44:2 happens to be the line chosen by Aquinas to challenge the argument that "spiritual sense [may be] found not only in Holy Scripture but also in profane literature (*ars poetica*)":

> *In nulla scientia humana industria inventa . . . potest inveniri nisi litteralis sensus; sed solum in ista scriptura, cuius spiritus sanctus est auctor, homo vero instrumentum; secundum illud psalm. Xliv, v. 2: lingua mea calamus scribae velociter scribentis . . . Fictiones poeticae non sunt ad aliud ordinatae nisi ad significandum; unde talis significatio non supergreditur modum litteralis sensus* (Quodlibet, n. 7, qu. 6, ar. 3.)
>
> [In no science devised by human ingenuity can one find more than literal sense; only in Scripture, whose author is the Holy Spirit, can man find the proper means (to genuine knowledge); as Psalm 44 says, "My tongue is the reed of a scribe swiftly writing.". . . Poetic fictions have no other aim than signification; their signification does not go beyond the mode of literal sense.]

Joyce's and Aquinas's citations of the same line from Psalm 44 operate at crosspurposes. In Aquinas, this line comes at the conclusion of the demonstration of the ineptitude of profane literature—the *infima doctrina*—to convey those spiritual meanings deployed instead by the doctrinal interpretation of the "allegorical or typical sense" of the Bible. Whereas Scripture, he claims, signifies beyond the reach of its literal sense, in profane literature tropic (or, more conforming to Aquinas's diction, "parabolic" [*parabolicus*]) meaning is never exorbitant of a passage's literal meaning. Aquinas believes that in profane literature the parabolic sense is part of the literal sense, or, as Eco would put it, the metaphorical sense emerges unmediatedly from the literal sense.[40] While the words of the Bible mean immediately one thing (historical or literal or parabolic) and mediately a distinct, spiritual thing,[41] a fiction from profane literature means immediately its own parable.[42]

In Joyce the citation seems to be aimed at the opposite purpose. Shem's tongue/ reed has the messianic power to return the use of the tongue, the full power of speech, or, figuratively, the gracious benevolence of *Logos,* to those unfortunate who were previously unable to express themselves in words (Luke 11:14). Joyce opposes multifarious, vernacular, common vociferation to the silent remoteness of Aquinas's spiritual sense. Shem, the incarnation of the profane letters of *Finnegans Wake,* must also be intended, therefore, as the messianic incorporation of the ultimate stage of scriptural inscription. He is the textual corpus—*altus prosator:* author, enactor, interpreter, *and* script—of the sacrificial type whereby the true meaning of Scripture manifests itself. In his existential and corporeal enactment of the scene of writing, the scriptural canon in its modernist stage cannot be distinguished any more from profane letters; the inverted scriptural Veronica—the *vera icona* of transaccidentation —is forever recycling its own decomposition.

Word and Flesh

The above aspects of *Finnegans Wake* bring to closure the bimillennial cycle of opposition between Word and Flesh that had been inaugurated for the consciousness of the West by the Pauline and Augustinian writings. This is the reason why Joyce's messianism manifests itself primarily as liturgy, as sacrificial enactment and *anamnesis;* its most radical affirmation, in *Finnegans Wake,* consists of the only text of the modern tradition that cannot be read, even in solitude, without being recited aloud, in the manner of an archaic epic narration, but, more relevantly here, in the manner of a liturgical canon whose recitation is existentially inseparable from its own reenactment.

Shem's biographic incorporation of the divine *Verbum* calls for an analogous liturgy on the part of the reader. Joyce's passages on transaccidentation cannot be read with the metaphysical confidence of the commentary that "considers the self-identity of the text, . . . carves out its contour [and] leaps over the text toward its presumed content."[43] To Joyce's reader pertains at this juncture the existential option of repeating or enacting anew Shem's biography of transaccidentation, in such a way (and with such a revisionistic thrust) that Joyce's agenda for the messianic self shall result radically differentiated from the conventional expectation of the "irreducible stratum of [a] signified."[44]

In *James Joyce's Pauline Vision,* Robert Boyle writes that "the thing we must be decontaminated from [in transaccidentation] is the body," so that we can "humanize [Shem's] ink."[45] In his treatment of transaccidentation, Boyle maintains that "the artist suffers a passing of accidents . . . in the artistic consecrated ink of the artist"— the artist referred to being indifferently either the Shem of transaccidentation or the Stephen Dedalus who "transmute[s] the daily bread of experience into the radiant body of everliving life" (*P,* 221).[46] Transaccidentation is the process, according to Boyle, but "consubstantiation" is the result whereby the self or soul of the artist is "huddled . . . under the ink until some reader . . . summons him forth."[47] Once the Eucharistic logic is transferred to the profane text, Boyle seems comfortable in reverting to the conventionally Thomist view of exegesis: in an episcopal fashion that may remind one of Jean-Luc Marion's Catholic phenomenology of Eucharistic liturgy (see chapter 1), the Joycean reader would "summon . . . forth" that which is already intentionally contained in Joyce's text, the irreducible stratum of its signified, the literal *factum* contained in the *figura.* This explains Boyle's indifferent attribution of transaccidentation to both Shem's bodily incorporation of "cyclewheeling history" and Stephen's "transmutation" of the bread of experience into a consecrated body.[48]

Boyle's view of the exegetic enterprise vis-à-vis Joyce's passages on transaccidentation is consistent with Aquinas's doctrine of typological interpretation. On the contrary, it must be thrown here in bold relief that transaccidentation is not just an episodic theme in Joyce's text, but also a proactive, existential model of readerly reception, that operates prospectively and retrospectively at once. The *vera icona* of transaccidentation, forever expanding and forever de-composing, must not be so much read or interpreted as it must be *celebrated* through the profanity (and the profanities) of an existential emulation. It is not recommendable to any and everybody, therefore, to engage in a Joycean liturgy of transaccidentation; to do so, one must don Shem's Veronica—his corpus, his body's *vera icona*—and face (or be-toward) one's ineluctable fate in death and decomposition. Far from being the superfluous ballast that, according to Boyle, one must be "decontaminated" from, one's own flesh becomes the protagonist of an autobiography of sacrificial *anamnesis*.

Shem "will[s] to show herword in flesh" (*FW*, 561:27) to his sister Isobel—also known as "Charis" and "Charissima," the "Mother of moth" (*FW*, 561:22, 27). In *Finnegans Wake* this tiny-breasted girl represents Jesus's mother, the virginal begetter of "herword in flesh." Her parents, Mr and Mrs Porter, may be seen in loving contemplation of her immaculate "dormitio," while "she may think [that] it hath happened to her" the miracle that, I submit, happens precisely to the imaginary maid of Stephen's "vampire quatrain": "you know what, as they [Mr and Mrs Porter] too what two dare not utter" (*FW*, 561:27–30).

With puberty comes responsibility, but in the messianic universe of *Finnegans Wake* the responsibility of abstinence that grounds the archaic tradition of primordial sacrifice, and opens the horizon of possibility for the constitution of human community, reaches a moment of dissipation, to be replaced hereafter by a festive and tolerant ethics of carnal concupiscence. The stercoraceously immolated Shem, the flesh-made-word that makes the Word perennially carnal, cannot "show herword in flesh" to his immaculate sister, the "mother of moth," without showing her the entire transaccidentated corpus of his scripturalized body, inclusive of "his bellbearing stylo" (*FW*, 186:15): this "stylo" is nothing but a belligerent "quillbone" (*FW*, 229:30) or phallus, tolling two festively testicular (or "ellipsoidal" *P*, 192) bells.

One may wonder if the miracle that Isobel "may think . . . hath happened to her," while she sleeps or pretends to sleep the sleep of immaculate death, has truly occurred—that same miracle that her "too" (two) parents "two" (too) dare not utter. Is this the night of the beginning of her menstrual cycle, in other words? It has to be, I should venture, if this is to be the night as well when Shem's transaccidentation into excremental scripture brings the essence of the divine to coincide with the basest secretions of mortal flesh, thereby turning Shem into a most pure expression of the sacred scapegoat, the holy savior made horrid and repellent; and the night when, furthermore, the scriptural type of the savior comes to coalesce with the elemental, virginal type of female fertility.

In *Pruning the Genealogical Tree*, I have defined this episode as the moment of copro-eschatology, when the dichotomous manifestation of good and evil is eclipsed.[49] But there occurs here also a moment of gynecoid-eschatology, and this is the moment of the resolved opposition between Eve and Mary. In her immaculate "dormition" as the "mother of moth," pubescent Isobel dreams of an absolution from the sentence or curse of the law of nature, an absolution extended to herself, to her "bellbearing" stylographic brother Shem, and to the entire lascivious and incestuous Porter family. It is a matter of collective rejoicing indeed, whenever the pale vampire of the menses, announced by her "redminers riots" (*FW*, 27:17–18), comes to kiss the Mallarmean lips of this exuberant, concupiscent, and concupiscible "handmaid of the moon." Freedom of choice and birth control have something futural and sacramental to them in the universe of *Finnegans Wake.*

Organic Bio-Graphy

The character of Shem stands for the sacred scapegoat who turns himself into a literal incorporation and excremental version, or better yet, revision, of the text of Scripture. The most decisive exegetic implication inherent to this incarnated scripture assumes the form of what Giuseppe Martella calls "bio-graphy": *Scrittura del corpo umano e di quello canonico della tradizione occidentale: epica letteraria del corpo umano simbolico* (Inscription of the human body and of the canonical body of Western tradition: literary epic of the symbolic human body).[50]

In the context of Shem's transaccidentation, this notion of bio-graphy may be taken to define a collusion of bio-graphic and bio-logic textuality, an organic sort of textuality that manifests itself as a permanent process of redrafting and reconfiguration. Bio-graphy signifies therefore the future-perfect enactment of its own result, that is, the future-perfect writing of the chronicle of a living organism: a chronicle-writing identical with the writing *of* (upon) this living organism *by* this living organism; a chronicle mediated, or told, or recalled, or inspired by a *logos* that, as it "weave[s] and unweave[s]" the body of this living organism, its "molecules shuttled to and fro" (*U,* 9:376–77), envisions and, at one and the same time, submits to constant revision the unfolding narrative of this organism's life and of its meaning. One is facing here a messianic exacerbation of Stephen Dedalus's analogy between molecular transformation of the body and tropic transfiguration of the persona.

But how can a chronicle be identical with the act of writing the chronicle's own text? And how can a chronicle envision a textuality always already identical with its own revision? The notion of bio-graphy circumscribes the interpretive field of an ever-changing perspective, one that shares with the tradition of Thomist hermeneutics, if little else, the all-encompassing exegetic dominant of Crucifixion. In Aquinas's practice of typological interpretation, the historical precipitation of Crucifixion provides the hermeneutic code or the "type of types" that translates the facts in the lives of Moses, of David, of Ezra, etc., into allegoric, moral, and anagogic lessons. Aquinas's hermeneutics corresponds to an unveiling practice of interpretation that frees the Word from the thickly epic, or *mythopoietic,* facade of wars, covenants, genealogies, love affairs, infatuations, and subterfuges (in one word, from common and ordinary experience), to reveal *it*—the Word Incarnate—as the sole protagonist and interpreter of Scripture. Luke: "And beginning with Moses and all the prophets, [Jesus] interpreted to [Cléopas and his traveling companion] the things concerning himself in all the scriptures" (24:27).

To Aquinas, then, the Old Testament is twice separated from its hermeneutics; first, by Jesus's interpretation of Scripture, and second, by Jesus's sacrificial enactment of the Word. When intended from the future-perfect perspective of bio-graphy, Crucifixion turns instead the double remove of this hermeneutic separation into the organic unity of a text whose protagonist, interpreter, and virtual redactor, or "dictator,"[51] is the Word—hence, *in nuce* the text itself. Within the Thomist logic of typological interpretation, one might confidently maintain that Jesus-on-the-Cross, as the type of all vetero-Testamentary types, is the embodiment of Scripture itself. However, as the instantaneously sacrificial reenactment of all his types and precursors, Jesus-on-the-Cross is also the demise of the typological principle that informs Scripture as literary form.

In this perspective, the theological stakes at play in the episode of the sacred scapegoat embodying the living Scripture of *Finnegans Wake* deserve to be further emphasized. Shem's bio-graphy is the subjective and objective writing of Shem, who manifests (or transaccidentates) himself as textual skin or cutaneous text. In turn, this living cutaneous text is the result of the act of writing whereby the protagonist of bio-graphy inscribes—and encrypts as well, in the manner of an extensive tattoo—a scripture, or Scripture *tout court,* upon himself. Lastly, this script is a logocentric and cuti-centric text that reenvisions and revises itself at the pace at which the molecules of Shem's skin will have woven and unwoven themselves.

Shem is the protagonist of a chronicle of events that he inscribes within the *livre de lui-même,*[52] turning thereby his own sacrificial body, and each and any single act performed by his body as well, into the instantaneous, future-perfect interpretation of his own chronicle: an interpretation that is interpretive simultaneity, a pure action that is immediate signification, a sudden narration that is constant retrospective anamnesis. This bio-graphy is sacramental. It amounts to an instance of the transaccidentation whereby the sacred scapegoat of Christian tradition communicates himself, via ingestion, with his own repulsive and impure excreta. It consists ultimately of an ever-evolving scripture, an uninterruptable canon, that will have been consecrated, or desecrated, or, more properly speaking, transaccidentated, via the self-replicative drift of its adaptive organicism.

EPILOGUE

NECROPOLITUDE

I remained in Coptos, Upper Egypt on the eastern bank of the Nile. I did not drink, eat, breathe—did not do anything at all. I was like one who is confined to the Underworld. I turned to my brother Ptah-nefer-ka and said, "My beloved Husband, it is vital that I see the Sacred Book. It is because of the Sacred Book that we suffer the pains that we will have suffered." Ptah-nefer-ka placed the Sacred Book in my hands. I recited one of the pages. My words became spellbinding. "How can we preserve the secret memory of these writings?" I asked my husband Ptah-nefer-ka, my older brother, a most excellent scribe and a man of great learning. He took a stash of papyrus leaves and transcribed every word contained in the Sacred Book, filling the leaves with the secrets of the Sacred Book. He then dissolved the leaves in a small basin. After they had been completely dissolved in the liquid, he drank the mixture. Thus he absorbed everything contained in the Sacred Book. Thoth, god of Writing, related [the theft of the Sacred Book] to the Sun. The Sun replied to Thoth: "For this act of thievery Ptah-nefer-ka's fate is now at the mercy of your judgment, as well as the fate of all his people." Because of the theft of the Sacred Book these sufferings have been laid out for us, sufferings that we tried to protect ourselves against by stealing the Sacred Book. When the boat reached the ravine of the Nile where our son Mehru had drowned, I stepped forward into the shadow of the royal boat and fell into the water. I let out an invocation to the Sun, and begged the diaphanous crowd gathered on the shore to save me, to no avail. The news of my drowning was reported to Ptah-nefer-ka, who then stepped forward into the shadow of the royal boat, read the Writings of the Sacred Book and made me rise to the surface. The power of the Sacred Book made me emerge from the waters that had killed me. My brother, my husband, asked me to recount to him in minute detail everything that happened to me, and the exact words that Thoth pronounced in front of the Sun when relating the theft of the Sacred Book. Then Ptah-nefer-ka returned with me to Coptos and had my body lowered to the Underworld.

Excerpts from The Tale of Setnau

The death of his own mother induces Stephen Dedalus to realize that the truth of his future poetry will not have been written in the language of ordinary and common experience.[1] He needs to invent a language expressive of the fecundity of his own ineluctable extinguishment in death. His adventures in *Ulysses* suggest that in order to deploy his poetic gift, Stephen ought to engage himself in a negative existence, unhinged from the logic of reciprocity in affective matters and retribution in economic matters. Stephen ought to write in the language expressive of this negative existence, but on June 16, 1904, he seems unable to do so.

On the same day we observe Leopold Bloom, on the verge of being overwhelmed by his desolate domestic situation, excavate out of the memories of his courtship of Molly the liturgy of their impossible, secretive symbiosis. This remembrance, in turn, supplies the nurturing, self-replicating host that vivifies his mourning for their lost son, Rudy. Bloom's every meal in *Ulysses* turns sacramental, a burial meal, reducing his domestic despair to a transitory misfortune vis-à-vis the exclusive, perennial, secret solidarity that Rudy's demise has bestowed on his and Molly's reciprocal attachment.

Stephen Dedalus and Leopold Bloom are negative characters whose predicaments adumbrate the existential urge to rebel against the tyranny of common, ordinary experience. Between the pole of the literal prescriptions of reciprocity and retribution and the pole of ironic reduction, which translates all flights of fantasy into figurative masks of the same literal prescriptions, Stephen and Bloom are in search of a third alternative. They both want to reconceive their own identity in the light of this third way. In the present study I have provided a tentative name to this sought-after alternative identity, that of messianic self, and an existential agenda, that of experiencing one's own inevitable death as cathartic for one's fellow mortals, collusive with the universal drive toward altruism and generosity. Such an agenda, eccentric to ordinary and common experience, yearns for the mystical condition, the state of intimacy with eternity experienced by our ancestors in their compulsive identification with the consecrated victim of holy sacrifice.

Joyce's two major protagonists object impulsively to the reduction of human existence to the signification and the significance attributed it by literal and/or metaphoric hermeneutics. Such an existential impulse may turn out to be rooted in our innate endowment of vestigial memories from the past of the species. I have discussed Vico's and Augustine's respective probings of the secrets of human interiority in order to test this very hypothesis, which enables me to argue that the premises for the existential alternative sought after by Stephen and Bloom are found in the hereditary endowment of our vestigial memories. These vestigial memories are the sepulchral embodiment of an obscure yet irresistible familiarity with our ancestors' cultic past. They contribute to the shaping of our biography in the guise of a necropolitan journey.

At the beginning of these closing remarks I have indulged in a long epigraph, in order to substantiate the interpretive outlook of the present discussion by means of a tangible vestige from our archaic past. The text of this epigraph is informed by an extraordinary, praeterhistorical sense of time that is homologous with the necropolitan logic informing the vestigial memories discussed principally in chapter 2. The original manuscript of the so-called *Tale of Setnau* consists of a papyrus in Demotic characters that was originally preserved in the Vice Regal Museum at Boulaq, Egypt, and is now catalogued as Cairo Museum Papyrus no 30646.[2] In 1865 Auguste Mariette brought it to the attention of Heinrich Brugsch, who published his French translation in a 1867 issue of the *Revue archéologique*. The first English translation was published by P. le Page Renouf in volume 4 of *Records of the Past* (1875), under the sanction of the Society of Biblical Archeology. The vital freshness of these two pioneering and still tentative translations had a much greater impact over the Western imagination of the Egyptian Cult of the Dead than the rigor of later, more philologically rigorous translations.

With the exception of the first two missing pages, whose contents are difficult to reconstruct,[3] the papyrus reports a self-contained novella referring to historical figures that lived during the 19th Dynasty: the son, daughter and grandson of Mer-ne-ptah, Ramses II's successor to the throne of Egypt.[4] The narrator is Ahura (also translated as Ahwere), Mer-ne-ptah's daughter and daughter-in-law. The events are told to Setnau, the fourth son of Ramses II,[5] who figures at first as the scribe who transcribes Ahura's narration, and becomes, in the second part of the story, the tale's ill-fated protagonist, bent on the self-destructive quest of the sacred book of Thoth. Ahura describes to him the events that led to her own death.

The problem with the translation of this manuscript is not so much that its story is told by a shade from the afterlife. Dante's poetics of non-referentiality, discussed especially in chapters 1 and 4 of the present study, affords elegant and, so to speak, painless solutions to the rendition of the voices from the afterlife. The principal problem and the source of colossal misconstructions shared by all extant translations is that Ahura's tale ventures into a temporal domain unexplored by Dante's shades. Ahura tells of future events that will have taken place even before the occurrence of events that should logically have preceded them. It is in Coptos, embalmed and buried in her own tomb, that Ahura reads the Sacred Book in search of the spell that will protect her from death, and it is her reading of the Sacred Book that triggers the events leading to her drowning and solemn burial.

Their still tentative knowledge of Demotic grammar and syntax enabled Brugsch and Page Renouf to reconstruct the structure of this tale with tolerable accuracy. Both archeologists betray, however, the limits of their respective translation in this, that to them it either relates the fantasy of mummies able to "mix . . . in the society of the living," or consists of the "mere recital of a dream."[6] The renderings resulting from either dissatisfactory premise ascribe to Ahura's shade an oneiric language consisting of condensations, dislocutions, and dislocations, while she speaks instead, I'm convinced, a necropolitan tongue whose verbal constructions are designedly meant to elude the hermeneutics of literal and figurative signification.

At the outset of the adventure leading to her death by water, Ahura introduces herself as a resident of the afterlife. Then she tells Setnau the story of her own death, but the plot's chronological sequence is impossible, just as improbably coincidental is the surrogate or substitutive role played by her son Mehru (also translated as Merib)—who, being the son of her brother, is her own brother, too—in her own dispatch to the afterlife. The causes of Ahura's descent to the underworld are also its effects. In the attempt to highlight the future-perfect nature of these impossibilities, my epigraph to this afterword consists of an amalgam of selected excerpts from the *Tale of Setnau*—the details of this amalgamation are explained at length in endnote number 1.

Ahura is obsessed with a problem of difficult solution: how can one preserve the memory of the past inscribed in the Sacred Book that holds the key to one's future? She asks this question of her brother and husband, Ptah-nefer-ka, a scribe and a man of great erudition who acts as her accomplice in the theft of the Sacred Book. Ptah-nefer-ka's lapidary answer is reminiscent of the analogous solution found in Ezekiel and John the Divine:[7] one must carry this memory within oneself, one must ingest it like a medicine or a poison. The answer of the priests from Coptos charged with Ahura's mummification will be basically the same, when they will wrap her embalmed corpse with bands inscribed with spells taken from the Book of the Dead.

The story of the theft of the Sacred Book unfolds backwards in time, in a regression, however, entirely consistent with the chronological progression inherent in the human memory of cathartic death. The past of Ahura's and Ptah-nefer-ka's misdemeanor coincides with the future perfect of their expiation of it. *It is because of the Sacred Book that we suffer the pains that we will have suffered,* Ahura tells her brother. And also: *Because of the theft of the Sacred Book these sufferings have been laid out for us, which we tried to protect ourselves against by stealing the Sacred Book.* This is the pattern of a ritual language impervious to the tyranny of facts, of decisions, of consequences, of causes and effects. Ahura's narration is the prophetic recollection of a future that has already taken place.

It is as if Ahura viewed her own existence as a sequel to her own death and decomposition. The last chapter of the present study, "Shem's Scripture," illustrates the analogous attitude vis-à-vis his necropolitan condition exhibited by Joyce's character in *Finnegans Wake*. In *Finnegans Wake* Joyce embarks upon a full-scale deconstruction of the tyranny of ordinary and common experience, as well as of its pertinent hermeneutics, literal and figurative. This deconstruction turns *Finnegans Wake* into the Bible of negative existence. Joyce thus dismantles the ordinary notions of identity and temporality by means respectively of character amalgamation and chronological destabilization.

I have described Joyce's procedure of character amalgamation in *Scriptural Poetics in Joyce's "Finnegans Wake."* In the first full paragraph of *Finnegans Wake* we learn for example that the patriarch of the *Wake*'s typical family, Humphrey (or Harold) Chimpden Earwicker (who is usually identified with the acronym HCE, and who corresponds, on the naturalistic level of narration, to a Mr Porter [*FW,* 30:2–7, 32.12–19]) has since time immemorial been doubling himself (in Dublin, his hometown, a city of "doublin" [*FW,* 3:8]) into his twin sons: "mishe mishe" (i.e., *Moses and Moses,* or, in Irish, *me and me,* which reads as the biblical *I Am Who I Am*),[8] "tauftauf" (*baptize baptize,* as a contraction of the German *taufen,* which may picture *St. John the Baptist and Jesus,* face to face), "thuartpeatrick" (i.e., *Sts. Patrick and Peter,* the latter alluded to via the neo–Testamentary phrase: "Thou are Peter"), "nathandjoe" (i.e., *Nathan and Joe,* and also Jonathan, an early reference to Swift, etc. [*FW,* 3:9–12]). The twins, usually identified as Shaun (the elder, "Jhem" [*FW,* 3:13] who corresponds to Jerry Porter on the naturalistic level of narration) and Shem (the cadet, "Shen" [*FW,* 3:13] who corresponds to Kevin Porter), are also diluted right away (or "amallagamated" [*FW,* 308, left column]) into the trio of Noah's sons, Shem, Japhet, and Ham, wine makers under the rainbow of the Covenant: "Rot a peck of pa's malt had Jhem or Shen brewed by arclight . . ." (*FW,* 3:12–13).[9]

A simple example of chronological destabilization is found in the "claybook" episode of *Finnegans Wake* (*FW,* 18:17–20:18) where the twins, Shem and Shaun (in the amalgamated personae of Mutt and Jute), engage in the excavation of the Book of Clay out of their family's "cemetery dump," their "swollen ancestral mound."[10] A punctual allusion to the Book of Kells, the celebrated manuscript of the four Gospels written in Insular Majuscule calligraphy,[11] Joyce's Book of Clay stands also for a comprehensive parody of ancient grave inscriptions, genealogical documents, and the Books of the Dead found in Egyptian tombs. The treatment of the "claybook" resurfaces for instance with the discussion of the Book of Kells as letter-litter at pp. 114 ff. Joyce calls it "a terricolous vivelyonview," that is, an interred or entombed Book of Life (*FW,* 18:29).[12] The Book of Clay is written according to the boustrophedonic principle, that is, in a continuous stream of characters running forward and backward on the page ("furrowards, bagawards"), "like yoxen [i.e., yoked oxen] at the turnpaht" (*FW,* 18:31–32). In *Essai sur l'origine des langues,* Jean-Jacques Rousseau attributes the boustrophedonic principle to the writing procedures of the ancient Greeks. As a principle of textual organization, Rousseau considers it "the most convenient to read" (*la plus comode à lire*),[13] superior to the traditional left-to-right texts, which "forces the eye to make a jump from the end of each line of writing to the beginning of the next line, as well as from the bottom of each page to the top of the next page."[14]

But Joyce's Book of Clay, which may be taken in turn for a figure of *Finnegans Wake* itself, pushes the comforts of the boustrophedonic principle one step farther than Rousseau. If the stream of characters from the Book of Clay—vowels, consonants, signs of punctuation—may be alternately read forward and backward, who is to say that entire passages from it should not be read the same way, starting from the end, backward, rather than forward from the beginning?

> Here say figurines billycoose arming and mounting. Mounting and arming bellicose figurines see here. (*FW,* 18:33–34)

The above citation from the "claybook" episode, displaying virtually the same sentence in two opposite linear arrangements, forward and backward, indicates that linguistic signification may be extracted from this sentence by reading it either way, backward or forward; moreover, it suggests that the coordinated performance of prospective and retrospective anticipation on the part of the reader would make both significations simultaneously valid. In the first of the two arrangements of the above sentence one envisages the "figurines billycoose" excavated from the ancestral mound by Shem and Shaun as amorous effigies, portrayed in the caressing attitudes of billing and cooing, embracing one another as they cross arms, or in the mounting position of sexual intercourse. In the second arrangement one envisages instead "bellicose figurines," belligerent effigies mounting their war horses and handling martial arms, ready to attack one another. By the coordinated mnemonic interplay of prospective and retrospective anticipation, the same etymologies come to reveal two opposite versions of their family's romance to Shem and Shaun.

The above citation may be taken to stand for an allegory of reading (à la Paul de Man)[15] applicable to *Finnegans Wake*. The linguistic ambivalence of two (or more) simultaneous significations destabilizes of course the temporal structure of our conventional reading habits, and with it our sequential notion of personal continuity. Augustine derived both our sense of self-containment and the sequential patterns of our reading habits from the faculty of memory, capable of mnemonic retention and proleptic anticipation.[16] But we just saw that the Book of Clay may be read both sequentially and antisequentially. This suggests that for the Wakean reader Augustine's discipline of reading by mnemonic retention and proleptic anticipation is complemented with a symmetrical practice of linguistic deferment. Engaged in retaining and projecting forward that which the text has imprinted in his/her memory, the reader must simultaneously engage in retaining and projecting backward that which the text will have imprinted in his/her memory. The reading performance delineated by this scheme may be labeled necropolitan, the reader's faculty of retention constantly holding on to that ultimate outcome that will have inevitably occurred, that is, the death of the reader and of signification itself. Furthermore, this ultimate occurrence would not function only as the outcome but also as the incipiency of the reading performance.

One cannot read *Finnegans Wake* without feeling the obscure and recurrent impression that one is not reading it for the first time. Given its procedures of character amalgamation and temporal destabilization, both rooted, as illustrated in my two brief examples, in the sepulchral burrow of our archaic past, one will never be done with reading *Finnegans Wake* in a conclusive, exhaustive, hermeneutic manner. One will have always only been reading it—in a responsive attitude to one's vestigial memories and their sepulchral intimations.

ACKNOWLEDGMENTS

Uncustomary as it may seem, my first expression of gratitude goes to the press's acquisitions editor, Barry Blose, whose far-seeing appreciation helped me envision the true potential of my project. The second colleague whose constant support and encouragement fall under the same motivational rubric is William Franke, who has stood by me in the course of a long journey of emancipation from the academe's *idées reçues*—prominent in this tired apparatus figuring the widespread idea that one does not write with a sense of obligation toward one's own readers but rather toward one's own employer. The third and last person in this group (but first in reticence) is Paola Gallo, my long-distance editor with Einaudi, the Turin-based publishing house whose fiction writers fed my culture and imagination as a young man. This book would have never seen the light without the distinct contributions of these three friends.

My four-year parenthesis at Stanford University gave me the opportunity to hear Robert Harrison's frequent dissertations on the afterlife and Thomas Sheehan's frequent discussions of St. Augustine, two subjects that play a fundamental role in this book. I owe it principally to Robert that I was repeatedly invited to teach subjects relating to the afterlife in Stanford's Introduction to the Humanities Program (IHUM). In this context I should mention Cheri Ross, IHUM's indefatigable associate director, who provided me with the most congenial environment to the preparatory reflections of this book.

My students have always been my best teachers, and in the spirit of this persuasion I wish to express my sincere devotion to Carolyn Sinsky, who shared her remarkable gifts with me during the completion of my final draft. Before stepping out of my Californian *isola felice* I should also acknowledge Brenda Machosky's vibrant bibliographic suggestions and Joseph Manning's providential guidance in my adventurous probings of Demotic script —rather exotic probings that, unbeknownst to me, were discreetly pointing at the next Cairene stage in my career.

The writings of three poets, namely Sarah (CB) Crosby-Baker, Rodney Koeneke, and Mary Kinzie, had a relevant effect, albeit intangible, on this book's arguments. Lucia Boldrini, Jennifer Fraser, and Sam Slote have pioneered the recent revival in the study of Joyce's literary relation to Dante, inspiring me to elaborate this book's existentialist approach to a promising and unexhausted discussion. In turn, the existentialist approach sprang from my reception, polemical by all means, of Thomas Carlson's vital treatment of the recent debate on negative theology. Even as an actor *dietro le quinte,* John Freccero remains the obligatory reference for any investigator of the Augustinian motifs in Dante, although no blame can be put on him regarding my own identification of analogous motifs in Joyce. In the summer and fall of 2002, Paola Pugliatti and Giuseppe Martella lent their benevolent ears to the inceptive soliloquies which generated my "vestigial theory" of language. Sean Latham's, Geert Lernout's, and Sebastian Knowles's responsiveness to my essay writing encouraged me to persevere in the concept of this book. I am grateful to Bucknell University Press for their permission to insert into chapter 8 an adapted and expanded version of sections 2 and 4 from chapter 3 of my *Rituals of Literature: Joyce, Dante, Aquinas, and the Tradition of Christian Epics* (2004). And a warm word of thanks goes to the resourceful project editor of my manuscript, Scott Evan Burgess.

My closing expression of gratitude is reserved for Thomas Altizer, whose discussions of Joyce had a profound impact on my own critical maturation through the years. I followed the example of his uncompromising rigor in seeking my own emancipation from the *lieus communs* that clog most critical and theoretical discourses—not excluded, I am bound to clarify, the logic of his dialectics.

GIAN BALSAMO

NOTES

Prologue

1. Mark Strand, "2002," *New York Review of Books,* December 19, 2002, 59.

2. See Michael Wood, "Experience's Ghosts," *New York Review of Books,* June 12, 2003, 71–73. Mark Strand is known for toying with the "element of vanity . . . even of posturing," which his writing undertakes to "overcome."

3. See Graham Greene, *The End of the Affair* (New York: Penguin, 1975), 135–47. In book 5, chapter 1, of *The End of the Affair,* Greene elaborates several irresistible paraphrases of the imagery of death from *Ulysses.* I have borrowed the tropes from some of his allusions.

4. Jacques Derrida, *The Gift of Death,* trans. David Wills (Chicago: University of Chicago Press, 1995), 7.

5. Maurice Blanchot, *La part du feu* (Paris: Gallimard, 1949), 331.

6. For the discussion of Augustine's views on memory and their affinity with the conceptions of memory that were "current in Joyce's time," see John S. Rickard, *Joyce's Book of Memory: The Mnemotechnic of "Ulysses"* (Durham, N.C.: Duke University Press, 1999), 101–3.

7. Augustinus, *Confessiones,* ed. Martinus Skutella, ed. corr. Curav. H. Juergens et W. Schaub (Bibliotheca Graecorum et Romanorum Teubneriana, Stutgardiae et Lipsiae: Teubner, 1996), Liber X, caps. 10, 25–27 (my translation).

8. Giambattista Vico, *La scienza nuova seconda,* ed. Fausto Nicolini, 2 vols. (Bari: Laterza, 1942), Libro I, Sez. 2, 22, 162; Libro II, Sez. 2, Capo 4, 445. Vico sketched the "idea of a dictionary of mental words, common to all nations," in the 1725 version of the *Scienza Nuova;* ibid., *Principi di una scienza nuova,* ed. Giuseppe Ferrari (Milan: Società Tipografica dei Classici Italiani, 1843), Libro 3, Capo 41.

9. Noam Chomsky, *New Horizons in the Study of Language and Mind* (Cambridge: Cambridge University Press, 2000), 32, 89, 178–79.

10. See Émile Durkheim, *Les formes élémentaires de la pensée religieuse: Le système totémique en Australie* (Paris: Félix Alcan, 1937), 451. See also Derrida, *The Gift of Death,* 6–10.

11. Derrida, *The Gift of Death,* 108–9.

12. Augustinus, *Confessiones,* Liber IV, cap. 11.

13. See *The Burial of Christ,* in *The Digby Plays,* ed. F. J. Furnivall. EETSes 70 (London: Oxford University Press, 1967), 180, lines 271–74. J. L. Baird and Coilin Owens have contributed an enlightening analysis of the correspondences between Shem's lurid inscription of his own body and the tradition of the medieval cycle drama, with particular reference to the Digby play *The Burial of Christ,* in "Shem as Crucified Word: FW 185–86,"

James Joyce Quarterly 14, no. 3 (Spring 1977): 252–53. I have derived my citations of *The Burial of Christ* from this article.

Chapter 1

1. John Freccero, "Moon Shadows: *Paradiso* III," in *Studies for Dante,* ed. Franco Fido, Rena A. Syska-Lamparska, and Pamela D. Stewart, 100 (Fiesole: Cadmo, 1998).

2. Erich Auerbach, *Mimesis: The Representation of Reality in Western Literature,* trans. Willard R. Trask (Princeton: Princeton University Press, 1991), 196–98, 277.

3. Thomas Carlson, *Indiscretion: Finitude and the Naming of God* (Chicago: University of Chicago Press, 1999), 257, 257n4.

4. Ibid., 19.

5. Ibid., 5. See also Derrida, *Given Time: I. Counterfeit Money,* trans. Peggy Kamuf (Chicago: University of Chicago Press, 1992), 34–70; Jean-Luc Marion, *Étant Donné: Essai d'une phénoménologie de la donation* (Paris: Presses Universitaires de France, 1997), 118–19, 326–35; ibid., *Dieu sans l'être* (Paris: Fayard, 1982), 204–20; ibid., "Sketch of a Phenomenological Concept of Gift," trans. John Conley, S. J. and Danielle Poe, in *Postmodern Philosophy and Christian Thought,* ed. Merold Westphal, 122 (Bloomington: Indiana University Press, 1999) (all translations from Marion's works are mine).

6. Lucia Boldrini, *Joyce, Dante, and the Poetics of Literary Relations: Language and Meaning in "Finnegans Wake"* (Cambridge: Cambridge University Press, 2001), 144. Boldrini leaves unresolved the issue of the veracity of Dante's reported experience in the afterlife. She does not exclude the possibility that Dante concretely undertakes the necropolitan journey, but only, in agreement with Giorgio Padoan, as the mystic vision of *elevatio ad coelum* (35, 149). See Giorgio Padoan, *Il Pio Enea e l'empio Ulisse* (Ravenna: Longo, 1977), 30–63.

7. Boldrini, *Joyce, Dante, and the Poetics of Literary Relations,* 148; Peter S. Hawkins, "Dante's *Paradiso* and the Dialectic of Ineffability," in *Ineffability: Naming the Unnameable from Dante to Beckett,* ed. Peter S. Hawkins and Anne Howland Schotter, 7 (New York: AMS Press, 1984).

8. Carlson, *Indiscretion,* 9, 19, 191–93, 256–57.

9. See Augustinus, *Confessiones,* Liber IV, cap. 12. Christ's descent to hell, first described in Nicodemus's apocryphal gospel, became an article of faith in the year 1215. See Robert M. Durling, trans. and annotator, and Ronald L. Martinez, annotator, *Inferno,* vol 1. of *"The Divine Comedy" of Dante Alighieri* (New York: Oxford University Press, 1996), 81 (notes to 4:47–50 and 4:52–63).

10. Freccero, *Dante: The Poetics of Conversion* (Cambridge: Harvard University Press, 1986), 25.

11. Augustinus, *Confessiones,* Liber IV, cap. 12.

12. Freccero, *Dante: The Poetics of Conversion,* 25, 104.

13. See Augustinus, *Confessiones,* Liber VII, cap. 12–13.

14. Phillip Cary, *Augustine's Inventions of the Inner Self: The Legacy of a Christian Soul* (Oxford: Oxford University Press, 2000), 109.

15. Ibid., 109. See Augustine, *De Trinitate,* in *Corpus Christianorum, Series Latina* (Turnhout: Brepols, 1954), 4:5.

16. Augustinus, *Confessiones,* Liber X, cap. 27.

17. John D. Caputo, "Toward a Postmodern Theology of the Cross," in *Postmodern Philosophy and Christian Thought,* 211.

18. Ibid., 213–14.

19. Caputo, "Apostles of the Impossible," 191, in *God, the Gift, and Postmodernism,* ed. John D. Caputo and Micheal J. Scanlon, 185–222 (Bloomington: Indiana University Press, 1999).

20. Brian Stock, *Augustine the Reader: Meditation, Self-Knowledge, and the Ethics of Interpretation* (Cambridge: Belknap Press of Harvard University Press, 1996), 13.

21. Augustinus, *Confessiones,* Liber IX, cap. 10.

22. Stock, *Augustine the Reader,* 222.

23. Ibid.

24. Augustinus, *Confessiones,* Liber X, cap. 8.

25. Stock, *Augustine the Reader,* 397n76.

26. Ibid., 223.

27. Martin Heidegger, *Being and Time,* trans. John Macquarrie and Edward Robinson (New York: Harper, 1962), 22–24.

28. Derrida, *Given Time,* 47–52.

29. Marion, *Dieu sans l'être,* 218–19, 250–51; ibid., *Étant Donné,* 328–35. One cannot help but recall at this juncture Derrida's critique of the "retrieval of the trace in parousia" as a constituent dimension in the "horizon of [Hegel's] absolute knowledge." Derrida treated this matter in *Of Grammatology,* trans. Gayatri Chakravorty Spivak (Baltimore: Johns Hopkins University Press, 1976), 26.

30. Marion, *Étant Donné,* 329, 329n1.

31. Ibid., *Dieu sans l'être,* 204n4, 220.

32. Ibid., 212–13.

33. Carlson, *Indiscretion,* 19–20, 231–32, 239.

34. See the introduction to Gian Balsamo, *Rituals of Literature: Joyce, Dante, Aquinas, and the Tradition of Christian Epics* (Lewisburg, Pa.: Bucknell University Press, 2004).

35. The doctrine of transubstantiation was intensely debated in the late Middle Ages by several of Aquinas's precursors, among them the heralds of the symbolic dimension of the Eucharist (such as Berengarius of Tours: *"Semel oblatus est Christus, sacrificium vero ecclesiae* exemplum *est sacrificii Christi"*) and the heralds of the realistic dimension (such as Pascasius Radbertus: *"Vera utique caro Christi quae crucifixa est et sepulta, vere illius carnis sacramentum quod per sacerdotem super altare in verbo Christi per Spiritum Sanctum divinitus consecratur"*), as well as Aquinas's own teacher, Albertus Magnus. But it is Aquinas who will be eventually identified by the Church as *Eucharistiae praeco et vates maximus.* For Aquinas's definition of transubstantiation, see *Summa Theologiae* 3, q. 75, a. 4, *responsio:* "And this actually happens by divine power in this sacrament. The complete substance of the bread is converted into the complete substance of Christ's body, and the complete substance of the wine into the complete substance of Christ's blood. Hence this change is not a formal change, but a substantial one. It does not belong to the natural kinds of change, and it can be called by a name proper to itself—'transubstantiation'" (translation from *Summa Theologiae,* vol. 58, trans. W. Barden [London: Blackfriars, 1965]). See Berengarius Turonensis, *De Sacra Coena adversus Lanfrancum* (New York: G. Olms, 1975), 131; Pascasius Radbertus, *De corpore et sanguine Domini,* cura et studio Bedae Paulus, O.S.B. (Turnholti: Typographi Brepols Editores Pontificii, 1969), 394m, p. 30; Pius XI, Encyclical letter *Studiorum ducem* (1923) (Washington, D.C.: National Catholic Welfare Conference, 1936).

36. See Rudolph Bultmann, "Paul's Demythologizing and Ours," in *The Writings of St. Paul,* ed. Wayne A. Meeks, 413 (New York: Norton, 1972); Alan F. Segal, *Paul the Convert: The Apostolate and Apostasy of Saul the Pharisee* (New Haven: Yale University Press, 1990), 168.

37. Stephen Sicari, *Joyce's Modernist Allegory: "Ulysses" and the History of the Novel* (Columbia: University of South Carolina Press, 2001), 63.

38. Augustinus, *Confessiones,* Liber IX, cap. 12.

39. Joyce, *Stephen Hero* (New York: New Directions, 1963), 186.

40. We owe the labeling of Joyce's writing endeavors as "underbred" to Virginia Woolf. See Richard Ellmann, *James Joyce* (London: Oxford University Press, 1983), 528.

41. William Butler Yeats, "The Autumn of the Body," in *Essays and Introductions* (New York: Collier, 1961), 193.

42. Roger Bellet, *Stéphane Mallarmé: L'encre et le ciel* (Seyssel: Champ Vallon, 1987), 94 (my translation). For Mallarmé's assimilation of theatrical representation to Catholic liturgy, see Francesco Piselli, *Mallarmé e l'estetica* (Milan: Mursia, 1969), 190–95.

43. See W. B. Stanford, *The Ulysses Theme: A Study in the Adaptability of a Traditional Hero* (Ann Arbor: University of Michigan Press, 1968), 215.

44. Kimberly J. Devlin, "Visible Shades and Shades of Visibility: The En-Gendering of Death in 'Hades,'" in *"Ulysses"—En-Gendered Perspectives: Eighteen New Essays on the Episodes,* ed. Kimberly J. Devlin and Marilyn Reizbaum, 82–84 (Columbia: University of South Carolina Press, 1999). Devlin discusses the economic role of the turn-of-the-century Dublin wife, in light of the consideration that "the material plight of [Stephen's] family seems . . . more precarious" after his mother's death than before.

45. Diane Stubbings, *Anglo-Irish Modernism and the Maternal: From Yeats to Joyce* (Houndmills: Palgrave, 2000), 54.

46. See Monic Robillard, *Le désir de la vierge: Hérodiade chez Mallarmé* (Geneva: Droz, 1993), 49. Robillard refers specifically to the *lecture maternante* (mothering reading) whereby the maternal muse in Mallarmé's *Don du poème* "gives life to the dead letter of the written text."

47. Derrida, *Glas,* trans. John P. Leavey Jr. and Richard Rand (Lincoln: University of Nebraska Press, 1990), 150–54.

48. As cited in Derrida, *Glas,* 151. *"Ne t'imagine pas que je dis des folies. / . . . Et surtout ne va pas, frère, acheter du pain."* See Stéphane Mallarmé, *Aumône* (my translation).

49. See the entry for 14 May 1867 in Stéphane Mallarmé, *Correspondance,* ed. Henri Mondor (Paris: Gallimard, 1959), 1:243.

Chapter 2

1. See Paul Ricoeur, *Time and Narrative,* trans. Kathleen McLaughlin and David Pellauer (Chicago: University of Chicago Press, 1984) 2:64ff.

2. Gian Balsamo, *Scriptural Poetics in Joyce's "Finnegans Wake"* (Lewiston, N.Y.: Edwin Mellen Press, 2002), 97–103, 137–44.

3. Hayden White, *Metahistory: The Historical Imagination in Nineteenth-Century Europe* (Baltimore: Johns Hopkins University Press, 1973), 30.

4. Sicari, *Joyce's Modernist Allegory,* 166 (my emphasis).

5. Boldrini, *Joyce, Dante, and the Poetics of Literary Relations,* 33 (my emphasis).

6. Hayden White, *Figural Realism: Studies in the Mimesis Effect* (Baltimore: Johns Hopkins University Press, 1999), 143.

7. For the autonoetic character of episodic memory, as contrasted with the noetic character of semantic memory, see Lars Nyberg, A. R. McIntosh, and Endel Tulving, "Functional Brain Imaging of Episodic and Semantic Memory with Positron Emission Tomography," *Journal of Molecular Medicine* 76 (1998): 48–53; Lars Nyberg and Endel Turving, "Classifying Human Long-Term Memory: Evidence from Converging Dissociations," *European Journal of Cognitive Psychology* 8, no. 2 (1996): 163–83. See also Andrew R. Mayes, Patricia A. Gooding, and Rob van Eijk, "A New Theoretical Framework for Explicit and Implicit Memory," in *Psyche* 3, no. 2 (June 1997).

8. Ricoeur, *Time and Narrative,* 3:153–54.

9. See for instance K. Anders Ericsson and Walter Kintsch, "Long-Term Working Memory," *Psychological Review* 102, no. 2 (1995): 211–45.

10. Carlson, *Indiscretion,* 247.

11. Augustinus, *Confessiones,* Liber IX, cap. x. See Stock, *Augustine the Reader,* 118.

12. Derrida, *Psyché: Inventions de l'autre* (Paris: Galilée, 1987), 540–45 (my translation).

13. Ibid.

14. Concerning this terminology see Heidegger, *Being and Time,* 34.

15. Carlson, *Indiscretion,* 160, 174.

16. For the application of Duns Scotus's portrayal of God to the discussion of the apophatic tradition, see Michael J. Scanlon, "A Deconstruction of Religion: On Derrida and Rahner," in *God, the Gift, and Postmodernism,* 226; Nicholas Lobkowicz, *Theory and Practice: History of a Concept from Aristotle to Marx* (Lanham, Md.: University Press of America, 1967), 74.

17. Augustinus, *Confessiones,* Liber IX, cap. x.

18. Augustine, Sermon 117:5: *"Ad mentem Deus pertinet, intelligendus est."* See also Phillip Cary, *Augustine's Invention of the Inner Self: The Legacy of a Christian Platonist* (Oxford: Oxford University Press, 2000), 167n72.

19. See Augustine, *Il maestro* (*De magistro*), trans. Massimo Parodi and Cristina Trovò (Milan: Biblioteca Universale Rizzoli, 1996), 41.

20. Hawkins, "Dante's *Paradiso* and the Dialectic of Ineffability," 9.

21. "Oh quanto è corto e come fioco / al mio concetto! E questo, a quel ch'i' vidi / è tanto, che *non basta a dicer 'poco'*" (*Paradiso,* 33:121–23 [my emphasis]).

22. Sam Slote, *The Silence in Progress of Dante, Mallarmé, and Joyce* (New York: Peter Lang, 1999), 37.

23. Giambattista Vico, *La scienza nuova seconda,* vol. 2, appendix 6, *Postille inedite,* 5–6, p. 331.

24. See Auerbach, *Scenes from the Drama of European Literature,* "Vico's and Aesthetic Historicism" (New York: Meridian, 1959), 197.

25. See Marcel Danesi, *Lingua, metafora, concetto: Vico e la linguistica conoscitiva* (Modugno: Edizioni del Sud, 2001), 45, 124–25.

26. Vico, *La scienza nuova seconda,* Libro I, Sez. 2, 22, 162; ibid., Libro II, Sez. 2, Capo 4, 445.

27. Marcel Danesi, introduction to *Giambattista Vico and Anglo-American Science* (Berlin: Mouton de Gruyter, 1995), 25.

28. Lorraine Weir, "Imagination and Memory in Vico and Joyce," in *Giambattista Vico and Anglo-American Science,* 246.

29. Chomsky, *Aspects of the Theory of Syntax* (Cambridge: MIT Press, 1965); ibid., *New Horizons in the Study of Language and Mind* (Cambridge: Cambridge University Press, 2000), 26.

30. Ibid., 100.

31. Ibid., 32.

32. For Augustine's notion of mental imprint, see Augustine, *Epistulae,* 162:4, in *Patrologia Latina* ed. J.-P. Migne, xxxiii, col. 706 (Paris, n.p.: 1844–64). See Auerbach, "Figura," in *Scenes from the Drama of European Literature: Six Essays,* trans. Ralph Manheim, 11–78 (New York: Meridian, 1959). As Auerbach remarks, the Augustinian views on mental imprints are influenced by Aristotle, *De memoria et reminiscentia,* 450a, 31. Discussions on Augustine's theory of memory are found in Paolo Rossi, *Clavis universalis: Arti della memoria e logica combinatoria da Lullo a Leibnitz* (Bologna, n.p.: 1983), 31–36; Dominique Doucet, "L'*Ars memoriae* dans les *Confessions,*" in *REA* 33 (1987): 49–69; Janet Coleman, *Ancient and Medieval Memories: Studies in the Reconstruction of the Past* (New York: Cambridge University Press, 1992), 80–116. Augustine discusses the subject of memory also in *De cura pro mortuis gerenda ad paulinum,* 4:6, in *Corpus Scriptorum Ecclesiasticorum Latinorum* (Vienna: 1866–), 41:630:12–16; ibid., *De catechizandis rudibus,* 2:3, in *Corpus Christianorum, Series Latina* 46:122–23:17–34; ibid., *De libero arbitrio,* 2:19:51, in *Corpus Christianorum, Series Latina* 29:271:30–35; ibid., *De quantitate animae,* 33:72, in *Corpus Scriptorum Ecclesiasticorum Latinorum,* 89:220:1–19.

33. Caputo, "Toward a Postmodern Theology of the Cross," 211.

34. Augustinus, *Confessiones,* Liber X, cap. 25–27.

35. Ibid., Liber X, cap. 10 (my translation).

36. Stock, *Augustine the Reader,* 13–14.

37. Ibid., 247. See also Augustine, *De trinitate,* Liber XV, cap. 10.

38. Calvin L. Troup, *Temporality, Eternity, and Wisdom: The Rhetoric of Augustine's "Confessions"* (Columbia: University of South Carolina Press, 1999), 88.

39. According to Derrida, the linguistic abdication to the transcendental signifier is inherent in the "implicit linguistic contract" which allows us to address the experience of the impossible. See Derrida, *Given Time,* 47–53.

40. Walter Burkert, *Creation of the Sacred: Tracks of Biology in Early Religions,* (Cambridge: Harvard University Press, 1996), 20.

41. Augustinus, *Confessiones,* Liber X, cap. 10.

42. In evolutionary theory, the term "phenotype" comprises the traits developed as a "reaction" of the genes inherited by an organism (genotype) to "external conditions that are relevant to it." See Richard Lewontin, *The Triple Helix: Gene, Organism, and Environment* (Cambridge: Harvard University Press, 2000,) 23, 48–49.

43. Donald Phillip Verene, *Vico's Science of Imagination* (Ithaca: Cornell University Press, 1981), 83–84, 89, 122–23.

44. Hayden White, *Tropics of Discourse* (Baltimore: Johns Hopkins University Press, 1986), 206. See my critique of ironic reductionism in the section "The Crisis of Irony." For an application of a White-like reductionism to both Joyce ad Dante, see Ernesto Grassi, "Joyce and Vico: The Demythologization of the Real," in *Vico and Joyce,* ed. Donald Phillip, 155 (Albany: State University of New York Press, 1987).

45. John O'Neill, "The Origins of Myth: Promethean or Orphic?" in *Giambattista Vico and Anglo-American Science,* 150.

46. John Bishop, *Joyce's Book of the Dark: "Finnegans Wake"* (Madison: University of Wisconsin Press, 1986), 373.

47. Webster's Dictionary of the English Language (1864), 1500.

48. See Émile Durkheim, *Les Formes élémentaires de la pensée religieuse,* 451.

49. Ibid.

Chapter 3

1. Thomas Aquinas, *Summa Theologiae,* 1, q. 1, a. 10, in vol. 3 of St. Thomae Aquinatis, *Opera Omnia,* ed. Roberto Busa (Stuttgart-Bad Cannstatt: Frommann-Holzboog, 1980); Ibid., *Quaestiones quodlibetales,* n. 7, q. 6, ar. 2, *responsio,* in *Opera Omnia,* 438–500.

2. Robert Alter, "Introduction to the Old Testament," in *The Literary Guide to the Bible,* ed. Robert Alter and Frank Kermode, 24–25, 35n8, 31, 13 (Cambridge: Harvard University Press, 1997); Robert Alter, trans. and comm., *Genesis* (New York: Norton, 1996), 115 (note to Genesis 24:11), 78 (note to Genesis 18:10), 126 (note to Genesis 25:21–23), xxvi.

3. Augustinus, *Confessiones,* Liber IX, cap. x (my translation).

4. For the role of eyesight, imaging, and recollection in the Platonic apprehension of truth, see John Sallis, *Being and Logos: The Way of the Platonic Dialogue* (Atlantic Highlands, N.J.: Humanities Press International, 1986), 84–91, 140–59, 383–85, 417–24, 448–55.

5. See Augustine, *Confessions,* in vol. 1 of *Nicene and Post-Nicene Fathers of the Christian Church,* ed. Philip Schaff, 1:137 (Edinburgh: T & T Clark, 1994); ibid., *Confessions,* trans. F. J. Sheed (Indianapolis: Hackett, 1993), 164; ibid., *Confessions,* trans. John K. Ryan (Garden City, N.J.: Image Books, 1960), 222; ibid., *Confessions,* trans. Rex Warner (New York: New American Library, 1963), 201.

6. Augustinus, *Confessiones,* Liber VII, cap. 20. Martha Nussbaum has aptly established the separation between the Plotinian, noetic asceticism of Augustine's earlier works, such as *De quantitate animae* and *De Genesi contra Manicheos,* and the passionate, introspective asceticism of the *Confessiones.* "Augustine's account of Christian ascent . . . situates [it] within humanity and renounces the [neo-Platonic] wish to depart from our own human condition." See Martha Nussbaum, *Upheavals of Thought* (Cambridge: Cambridge University Press, 2001), 547. My objection to Nussbaum's position is not specific to her presentation of Augustine but epistemological. The project of ethical philosophy described in *Upheavals of Thought* is predicated on the quest of a practice of love conducive to accountability in human affairs, such accountability being identified with our capacity for compassion, reciprocity, and individual recognition (479–80). Nussbaum fails to problematize the phenomenal character of the state of human affairs she wants to regulate by means of loving accountability; this state of affairs is experienced, mostly outside the U.S. but also by large sections of the American population, as eminently conducive to the individual biographies of oppression and alienation which Nussbaum would like to see exorcized.

7. An intimation that the philosophical premises for an existentialist conversion of Platonic transcendence are found in Plato himself is provided by Martha Nussbaum in her discussion of the *Symposium.* In contrasting the existentialist thrust in the speech of Alcibiades with the epistemic thrust of Socrates's definition of Eros and Beauty, Nussbaum points out how these two views are informed by contrasting conceptions of light and vision. See Nussbaum, *The Fragility of Goodness: Luck and Ethics in Greek Tragedy and Philosophy* (Cambridge: Cambridge University Press, 1986), 193.

8. See Durling and Martinez, *Inferno,* 81 (notes to 4:47–50 and 4:52–63). As mentioned previously, Christ's descent to hell is first described in Nicodemus's apocryphal gospel, and becomes an article of faith in 1215.

9. The *trasmutar sembiante* of Beatrice in *Paradiso* (5:88) may be taken as another instance of a Dantesque transmutation which is exuberant of ordinary existence and connotative/denotative language. In paradise, human subjectivity is presented to Dante as a mere illusion, the empty form staged by the celestial beings for the benefit of his own limited, terrestrial imagination; Dante's imagination could not otherwise conceive the collapse of individual differentiation in paradise, which notion the human mind can only comprehend intellectually, not conceive imaginatively. Whenever Beatrice directs her desiring gaze at the light of the Empyrean, her celestial features transcend the corporeal ones she adopts in her direct communications with Dante. The intensity of her transcendence of human features varies according to circumstances, being somewhat proportional to the intensity of her desiring gaze; yet it is not the expression of a desiring self, the very principle of selfhood having collapsed in paradise, together with the drives of subjective, deliberative intentionality.

10. See Augustine, *De trinitate,* Liber XV, cap. 10.

11. St. Augustine's journey unto death anticipates Pseudo-Dionysius's "surpassing [of] speech" of at least one century. (See Pseudo-Dionysius, *Divine Names,* in *Complete Works,* trans. Colm Luibheid, 49 [New York: Paulist Press, 1987]). The entire tradition of apophatic or mystical theology is informed by the notion of the journey toward God—the title of St. Bonaventura's *Itinerarum ad Mentis Deum* helps in the validation of this thesis. Most modern interpreters of the apophatic tradition, misled by neo-Platonic rhetorics of ascent, desensitization, and interior vision, have systematically failed to identify the existential character of the fundamental stations of the journey unto death.

12. See Robert Scholes, "Stephen Dedalus, Poet or Esthete?" in *"A Portrait of the Artist as a Young Man": Text, Criticism, and Notes,* ed. Chester G. Anderson, 480 (New York: Viking, 1968); Bernard Benstock, "The Temptation of St. Stephen: A View of the Villanelle," *James Joyce Quarterly* 14, no. 1 (Fall 1976): 37. I agree with Robert Scholes that Stephen must undergo the transition from "esthete" to "poet," but Scholes's argument that "The Villanelle of the Temptress" marks such a transition seems fragile (480). I find more persuasive Bernard Benstock's view that Stephen's villanelle is just an element in the ramified illustration of the creative process that leads to its creation, and serves primarily to grasps the character of this process. Benstock maintains that it is questionable "whether [the villanelle] is intrinsically a good poem," signaling therefore the transition detected by Scholes, because, being "written by a fictional poet," it lacks the contextual connotations (literary and biographic) that are indispensable to critical debate.

13. See Jean-Paul Hameury, *L'échec de Mallarmé* (Bédée: Folle Avoine, 1998), 39.

14. Regarding the three successive stages of *L'Après-midi d'un Faune,* see Lloyd James Austin, *Essais sur Mallarmé,* ed. Malcolm Bowie (Manchester: Manchester University Press, 1995), 183.

15. On Stephen's "nocturnal emission" as "a statement of the obvious," see Benstock, "The Temptation of St. Stephen," 34. See also See David Weir, "A Womb of His Own: Joyce's Sexual Aesthetics," *James Joyce Quarterly* 31, no. 3 (Spring 1994): 218.

16. Balsamo, *Scriptural Poetics in Joyce's "Finnegans Wake,"* 18–28.

17. See Freccero, "Moon Shadows: *Paradiso* III," 100.

18. See Sicari, *Joyce's Modernist Allegory,* 157–58.

19. See *Paradiso* 4:28. The term "in-numenated" is my translation of Dante's neologism *indiati,* obtained by the superposition of *in,* a prepositional adverb of place, with *dio,* Italian for god (or the Latin *numen*), and with *ati,* a past participial plural desinence.

20. Freccero, *Dante: The Poetics of Conversion*, 106.

21. Ibid., 100.

22. Ibid., 99.

23. Ibid., 101, 106, 211, 221.

24. See Durling and Martinez, *Inferno*, 81 (notes to 4:47–50 and 4:52–63).

25. Augustinus, *Confessiones*, Liber IV, cap. 12.

26. Augustine, *De libero arbitrio*, Liber III, cap. 25:74, in Augustine, *Earlier Writings*, ed. J. H. S. Burleigh (Philadelphia: Westminster, 1953), 113–217; Dante, *Paradiso* 4:1–9. See the "moral argument" on *libero arbitrio* and individual responsibility in P. Montanari, "Prefazione," ix–xl, in Agostino, *De libero arbitrio*, trans. P. Montanari, Bag 21 (Florence: n.p., 1939); Montanari, "Il problema della libertà in Agostino," *Rivista di filosofia neo-scolastica* 29 (1937): 359–87.

27. Hayden White, *Metahistory: The Historical Imagination in Nineteenth-Century Europe*, 37.

28. Ibid., *Figural Realism*, 11, 15.

29. Margot Norris, "Narration under a Blindfold: Reading Joyce's 'Clay,'" in *James Joyce's "Dubliners,"* ed. Harold Bloom, 156 (New York: Chelsea House, 1988).

30. Charles S. Singleton, *Dante Studies I: Elements of Structure* (Cambridge: Harvard University Press, 1957), 62.

31. See Freccero, *Dante: The Poetics of Conversion*, 20–24.

32. Benvenuto da Imola, *Commentum super Dantis Aldigherii Comoediam*, ed. I. F. Lacaita (Florence: n.p., 1887), 2:293. See also David Thompson, *Dante's Epic Journey* (Baltimore: Johns Hopkins University Press, 1974), 14–50. According to Benvenuto da Imola, in Dante's days even children were aware of Odysseus's happy return.

33. Boldrini, *Joyce, Dante, and the Poetics of Literary Relations*, 130. See my discussion of Joyce's poetics of intertextual filiation in *Scriptural Poetics in Joyce's "Finnegans Wake,"* 26–27, and ch. 3, sec. 1 in *Rituals of Literature*.

34. Durling and Martinez, *Inferno*, 93.

35. Augustine, *Confessions*, trans. William Watts (Cambridge: Harvard University Press, 2000), Liber VIII, cap. 12.

36. Credit must be given to Robert Harrison for his suggestion of the intertextual connection between Augustine's and Dante's respective closing of the book.

37. See my illustration of Joyce's poetics as disengaged from the logic of origin, or *arche*, and destination, or *telos*, in *Scriptural Poetics in Joyce's "Finnegans Wake,"* 21–22.

38. See Freccero, *Dante: The Poetics of Conversion*, 211, 221. See also Freccero, "Moon Shadows: *Paradiso* III," 92.

39. Boldrini, *Joyce, Dante, and the Poetics of Literary Relations*, 144.

40. See Sicari, *Joyce's Modernist Allegory*, 68; Brook Thomas, *James Joyce's "Ulysses": A Book of Many Happy Returns* (Baton Rouge: Louisiana State University Press, 1982), 281. The redemptive journey unto death is at play in the very beginning of Paul's missionary career, described in Acts 9. The journey to Damascus is an essential figural component in Saul's vision of Christ, his immediate death to paganism, and his rebirth as Paul the Apostle. The metaphor of death will subsequently pervade most of his doctrine, from the metaphor of death to the Law and to the flesh (Galatians 2) to the metaphor of baptism as death to racial, social, and gendered distinctions (Galatians 3), from the metaphor of individual crucifixion as death to the world (Galatians 6) to the metaphor of individual death in Adam and resurrection in Christ (1 Corinthians 15), etc.

41. Dante Alighieri, *Vita Nuova*, in *Tutte le Opere*, ed. Fredi Chiappelli (Milan: Mursia, 1965), 42:1–2.

42. Slote, *The Silence in Progress of Dante, Mallarmé, and Joyce*, 6, 9.

43. Ibid., 9.

44. Robert Adams Day, "How Stephen Wrote His Vampire Poem," *James Joyce Quarterly* 17, no. 2 (Winter 1980): 186.

45. Douglas Hyde, ed. and trans., *The Love Songs of Connacht* (Dublin: Irish University Press, 1974), 20–21.

46. Maurice Blanchot, *La part du feu*, 41 (my translation); cited in Slote, *The Silence in Progress of Dante, Mallarmé, and Joyce*, 75.

47. A vessel that Boldrini might perceive as both "polysemic" vehicle and vehicular *integumentum*. See Boldrini, *Joyce, Dante, and the Poetics of Literary Relations*, 127.

48. Joyce, "Drama and Life" and "Ibsen's New Drama" in *The Critical Writings of James Joyce*, ed. Mason Ellsworth and Richard Ellmann (Ithaca: Cornell University Press, 1989), 38–67.

49. See Nussbaum, *Upheavals of Thought*, 687.

50. Joyce, *Stephen Hero*, 186.

Chapter 4

1. Hugh Kenner, *Dublin's Joyce* (Boston: Beacon Press, 1962), 355.

2. Ibid., *Joyce's Voices* (Berkeley: University of California Press, 1978), 17.

3. Norris, "Narration under a Blindfold," 148–49.

4. Kenner, *Joyce's Voices*, 15.

5. It was Gretta, also a pillar of this society, and not the Misses Morkan, who nursed Gabriel's mother "during all her last long illness in [Gabriel's and Gretta's] house at Monkstown" ("The Dead," 187).

6. For the "increased use of free indirect style" at the end of "The Dead," see John Paul Riquelme, "Joyce's 'The Dead': The Dissolution of the Self and the Police," in *ReJoycing: New Readings of "Dubliners,"* ed. Rosa M. Bollettieri and Harold F. Mosher Jr., 125 (Lexington: University Press of Kentucky, 1998).

7. In the unveiling of the Dantesque intertextuality pertinent to the ubiquitous reflections and self-reflections in "The Dead," Florence Walzl contends the primacy to Virginia Moseley, whose central insight is mentioned later. Walzl refers to the window in the Gresham Hotel room as "a reflecting window . . . highly Dantean in its concept." See Florence L. Walzl, "Gabriel and Michael: The Conclusion of 'The Dead,'" in *James Joyce, "Dubliners,"* ed. Robert Scholes and A. Walton Litz, 436 (New York: Viking, 1976). This article was originally delivered at a 1964 conference and published in a different version in the *James Joyce Quarterly* (Fall 1966).

8. Freccero, "Moon Shadows: *Paradiso* III," 100.

9. If *Dubliners* as a whole may be taken as Joyce's implementation of the "extreme version of realism" known as naturalism, the brusque introduction of the theme of the necropolitan journey at the closure of its last story is the harbinger of Joyce's "larger and ultimate ambition." See Sicari, *Joyce's Modernist Allegory*, 14.

10. See Friedrich Nietzsche, *The Birth of Tragedy*, in *"The Birth of Tragedy" and "The Case of Wagner" by F. Nietzsche*, trans. Walter Kaufmann, 36–37, 39–40, 72–74 (New York: Vintage, 1967). Oscar Wilde offered a modern parody of the demise of the *principium individuationis* in *The Picture of Dorian Gray*, a novel Joyce admired with reservations. See Ellmann, *James Joyce*, 233.

11. See Augustine, *Confessions,* with a translation by William Watts (Cambridge: Harvard University Press, 2000), vol. 2, Liber X, cap. 6, p. 90.

12. Ibid., vol. 1, Liber VII, cap. 3, p. 343.

13. Ibid., vol. 1, Liber VIII, cap. 10, p. 451.

14. See Augustine, *De immortalitate animae,* in *Patrologia Latina* ed. J. P. Migne, 32: 1023A.

15. All citations from Dante's *Commedia* come from Dante Alighieri, *"La divina commedia,"* 3 vols., ed. Carlo Grabher (Bari: Laterza, 1964) (the translations are mine unless otherwise specified).

16. Freccero, *Dante: The Poetics of Conversion,* 211, 221. See also Freccero, "Moon Shadows: *Paradiso* III," 92.

17. See Freccero "Moon Shadows: *Paradiso* III," 95, for the rendering of Dante's *postille debili* as "surface tracings."

18. See Virginia Moseley, "'Two Sights for Ever a Picture' in Joyce's 'The Dead,'" in *College English* 26 (March 1965): 431–33.

19. I have adopted here Allen Mandelbaum's translation, with one modification. Like other interpreters before him, Maldelbaum attributes a double valence to Dante's *in sù* (27:70); he translates it both as a predicate of *etera* (that ether there—a beautiful alliteration) and as an adverbial modifier of *fioccar* (were flaking up to the Empyrean). I have chosen to limit the valence of *in sù* to one single instance, as an attribute of ether. Dante was wary of abusing signifiers of directionality, given the ambivalent spatiality of paradise. See Allen Mandelbaum, trans., *"The Divine Comedy" of Dante Alighieri: "Paradiso"* (New York: Bantam, 1986).

20. See, respectively, Garry Martin Leonard, *Reading "Dubliners" Again: A Lacanian Perspective* (Syracuse, NY: Syracuse University Press, 1993), 307–8; Riquelme, "Joyce's 'The Dead,'" 139; Walzl, "Gabriel and Michael," 424, 442; Donald T. Torchiana, *Backgrounds for Joyce's "Dubliners"* (Boston: Allen & Unwin, 1986), 249.

21. Kenner, *Dublin's Joyce,* 66–67.

22. One of Joyce's stupendous letters to Grant Richards (May 5, 1906) describes the style adopted in the composition of *Dubliners* as "a style of scrupulous meanness." See Joyce, *Dubliners,* eds. Robert Scholes and A. Walton Litz, 269.

23. Norris, "Narration under a Blindfold," 160.

24. David Leon Higdon, "Gendered Discourse and the Structure of Joyce's 'The Dead,'" in *ReJoycing,* 179–80.

25. Kenner, *Joyce's Voices,* 15–16.

26. Leonard, *Reading "Dubliners" Again,* 297; Riquelme, "Joyce's 'The Dead,'" 127. Basing his argument on an outlandish citation from Elizabeth Post's *Emily Post's Etiquette,* David Higdon argues the specious point that Gabriel's gift of a coin "is less a muted sexual insult than it is a gross violation of the etiquette." See Higdon, "Gendered Discourse and the Structure of Joyce's 'The Dead,'" 181–82.

27. Torchiana, *Backgrounds for Joyce's "Dubliners,"* 249–50.

28. Kenner, *Dublin's Joyce,* 118.

29. Walzl, "Gabriel and Michael," 433.

30. Leonard, *Reading "Dubliners" Again,* 295.

31. Balsamo, *Pruning the Genealogical Tree: Procreation and Lineage in Literature, Law, and Religion* (Lewisburg, Pa.: Bucknell University Press, 1999), 57–71.

32. Joyce, *A Portrait of the Artist as a Young Man,* 215.

33. Auerbach, *Mimesis,* 202.

34. My argument parallels Freccero's polemic with Auerbach. See Freccero, *Dante: The Poetics of Conversion,* 259. Auerbach's view that "both figure and fulfillment possess . . . the character of *actual historical events and phenomena*" is warranted by the assumption that in Dante the praeterhistorical is a pretext for the affirmation of the concretely historical. Paradoxical as it may sound, I should venture that Auerbach is just one little step away from reversing the patristic tradition, arguing that historical contingency is the *forma perfectior* of its own tropes. See Auerbach, *Mimesis,* 197, 201–2 (my emphasis).

35. White, *Tropics of Discourse,* 206; ibid., *Metahistory,* 37; ibid., *Figural Realism,* 11, 15.

36. Freccero, *Dante: The Poetics of Conversion,* 99.

37. Ibid., 101, 106, 211, 221.

38. Lucia Boldrini, "The Artist Pairing His Quotations: Aesthetic and Ethical Implications of the Dantean Intertext in *Dubliners,*" in *ReJoycing,* 238–39.

39. Ibid., 237.

40. Stephen Dedalus himself, for instance, undergoes an equivalent, if slightly less immediate, transition from the vision of infernal watchers hiding in his bedroom to the vision of paradisiac watchers traversing the "heavenly bodies" above him. Joyce, *A Portrait of the Artist as a Young Man,* 136, 172, respectively.

41. See Charles S. Singleton, trans. and ed., *"The Divine Comedy" of Dante Alighieri: "Paradiso": Commentary* (Princeton: Princeton University Press, 1991), 434n67–72; Dante Alighieri, *Paradiso,* ed. Carlo Grabher, 340n67–72.

42. Dante Alighieri, *Vita nuova,* in *Tutte le Opere,* canzone 23, lines 25–27.

43. Later Dante goes to wake the corpse of Beatrice. Her face "seem[s] to be saying: 'I've gone to see the principle of peace.'" Released from his anguish, Dante implores Beatrice with the words: "Sweetest Death, come to me, . . . don't you see the intensity of my desire for you" (my translation).

44. Joyce, *A Portrait of the Artist as a Young Man,* 170–71 (my emphasis).

45. Ibid., 169–70.

46. Ibid., 217, 171, 35.

47. See Ellmann, *James Joyce,* 319; Mary T. Reynolds, *Joyce and Dante: The Shaping Imagination* (Princeton: Princeton University Press, 1981), 142.

48. Joyce, *A Portrait of the Artist as a Young Man,* 172 (my emphasis).

49. Kenner, *Dublin's Joyce,* 355.

50. Ibid., 355.

51. Boldrini, "The Artist Pairing His Quotations," 242.

52. See ch. 1 in Boldrini, *Joyce, Dante, and the Poetics of Literary Relations.* Boldrini devotes a brilliant chapter to the discussion of this discordant analogy.

53. Chambers, "Gabriel Conroy Sings for His Supper, or Love Refused," in *James Joyce's "Dubliners,"* ed. Harold Bloom, 115 (New York: Chelsea House, 1988). To be fair, I should mention that Chambers considers also the possibility for Gabriel of a metaphorical journey into "the heart of the storm" of the passionate existence that he has refused himself thus far" (115).

54. Torchiana, *Backgrounds for Joyce's "Dubliners,"* 249–50.

55. Leonard, *Reading "Dubliners" Again,* 308.

56. Sicari, *Joyce's Modernist Allegory,* 237–38n1.

57. *Paradiso* 27:76–84: *"Onde la donna, che mi vide assolto / de l'attendere in su, mi disse: 'Adima / il viso, e guarda come tu se' vòlto.' / Da l'ora ch'io avea guardato prima / i' vidi mosso me per tutto l'arco / che fa dal mezzo al fine il primo clima; / sì ch'io vedea di là da Gade il varco / folle d'Ulisse, e di qua presso il lito / nel qual si fece Europa dolce carco."*

58. See also *Paradiso* 23:103–5, where Gabriel defines himself as "angelic love": *"Io sono amore angelico che giro / l'alta letizia che spira dal ventre / che fu albergo del nostro disiro."* (Carlo Grabher identifies the speaker with Gabriel; see Grabher, ed., *Paradiso,* 296n91–96, 297n103–8).

59. See Grabher, ed., *Inferno.* In *Inferno* 7:13, the noun *strupo* must be intended as a meta-thesis of *stupro,* literally signifying therefore Lucifer's "rape" of the heavens. I have chosen this literal translation, against the variously tamed renderings from the available translations.

60. Ellmann, *James Joyce,* 399.

61. Seamus Deane, "Dead Ends: Joyce's Finest Moments," in *Semicolonial Joyce,* ed. Derek Attridge and Marjorie Howes, 36 (Cambridge: Cambridge University Press, 2000).

62. See Kenner, *Dublin's Joyce,* 38, 43–45.

63. Riquelme, *Teller and Tale in Joyce's Fiction: Oscillating Perspectives* (Baltimore: Johns Hopkins University Press, 1983), 128–29.

64. Walzl, "Gabriel and Michael," 431.

65. Ibid., 443.

66. Ellmann, *James Joyce,* 359.

67. Joyce, *Stephen Hero,* 186 (my emphasis).

68. Ibid., "Drama and Life," 43.

Chapter 5

1. Benstock, "The Temptation of St. Stephen," 37; Weir, "A Womb of His Own," 218.

2. Benstock, "The Temptation of St. Stephen," 34.

3. See my discussion in Balsamo, *Pruning the Genealogical Tree,* 135.

4. See Joyce, *Dubliners,* 31.

5. Sicari, *Joyce's Modernist Allegory,* 40, 63.

6. See Nehama Aschkenasy, "Biblical Females in a Joycean Episode," in *Modern Language Studies* 15, no. 4 (Fall 1985): 29.

7. See Benstock, "The Temptation of St. Stephen," 35. Benstock argues that the nocturnal emission that triggers Stephen's composition of "The Villanelle of the Temptress" is followed, before the poem is completed, by an episode of "purposeful masturbation."

8. John Gordon, "Notes in Response to Michael Seidel's '*Ulysses*'s Black Panther Vampire,'" *James Joyce Quarterly* 15, no. 3 (Spring 1978): 231.

9. Balsamo, *Pruning the Genealogical Tree,* 72.

10. Michael Seidel, "*Ulysses*'s Black Panther Vampire," *James Joyce Quarterly* 13, no. 4 (Summer 1976): 419.

11. See pt. 3, ch. 2 in Balsamo, *Rituals of Literature.*

12. Vincent J. Cheng, "Stephen Dedalus and the Black Panther Vampire," *James Joyce Quarterly* 24, no. 2 (Winter 1987): 164.

13. Joyce, *Letters,* ed. Richard Ellmann (New York: Viking, 1966), 2:48–50.

14. Three times Stephen alludes to himself as the lapwing or *garrula perdix* of Ovid, which in "Scylla and Charybdis" stands for Osric's servile obsequiousness to Hamlet (*U,* 9:954, 9:976, 9:980). See Balsamo, *Pruning the Genealogical Tree,* 131–32.

15. Slote, *The Silence in Progress of Dante, Mallarmé, and Joyce,* 74, 83.

16. See pt. 2, ch. 4 in Balsamo, *Pruning the Genealogical Tree.*

17. Slote, 2–5, 77.

18. See Don Gifford, *Ulysses Annotated: Notes for James Joyce's "Ulysses,"* revised and expanded edition (Berkeley: University of California Press, 1988), 147.

19. See Balsamo, *Pruning the Genealogical Tree,* 110–13.

20. Ibid., 103–4, 112–13.

21. Balsamo, *Pruning the Genealogical Tree,* 78–82.

22. Augustinus, *Confessiones,* Liber IX, cap. 9. This transformative reversal will be reflected in the biblical echoes of a parodic passage from the "Oxen of the Sun" episode, wherein Stephen attributes God's debasement to the condition of a "slave of servants" to the sinfulness of the Irish (*U,* 14:367–71).

23. Augustinus, *Confessiones,* Liber IX, cap. 9.

24. Ibid., Liber IX, cap. 10.

25. In "Proteus" Stephen Dedalus assimilates the "rhythm" of the waves with Yeats's "Who Goes with Fergus" (*U,* 1:239–45), which is written in four-footed lines of acatalectic (i.e., regular, or missing no final foot) iambs. By refusing to look at the visual manifestation (*Nebeneinander*) of the waves, Stephen enables himself to perceive the waves' potential for chrono-poetic representation (*Nacheinander*).

26. Augustinus, *Confessiones,* Liber VII, cap. 12, p. 142.

27. See Marcel Proust, *Contre Sainte-Beuve,* ed. Pierre Clarac et Yves Sandre (Paris: Gallimard, 1971), 819n1. Proust's long and harsh polemic against Sainte-Beuve's biographical criticism starts in 1905 with the article *"Sur la lecture."*

28. Sicari, *Joyce's Modernist Allegory,* 46.

29. Gifford, *Ulysses Annotated,* 31.

30. See Gifford, *Ulysses Annotated,* 56. Kevin Egan, who in *Ulysses* stands for the Fenian Joseph Casey, was detained in the Clerkenwell prison with Richard Burke, an Irish-American Fenian, at the time of the plot "to blast the wall of the prison yard." In this episode, narrated by Kevin Egan to Stephen Dedalus in Paris, the "shattered glass and toppling masonry" belong to the Clerkenwell prison.

31. Cited in Sicari, *Joyce's Modernist Allegory,* 41. The affirmation that "Imagination has nothing to do with memory" is found in Blake's annotations to Wordsworth's poems.

32. Devlin, "Visible Shades and Shades of Visibility," 80.

33. Samuel Taylor Coleridge, "The Rime of the Ancient Mariner," line 463, in *The Norton Anthology of Poetry,* 4th ed., ed. M. Ferguson, Mary Jo Salter, Jon Stallworthy, 744–59 (New York: Norton, 1996).

34. Balsamo, *Scriptural Poetics in Joyce's "Finnegans Wake,"* 90.

35. See Gifford, *Ulysses Annotated,* 205. Yeats adopted the above phrase from Villiers de L'Isle-Adam's play *Axel* as an epigraph for his 1897 *The Secret Rose,* which he dedicated to AE (i.e., George William Russell).

36. Sicari, *Joyce's Modernist Allegory,* 137.

37. Augustinus, *Confessiones,* Liber XI, cap. 20.

38. Ibid., Liber X, cap. 6, my emphasis, my translation.

39. Ibid., Liber XI, cap. 20 and Liber XIII, cap. 11.

40. Augustine, *De immortalitate animae,* 32:1023A.

41. See Colleen Jaurretche, *The Sensual Philosophy: Joyce and the Aesthetics of Mysticism* (Madison: University of Wisconsin Press, 1997), 63–64; Stock, *After Augustine: The Meditative Reader and the Text* (Philadelphia: University of Pennsylvania Press, 2001), 21–22, 55–56; ibid., *Augustine the Reader*, 236; Mary Carruthers, *The Book of Memory: A Study of Memory in Medieval Culture* (Cambridge: Cambridge University Press, 2002), 64.

42. Stock, *Augustine the Reader*, 260.

43. See Jean-Michel Rabaté, *James Joyce Authorized Reader* (Baltimore: Johns Hopkins University Press, 1991), 160–64; Boldrini, *Joyce, Dante, and the Poetics of Literary Relations*, 160.

44. See Dante Alighieri, *Convivio*, in *Tutte le opere di Dante*, ed. Fredi Chiappelli, trattato IV, 3 and 4 (Milan: Mursia, 1965).

45. Ibid., 5. In Dante's diction, *autentin*, which in macaronic Greek signifies an auto-*ens* or self-constituting agency.

46. See Aquinas, *Summa Theologiae*, 1–2, q. 101, a. 2, ad 2. This disquisition betrays Dante's adherence in the *Convivio* to the Thomist debate on poetry as "inferior doctrine" (*infima doctrina*), a position which induces Dante to espouse the primacy of philosophical reflection and reject the "deficiency in truth" (*defectum veritatis*) intrinsic to the fictions of poetry. With the *Commedia*, after the philosophical parenthesis of the *Convivio*, Dante will return to a renewed and reinvigorated conception of his poetic craft.

47. See Dante, *Convivio*, trattato IV, 6. Dante insinuates that the uppercase A revolves itself into an uppercase U by a 180 degree inversion accompanied by a dropping of the horizontal bar; the uppercase U stretches itself into the straight perpendicular line of an uppercase I; the uppercase I prolongs the two bars at its base and its top, and adds a third horizontal bar to turn itself into an uppercase E; the uppercase E bends its straight lines into the circle of an uppercase O, dropping at the same time the horizontal bar in its middle.

48. Robertus De Basevorn, *Forma praedicandi*, XLVIII, p. 311–12 (my translation and my added biblical references when missing from the original); see Thomas Marie Charland, O. P., ed., *Artes praedicandi: Contribution à l'histoire de la rhétorique au moyen âge* [Paris: J. Vrin; Ottawa: Institute d'études médiévales, 1936], 231–14. "There are five vowels, *a e i o u*, which make up all the words [of the sermon]. Hence Christ's five wounds [shall] make up any sound [in the sermon], whether sorrowful or joyful. Visualize [therefore] the *a* and the *e* in [Christ's] hands, as in [Jerome 31] 'Attraxi te miserans, etc.' and Isahia [49] 'Ecce in *manibus* meis descripsi te'; the *i* in his side, where the spear pierced the skin in a straight line . . . as in Genesis [6] and John [20] 'Infer digitum tuum huc et mitte in *latus* meum, et noli esse incredulus, etc.'; . . . the *o* and the *u* in his feet, as in [Psalm 8] 'Omnia subjecit Deus sub *pedibus* ejus.' Thus as you go forward [in your sermon], you may claim as a matter of fact that, [Job 23] 'Uestigia ejus seculus est *pes* meus.'"

49. Augustinus, *Confessiones*, Liber IX, cap. 10.

50. Ibid.

51. See also ibid., Liber IV, caps. 10–11. A detailed treatment of this issue is found in ch. 8 of Stock, *Augustine the Reader*, 207–42.

52. Reynolds, *Joyce and Dante*, 207.

53. Buck, author of the sophomoric "Ballad of the Laughing Jesus," and not Stephen, is invited to the soirée in honor of young poetic talents at George Moore's residence that evening.

54. Augustinus, *Confessiones,* Liber IX, cap. 10.

55. Derrida, *Given Time,* 56–59.

56. Augustinus, *Confessiones,* Liber X, cap. 10 (my translation).

57. Cited in Ellmann, *James Joyce,* 340.

Chapter 6

1. See Balsamo, *Pruning the Genealogical Tree,* 56. The maternal attributes of the sea emerged already from Stephen's conversation with Buck Mulligan on the roof of the Martello Tower in "Telemachus."

2. Gordon, "Notes in Response to Michael Seidel's '*Ulysses*'s Black Panther Vampire,'" 231.

3. See David Hayman, *Joyce et Mallarmé,* 2 vols. (Paris: Lettres Modernes, 1956), 1:26. According to David Hayman, Joyce had read Mallarmé by the age of seventeen in his own copy of Verlaine's *Les Poètes Maudits,* where one may find Verlaine's comment on "*L'après-midi d'un faune.*"

4. Stéphane Mallarmé, in *Oeuvres complètes,* ed. Carl Paul Barbier and Charles Gordon Millan (Paris: Flammarion, 1983), 176. See Mallarmé, *Correspondances,* 1:247: "At times I wish I could go and be a beggar in Africa!" (my translation).

5. Ibid., *L'après-midi d'un faune,* trans. Frederick Morgan, in *An Anthology of French Poets from Nerval to Valéry in English Translation,* ed. Angel Flores (New York: n.p., 1958), 156, as cited in Gifford, *Ulysses Annotated,* 63.

6. Francesco Piselli, *Mallarmé e l'estetica,* 61 (my translation).

7. Lloyd James Austin, *Essais sur Mallarmé,* ed. Malcolm Bowie (Manchester: Manchester University Press, 1995), 194 (my translation).

8. Roger, Bellet, *Stéphane Mallarmé: L'encre et le ciel* (Seyssel: Champ Vallon, 1987), 87 (my translation).

9. Carl Paul Barbier and L. A. Joseph, eds., *Documents Mallarmé* (Paris: Nizet, 1977), 6:261–64.

10. See Gifford, *Ulysses Annotated,* 63.

11. See Joyce, *Stephen Hero,* 32; Hayman, *Joyce et Mallarmé,* 26.

12. See Stuart Gilbert, *James Joyce's "Ulysses"* (New York: Vintage, 1958), 133.

13. Cited in ibid.

14. Balsamo, *Pruning the Genealogical Tree,* 63–66.

15. William Blake, *Complete Writings,* ed. Geoffrey Keynes (London: Oxford University Press, 1967), 749, lines 57–58.

16. Augustinus, *Confessiones,* Liber IX, cap. 10; Liber IV, cap. 11 (my translation).

17. Yeats, "To Ireland in the Coming Times," from *The Rose,* in *The Variorum Edition of the Poems by W. B. Yeats,* ed. P. Allt and R. K. Alspach (New York: Macmillan, 1957), line 11.

18. See Charles S. Singleton, ed. and trans., *"The Divine Comedy" of Dante Alighieri: "Purgatorio"* (Princeton: Princeton University Press, 1991), 1:7–12. Dante's invocation to Calliope alludes to Ovid's description of Calliope's poetic performance in the *Metamorphoses: . . . surgit . . . Calliope . . . atque haec percussis subiungit carmina nervis* (Calliope . . . rose . . . then boldly struck the chords, . . . setting her theme to music); from Ovid, *Metamorphosen* (Dublin: Weidmann, 1969) 5:338–40. For the translation see A. E. Watts, trans., *"The Metamorphoses" of Ovid,* (Los Angeles: Los Angeles University Press, 1954), 105. See also my treatment of this set of intertextual allusions in Balsamo, *Pruning the Genealogical Tree,* 72–73.

19. See Ovid, *Metamorphosen,* 5:365–84.

20. Yeats, "Who Goes with Fergus?" in *Major British Writers,* ed. G. B. Harrison (New York: Harcourt, Brace & World, 1967), 991.

21. Mary Kinzie, *A Poet's Guide to Poetry* (Chicago: University of Chicago Press, 1999), 172–73.

22. See James Richardson, *Vanishing Lives: Style and Self in Tennyson, D. G. Rossetti, Swinburne, and Yeats* (Charlottesville: University Press of Virginia, 1988), 231–35.

23. Boccaccio, *Il Decameron,* ed. Attilio Momigliano and Edoardo Sanguineti (Turin: Petrini, 1965), 226–28. Stephen's reflection on the "houses of decay" alludes to an episode from the ninth novella of the sixth *giornata* in Boccaccio's *Decameron.* A band of noisy youth surrounds Guido Cavalcanti while he takes a meditative stroll among the tombs of San Giovanni in Florence. To evade their derision, Guido intimates that the surrounding tombs are these youth's own homes.

24. Jennifer Margaret Fraser, *Rite of Passage in the Narratives of Dante and Joyce* (Gainesville: University Press of Florida, 2002), 106–7. See also Frances E. Restuccia, *Joyce and the Law of the Father* (New Haven: Yale University Press, 1989), 51.

25. Dante, *Paradiso,* 23:73–74 (my translation).

26. Ibid., 13:133–35: *ch'i' ho veduto tutto il verno prima / lo prun mostrarsi rigido e feroce, / poscia portar la rosa in su la cima.* St. Thomas is here alluding to the tropes of the rose and the thorn from St. Bernard's homily of the Blessed Virgin Mary. See Gifford, *Ulysses Annotated,* 415; Weldon Thornton, *Allusions in "Ulysses": An Annotated List* (Chapel Hill: University of North Carolina Press, 1987), 328–29.

27. See Dante, *Paradiso* 5:7–12, 33:97–105.

28. Already in *Stephen Hero,* Stephen Daedalus interest in Yeats's "The Adoration of the Magi" exposed him to Yeats's ideas about the maternal figure. See Joyce, *Stephen Hero,* 178–79. See Yeats, *Mythologies* (London: Macmillan, 1959), 310.

29. See Elizabeth B. Cullingford, "At the Feet of the Goddess: Yeats's Love Poetry and the Feminist Occult," in vol. 9 of *Yeats Annual,* ed. D. Toomey (London: Macmillan, 1992), 53.

30. Diane Stubbings, *Anglo-Irish Modernism and the Maternal: From Yeats to Joyce* (Houndmills: Palgrave, 2000), 54–55.

31. Yeats, "Into the Twilight," in *The Varorum Edition of the Poems by W. B. Yeats,* ed. P. Allt and R. K. Alspach (New York: Macmillan, 1957), 48, line 5.

32. R. Kearney, "Myth and Motherland," in *Ireland's Field Day,* ed. Field Day Theatre Company (London: Hutchison, 1985), 70.

33. Julia Kristeva, "*Stabat Mater*" in *The Kristeva Reader,* edited and introduced by Toril Moi (New York: Columbia University Press, 1986) 183; Nina Auerbach, *Woman and the Demon: The Life of a Victorian Myth* (Cambridge: Harvard University Press, 1982), 185. See Stubbings, *Anglo-Irish Modernism and the Maternal,* 206n15.

34. Fraser, *Rite of Passage in the Narratives of Dante and Joyce,* 133.

35. Stubbings, *Anglo-Irish Modernism and the Maternal,* 153.

36. Kinzie, *A Poet's Guide to Poetry,* 172.

37. Yeats, "Easter 1916," in *Major British Writers,* 995, lines 57–64.

38. Luke 1:38.

39. Ibid.

40. Stubbings, *Anglo-Irish Modernism and the Maternal,* 155–56.

41. Tibor Wlassics defines Stephen's quatrain as a pastiche in "Nota su Dante nell'*Ulisse*," in *Rivista di letterature moderne e comparate* 24, no. 2 (1971): 151–54.

42. See Douglas Hyde, ed. and trans., *The Love Songs of Connacht*, 21. "And my love came behind me C / He came from the South; / His breast to my bosom, / His mouth to my mouth."

43. See Adams Day, "How Stephen Wrote His Vampire Poem," 184, 193. Adams Day has wondered how Stephen's lofty sources of inspiration may be reconciled with his choice to write a parody of these verses by Hyde, when all evidence shows that Stephen despised Hyde's rendering of *The Love Songs of Connacht*. To explain this apparent paradox, Day refers to Joyce's 1902 review of William Rooney's *Poems and Ballads*. Although this review is "highly unfavorable," Joyce has words of praise for Rooney's translation of a poem by Douglas Hyde. It is "a piece . . . which seems to have come out of a conscious personal life. It is a translation of some verses by Dr. Douglas Hyde, and . . . yet I cannot believe that it owes more than its subject to its original. . . . It seems to come out of a personal life which has begun to realize itself." Adams Day applies the logic of Joyce's opinion to Stephen's choice of Hyde's verses: "Even the dross of someone like Hyde [can be transmuted into] lines of living verses."

44. Ibid., 188; Cheng, "Stephen Dedalus and the Black Panther Vampire," 164; Gordon, "Notes in Response to Michael Seidel's '*Ulysses*'s Black Panther Vampire,'" 230.

45. Adams Day, "How Stephen Wrote His Vampire Poem," 187.

46. Emma stands for the Emma Clery from *Stephen Hero*. As Bernard Benstock remarks, in *A Portrait of the Artist*, Emma has "lost her surname," and even her Christian name is mostly absent, except for the exception of "a single incident." Now Stephen refers to her as E.C., "a poetic designation, the sort of sacred subterfuge attributed to the Romantic Poets." See Benstock, "The Temptation of St. Stephen," 31.

47. John P. Frayne, ed., *Uncollected Prose, by W. B. Yeats* (New York: Columbia University Press, 1970), 1:130–37.

48. Patrick J. Keane, *Yeats, Joyce, Ireland, and the Myth of the Devouring Female* (Columbia: University of Missouri Press, 1988), x–xi.

49. Stephen's "wet sign" is usually identified with Horatio's designation of the moon as the "moist star" in Shakespeare's *Hamlet* (1.1.118), and also with the "watery star" of Shakespeare's *The Winter's Tale* (1.2.1). See Thornton, *Allusions in "Ulysses,"* 62.

50. Ewa Ziarek, "Working the Limit: (m)other, text, abject in *Ulysses*," in *Images of Joyce*, ed. Clive Hart, C. George Sandulescu, Bonnie K. Scott, and Fritz Senn, 2:639–40 (Gerrards Cross: Colin Smyth, 1988).

51. See Enda Duffy, "Interesting States: Birthing and the Nation in 'Oxen of the Sun,'" in *"Ulysses"—En-Gendered Perspectives*, 216–17, concerning the early-twentieth-century Irish debate on "the relation between population growth and a 'healthy' nation."

52. Cheryl Herr, "Old Wives' Tales as Portals of Discovery in 'Proteus,'" in *"Ulysses"— En-Gendered Perspectives*, 38.

53. For a discussion of the milkwoman as "linked with the Otherworld tradition in Irish literature," see Caitriona Moloney, "The Hags of *Ulysses*: The 'Poor Old Woman,' Cathleen Ni Houlihan, and the Phallic Mother," *James Joyce Quarterly* 34, nos. 1 and 2 (Fall 1996 and Winter 1997): 116–17.

54. Stubbings, *Anglo-Irish Modernism and the Maternal*, 57, 148–49, 153.

55. Dante, *Convivio*, in *Tutte le opere*, treatise 3, 15, lines 15–18.

56. Jaroslav Pelikan, *Mary through the Centuries: Her Place in the History of Culture* (New Haven: Yale University Press, 1996), 132.

57. Thomas J. J. Altizer, *History as Apocalypse* (Albany: State University of New York Press, 1985), 126 (my emphasis); Dante, *Paradiso,* 32:85–87.

58. Pelikan, *Mary through the Centuries,* 139.

59. Ibid.

60. Ibid., 141.

61. In the essay "Leonardo da Vinci," for instance, Walter Pater describes *La Gioconda* as a vampire who "has been dead many times, and learned the secrets of the grave." See Walter Pater, *The Renaissance: Studies in Art and Poetry* (London: Macmillan, 1877), 135.

62. See, for instance, Mallarmé's autumn 1864 letter to Henri Cazalis, *Correspondances,* 1:137–38.

63. Robillard, *Le désir de la vierge,* 80–81.

64. See Stéphane Mallarmé, *Collected Poems,* trans. Henry Weinfield (Berkeley: University of California Press, 1994), 24. The present, modified version of Henry Weinfield's translation privileges lexical accuracy at the expense of rhyme and meter. *"Je t'apporte l'enfant d'une nuit d'Idumée! / Noire, à l'aile saignante et pâle, déplumée, / Par le verre brûlé d'aromates et d'or, / Par les carreaux glacés, hélas! mornes encor / L'aurore se jeta sur la lampe angélique, / Palmes! et quand elle a montré cette relique / A ce père essayant un sourire ennemi, / La solitude bleue et stérile a frémi. / O la berceuse avec ta fille et l'innocence / De vos pieds froids, accueille une horrible naissance / Et, ta voix rappelant viole et clavecin, / Avec le doigt fané presseras-tu le sein / Par qui coule en blancheur sibylline la femme / Pour des lèvres que l'air du vierge azur affame?"* Mallarmé, *Oeuvres Complètes,* 192.

65. Mallarmé, *Correspondances,* 1:142 (my translation).

66. *"Et surtout ne va pas, frère, acheter du pain."* See Mallarmé, *Aumône,* as cited in Derrida, *Glas,* 151 (my translation).

67. Mallarmé, *Correspondances,* 1:240.

68. Bellet, *Stéphane Mallarmé: L'encre et le ciel,* 94 (my translation).

69. Robillard, *Le désir de la vierge,* 48.

70. Stock, *Augustine the Reader,* 24.

71. Mallarmé, *Correspondances,* 1:166 (my translation).

72. Ibid., 1:154 (my translation). See also Robillard, *Le désir de la vierge,* 10.

73. Robillard, *Le désir de la vierge,* 185, 49.

74. See Mallarmé's 31 December 1865 letter to Villiers de l'Isle-Adam, *Correspondances,* 1:193 (my translation).

75. Derrida writes that "Idumaea, the land of the Edomites [descendants of Esau], would be the pre-Adamic kingdom: Before Esau was replaced by Jacob, who received his blind father's blessing, the kings of Idumaea were supposed to reproduce themselves without sex and without women." See Derrida, *Given Time,* 59 (I have modified the translation slightly).

76. See for instance Pater, *The Renaissance,* 77.

77. Virgil, *Aeneis* (Turin: Einaudi, 1989), 6:74–75.

78. See Mallarmé, *Brise marine,* in *Oeuvres complètes,* 176, line 7 (my translation). Mallarmé worked simultaneously on "Gift of the Poem" and "Sea Breeze."

79. Freccero, *Dante: The Poetics of the Afterlife,* 247.

80. The present and the previous paragraph reproduce the contents of two corresponding paragraphs from Balsamo, *Pruning the Genealogical Tree,* 58–59.

81. Mallarmé, *Correspondances,* 1:166.

82. Slote, *The Silence in Progress of Dante, Mallarmé, and Joyce,* 74, 83.

83. Derrida, *Given Time,* 59.

84. Maurice Blanchot, *La part du feu,* 329: "Dans la parole meurt ce qui donne vie à la parole."

85. Stubbings, *Anglo-Irish Modernism and the Maternal,* 57–58.

86. See Blanchot, *La part du feu,* 311: "*L'écrivain ne peut pas se retirer an lui-même, ou il lui faut renoncer à écrire.*"

87. Daniel 8:17, 12:9, 7:14.

88. This is an allusion to Dante's epithet in Canto 33 of the *Paradiso*: Mary, "daughter of her own son" (33:1).

89. See Balsamo, *Pruning the Genealogical Tree,* 68.

Chapter 7

1. See Kinzie, *A Poet's Guide to Poetry,* 433.

2. Edward Lear, *A Book of Nonsense* (New York: Knopf, 1992), 174, 204.

3. Jean-Pierre Vernant, "A General Theory of Sacrifice and the Slaying of the Victims in the Greek *Thusia,*" in *Mortals and Immortals,* ed. Froma I. Zeitlin (Princeton: Princeton University Press, 1991), 294.

4. Walter Burkert, *Creation of the Sacred,* 152–55.

5. See pt. 1, ch. 2 in Balsamo, *Rituals of Literature.*

6. See, for instance, E. L. Schieffelin, "Reciprocity and the Construction of Reality," *Man* 15 (1980): 502–17.

7. Burkert, *Creation of the Sacred,* 150–52.

8. See Durkheim, *Les formes élémentaires de la vie religieuse,* 451.

9. See Robert Hertz, "*Contribution à une étude sur la représentation collective de la mort,*" in *Année sociologique,* 1st series, tome X, 1907; reprinted in Robert Hertz, *Sociologie religieuse et folklore* (Paris: Presses Universitaires de France, 1970), 8, 23–24.

10. Vico, *Scienza nuova,* 404.

11. Sigmund Freud, *Totem and Taboo,* trans. James Strachey (New York: Norton, 1989), 186–88.

12. See Karen Lawrence, "Legal Fiction or Pulp Fiction in 'Lestrygonians,'" in *"Ulysses"—En-Gendered Perspectives,* 104.

13. Nussbaum, *Upheavals of Thought,* 709.

14. See José Lanters, "Old Worlds, New Worlds, Alternative Worlds: *Ulysses, Metamorphoses* 13, and the Death of the Beloved Son," *James Joyce Quarterly* 36, no. 3 (Spring 1999): 531.

15. Friedrich Nietzsche, *The Birth of Tragedy,* ed. Walter Kaufmann (New York: Vintage, 1967), 132–33.

16. Daniel Ogden, "Cleisthenes of Sycyon," *Classical Quarterly* 43, no. 2 (1993): 357–58.

17. Jan Bremmer, "Scapegoat Rituals in Ancient Greece," *HSCP* 87 (1983): 303–5.

18. Burkert, *Creation of the Sacred,* 53.

19. Cheryl Herr, "Old Wives' Tales as Portals of Discovery in 'Proteus,'" in *"Ulysses"—En-Gendered Perspectives,* 38.

20. Ibid., 37–38.

21. See Enda Duffy, "Interesting States," in *"Ulysses"—En-Gendered Perspectives,* 218.

22. See for instance Marcel Mauss, "L'expression obligatoire des sentiments," in *Journal de psychologie normal et pathologique*, vol. 18 (Paris: Alcan 1921), 430n1.

23. See Devlin, "Visible Shades and Shades of Visibility," in *"Ulysses"—En-Gendered Perspectives,* 78. In discussing this passage, Kimberly Devin inaccurately "juxtaposes [in it] child-birthing and physical toil," as the two principal tasks which Bloom's thought would assign to women. The "physical toil" of this passage does not pertain to generic labor, but rather to the reversal of the labor of delivery onto the toils pertinent to the disposition of the corpse.

24. John Z. Bennett, "Unposted Letter: Joyce's Leopold Bloom," in *Critical Essays on James Joyce's "Ulysses,"* ed. Bernard Benstock, 95 (Boston: G. K. Hall & Co., 1989).

25. See Lawrence, "Legal Fiction or Pulp Fiction in 'Lestrygonians,'" in *"Ulysses"—En-Gendered Perspectives,* 106.

26. See R. M. Adams, "Hades," in *James Joyce's "Ulysses": Critical Essays,* ed. Clive Hart and David Hayman, 95 (Berkeley: University of California Press, 1974).

27. Lawrence, "Legal Fiction or Pulp Fiction in 'Lestrygonians,'" in *"Ulysses"—En-Gendered Perspectives,* 105–6.

28. Devlin, "Visible Shades and Shades of Visibility," in *"Ulysses"—En-Gendered Perspectives,* 72–73.

29. Kristeva, *Powers of Horror: An Essay on Abjection,* trans. Leon S. Roudiez (New York: Columbia University Press, 1982), 109.

30. Lawrence, "Legal Fiction or Pulp Fiction in 'Lestrygonians,'" in *"Ulysses"—En-Gendered Perspectives,* 106.

31. Patrick McGee, "Gesture: The Letter of the Word," in *Critical Essays on James Joyce's "Ulysses,"* 318.

32. Plato, *Symposium,* trans. Seth Benardete (Chicago: University of Chicago Press, 2001), 189E–90A, p. 19.

33. Ibid., 191A–B, p. 20.

34. Cited in Lawrence, "Legal Fiction or Pulp Fiction in 'Lestrygonians,'" in *"Ulysses"—En-Gendered Perspectives,* 109.

35. See my discussion in Balsamo, *Scriptural Poetics in Joyce's "Finnegans Wake,"* 7–11.

36. Lawrence, "Legal Fiction or Pulp Fiction in 'Lestrygonians,'" in *"Ulysses"—En-Gendered Perspectives,* 108–9.

37. Ibid.

38. Ibid., 108

39. Regarding this analogy I disagree with Lawrence, who contrasts the "transfer of pulp from Molly's mouth to Bloom's [and] the terrifyingly vampiric 'mouth to mouth' kiss in Stephen's poem." See Lawrence, "Legal Fiction or Pulp Fiction in 'Lestrygonians,'" in *"Ulysses"—En-Gendered Perspectives,* 109.

40. Ibid., 108.

41. See Augustine, *Enarrationes in psalmos,* 46:1, in Corpus Christianorum Series Latina 38:529 (Turnhout: Brepols, 1954–) and *De trinitate,* 11:7, in Corpus Christianorum Series Latina 50:377:76; Ezekiel 3:1–3; Revelation 10:9–11.

Chapter 8

1. See also Richard Ellmann, *Ulysses on the Liffey* (New York: Oxford University Press, 1972), 139: "Joyce is establishing a secret parallel and opposition: the body of God and the body of woman share blood in common."

2. Robert Boyle, "Miracle in Black Ink: A Glance at Joyce's Use of His Eucharistic Image," *James Joyce Quarterly* 10 (Fall 1972): 47, 54–55.

3. Ibid., 47.

4. David Hayman *A First-Draft Version of "Finnegans Wake"* (Austin: University of Texas Press, 1963), 108. Hayman reports an early fragmentary version of the relevant passage from *Finnegans Wake,* wherein is found the phrase, ". . . writes universal history on his own body (parchment)."

5. Boyle, "*Finnegans Wake,* Page 185: An Explication," *James Joyce Quarterly* 4 (Fall 1966): 3–4.

6. Boyle, "Miracle in Black Ink," 56–57.

7. Vulgate, Psalm 44:1; Authorized Version, Psalm 45:1.

8. Boyle, "Miracle in Black Ink," 56–57.

9. Bernardus Silvestris writes in *Commentum: Integumentum est genus demonstrationis sub fabulosa narratione veritatis involvens intellectum; unde etiam involucrum dicitur.* Cf. Bernardus Silvestris, *Commentum super sex libros Eneidos Virgilii,* ed. Julian Ward Jones and Elizabeth Frances Jones (Lincoln and London: University of Nebraska Press, 1977), 3, lines 14–15. See also Edouard Jeauneau, "L'usage de la notion d'integumentum à travers le Gloses de Guillaume de Conches," in *Archives d'histoire doctrinale et littèraire du Moyen Age* 24 (1957); cited in Nicoló Mineo, *Profetismo e Apocalittica in Dante: Strutture e temi profetico-apocalittici in Dante dalla Vita Nuova alla Divina Commedia* (Catania: Facoltá di Lettere e Filosofia, 1968), 318n73.

10. Gregorius Magnus, *Moralia in Job,* trans. Dom André de Gaudemaris (Paris: Éditions du cerf, 1975), Praefactio, 517a–b: *Auctor libri [est] [Spiritus Sanctus] qui scribenda dictavit . . . in illius opere inspirator extitit, et per scribentis vocem imitanda ad nos ejus facta transmisit* (The author of the book [of Job] is the Holy Spirit who dictated it since it was to be written . . . the inspirator is manifest through the influence [of the Holy Spirit], who, by means of the voice of the scribe, gave us these examples [from the story of Job] to imitate) (my translation).

11. See Isidorus of Seville, *De ecclesiasticis Officiis* ed. Christopher M Lawson (Turnholti: Brepols, 1989) (in *Corpus Christianorum, Series Latina* vol. 113), 1:12, lines 99–103 (my translation). Isidore of Seville writes in *De ecclesiasticis Officiis,* for instance: *Scriptores sacrorum librorum diuina inspiratione loquentes . . . Auctor autem earundem scripturarum spiritus sanctus esse creditur; ipse enim scripsit qui per prophetas suos scribenda dictauit.* (The writers of the sacred books speak through divine inspiration. . . . The Holy Spirit takes credit as the author of those scripts; in truth He is the writer, since He dictated that which his prophets were to inscribe).

12. Burkert, *Creation of the Sacred,* 53.

13. Galatians 3:13.

14. Luke 22:19–20.

15. Thomas Aquinas, *Summa Theologiae,* 3, q. 76, a. 1, ad 1. I have modified the translation from *Summa Theologiae,* vol. 58, *The Eucharistic Presence,* trans. William Barden (London: Blackfriars, 1965).

16. Aquinas, *Summa Theologiae,* 3, q. 76, a. 1, ad 1.

17. In the *Summa Contra Gentiles,* Aquinas identifies the death of the Word of God with the death of God himself. Cf. Aquinas, *Summa Contra Gentiles,* trans. R. Bernier and F. Kerouanton (Paris: Lethielleux, 1957), 4, 34: *Omni passio quae in corpore ollius hominis facta fuit,*

potest Verbo Dei attribui. Recte igitur dici potest quod Verbum Dei, et Deus, est passus, crucifixus, mortuus et sepultus (198).

18. *Christus resurgens ex mortuis jam non moritur* (Aquinas, *Summa Theologiae*, 3, q. 76, a.1, ad 1.) The predicate *resurgens* signifies active purposiveness on the part of the resurrected Christ, which I have opted to render as "having risen." It seems to me that passive renderings such as that found in Barden's translation (*Summa Theologiae*, vol. 58) (raised), however evocative of the current English translations of Romans 6:9, corrupt Aquinas's intended meaning.

19. Boyle, "Miracle in Black Ink," 52.

20. Saint Augustine, *De civitate dei*, trans. David S. Wiesen (Cambridge: Harvard University Press, 1968), vol. 3, bks. 10, 6, 20 (translation modified).

21. Altizer, "The Primordial Sacrifice," personal communication.

22. See Boldrini, *Joyce, Dante, and the Poetics of Literary Relations*, 76.

23. Boyle, "Miracle in Black Ink," 58.

24. "Not even then could such an antinomian [i.e., Shem] be true to type" (*FW*, 172: 17–18). See also *FW* 139:29–30: "Which title is the true-to-type motto-in-lieu for that Tick for Teac thatchment [i.e., the escutcheon or Arms of the City of Dublin]." If "true-to-type" must be an attribute of a "motto-in-lieu" or homonym, then it is rather impossible for an "antinomian" to be true to type.

25. Thomas Aquinas, *Quaestiones quodlibetales*, n. 7, q. 6, ar. 2, *responsio*, in *Opera Omnia*, 438–500 (my emphasis, my translation).

26. Ellmann, *Oscar Wilde* (New York: Vintage, 1988), 311. Ellmann mentions Wilde's "veneration" for and "idolization" of Balzac (213, 289).

27. See Balzac, *La peau de chagrin*, in *La comédie humaine*, ed. P. Citron (Paris: Gallimard, 1976), 82n1, 83. Whereas the exact identification of the nature of the *chagrin* is a matter of etymological contention, as Pierre Citron explains in his edition of *La Peau de chagrin*, the *peau de chagrin* may be obtained from the hide of a variety of animals, including horses, donkeys, and goats. But in Balzac's story the hide is clearly attributed to an onager.

28. Pierre Citron, introduction to *La comédie humaine*, 25.

29. For the prospective repetition and retrospective revision of biblical types in *Ulysses* and in *Finnegans Wake*, see parts 2 and 3 of Balsamo, *Scriptural Poetics in Joyce's "Finnegans Wake."*

30. See Boyle, "Portrait of the Artist as Balzacian Wilde Ass," in *A Conceptual Guide to "Finnegans Wake,"* ed. Michael H. Begnal and Fritz Senn, 76 (London: Pennsylvania State University Press, 1974).

31. Boyle, "Miracle in Black Ink," 55, 58.

32. See Freccero, *Dante's Cosmos*, Bernardo Lecture Series 6 (Binghamton: Center for Medieval and Renaissance Studies, SUNY, 1998), 7–12. The Miltonic contiguity of crystal and chaos parallels somewhat the Dantesque contiguity of *Primum Mobile* and Empyrean described in Canto 2 of *Paradiso* (112–14; see also *Paradiso* 1:122–23). But only a rigidly Ptolemaic apprehension of Dante's universe could misplace the crystal boundaries of the *Primum Mobile* at the borders of Dante's planetary system. The mirroring dialectic between planetary spheres and heavenly spheres developed by Dante in *Paradiso* disallows such a misapprehension. When Beatrice defines God with the words *il sol de li angeli* (the sun of the angels) (*Paradiso* 10:53), her heliocentric trope is in evident conflict with the geocentric order dominant in medieval astronomy. The structure of Dante's planetary spheres is

Ptolemaic, but the structure of his heavenly spheres is Copernican, the sun-God being at the center and the spheres losing entropically speed (rather than increasing it, as do the planetary spheres farther away from the earth) as they grow distant from the center.

33. See Dante, *Convivio,* 2:3:7–8, 2:3:11, 2:14:14, and the epistle to *Cani Grandi de la Scala (Epistula XIII.,* in *Tutte le opere,* p. 866, sentence no. 68), for the crystalline essence of the Empyrean *Primum Mobile,* and its luminous impregnation of all other layers of the material and immaterial universe.

34. Durling and Martinez, *Time and the Crystal: Studies in Dante's Rime Petrose* (Berkeley: University of California Press, 1990), 253.

35. See Roger Dragonetti, *Dante, pélerin de la sainte Face,* Romanica gaudensia, no. 11, Ghent, 379.

36. Durling and Martinez, *Time and the Crystal,* 253.

37. See Gifford, *Ulysses Annotated,* 218 (note to 9:376–78).

38. Ovid, *Les Métamorphoses,* ed. and trans. Georges Lafaye (Paris: Les Belles Lettres, 1972), 3:15:878–79 (my emphasis).

39. Boyle, "*Finnegans Wake,* Page 185: An Explication," 13.

40. Umberto Eco, *Il problema estetico in Tommaso d'Aquino* (Milan: Bompiani, 1970), 186.

41. The spiritual sense of the Bible is divided by Aquinas into allegorical, moral, and anagogic sense. *Summa Theologiae,* 1, q. 1, a. 10.

42. See Thomas Aquinas, *Quaestiones quodlibetales,* n. 7, q. 6, a. 3: "Poetical fictions have only one function, that of signifying; hence, their signification does not go beyond the mode of the literal sense." (my translation); *Summa Theologiae* 1, q. 1, a. 10: "The parabolical sense is contained in the literal sense, for words can signify something properly and something figuratively; in the last case the literal sense is not the figure of speech itself, but the object it figures. When Scripture speaks of the arm of God, the literal sense is not that he has a physical limb, but that he has what it signifies, namely the power of doing and making." Translation from St. Thomas Aquinas, *Summa Theologiae,* vol. 1, *Christian Theology,* trans. Thomas Gilby (London: Blackfriars, 1964).

43. Derrida, *Of Grammatology,* trans. Gayatri Chakravorty Spivak (Baltimore: Johns Hopkins University Press, 1976), 159–60.

44. Ibid., 160.

45. Boyle, *James Joyce's Pauline Vision: A Catholic Exposition* (London: Feffer & Simons, 1978), 49, 115n5.

46. Boyle, "Miracle in Black Ink," 57.

47. Ibid., 57, 116n14.

48. See Gifford, *Joyce Annotated: Notes for "Dubliners" and "A Portrait of the Artist as a Young Man,"* (Berkeley: University of California Press, 1982), 265; Reynolds, *Joyce and Dante,* 180–83. For the source of Stephen's "transmutation," it is of course customary to refer to Yeats's "Rosa Alchemica." However, Mary Reynolds has convincingly shown that Joyce, in the final revisions of *A Portrait of the Artist as a Young Man,* deliberately obscured the entire range of early influences emerging from *Stephen Hero* (i.e., Shakespeare, Ibsen, D'Annunzio, Yeats, and Pater) in order to highlight the Dantesque elements. Terms such as *transmutare (Inferno,* 25:142) or *trasumanar (Paradiso,* 1:70) were familiar to Joyce and to Stephen Dedalus from their respective readings of Dante.

49. Balsamo, *Pruning the Genealogical Tree,* 138.

50. Giuseppe Martella, *"Ulisse": Parallelo biblico e modernità* (Bologna: CLUEB, 1997), 56–57 (my translation).

51. Cf. Gregorius Magnus, *Moralia in Job,* Praefactio, 517a–b; Isidorus of Seville, *De ecclesiasticis officiis,* 1:12, lines 99–103.

52. This expression, derived from Mallarmé's meditation, "Hamlet et Fortinbras," is used by Richard Best, assistant director of Dublin's National Library, in the "Scylla and Charybdis" discussion on Shakespeare"s authorship of *Hamlet* (*U,* 9:114).

Epilogue

1. The facsimile of the papyrus in Demotic characters that is conventionally identified as "Setnau" (or "Setne I") is reproduced in plates 29–32 ("Papyrus no. 5") from Auguste Mariette, *Les papyrus égyptiens du Musée de Boulaq* (Paris: Librairie A. Franck, 1871), Tome Premier, Papyrus no. 1–9. The above version of the "Tale of Setnau" consists of my poetic adaptation of selected excerpts from plate 29 (lines 39–40) and plate 30 (lines 3–4, 6–7, 13–16), where I propose a future-perfect solution to the dissatisfactory chronology that entangles all extant translations. The cycle of Setnau was revealed to the archeological world in a 1867 French translation by Heinrich Karl Brugsch, *Le roman de Setnau,* in *Revue archéologique* (Paris: Leleux, 1867), 161–79, and a 1875 English translation by P. Le Page Renouf, *The Tale of Setnau,* in *Records of the Past,* vol. 4, *Egyptian Texts* (London: Samuel, Bagster and Sons, 1875), 129–48. When compared with these two early renderings, the translations of "Setne I" found in E. Bresciani, *Letteratura e poesia dell'antico Egitto* (Turin: n.p., 1969), 615–26, and Bernard Lewis, ed. and intro., *Land of Enchanters: Egyptian Short Stories from the Earliest Times to the Present Day* (London: Harvill Press, 1948), 67–83, bear witness to the astounding progress later made in our understanding of Demotic script. However, my dissatisfaction with the linear chronology of extant translations applies no less to the more recent than to the earlier ones. For my poetic adaptation I have referred mainly to Brugsch's and Renouf's respective versions, whose tentative renderings of the Demotic original have the advantage of a vital freshness that is lost to subsequent translations.

2. See Miriam Lichtheim, *Ancient Egyptian Literature: A Book of Reading,* vol. 3, *The Late Period* (Berkeley: University of California Press, 1980), 125.

3. A tentative reconstruction based on Cairo Papyrus no. 30692, which consists of either "a part of the missing beginning or a variant of it," may be found in Lichtheim, *Ancient Egyptian Literature,* 3:127.

4. See Brugsch, *Le roman de Setnau,* 163; John A. Wilson, *The Culture of Ancient Egypt* (Chicago: University of Chicago Press, 1957), 320.

5. Lichtheim, *Ancient Egyptian Literature,* 3:125.

6. Renouf, *The Tale of Setnau,* 131. Brugsch-Bey, *Le roman de Setnau,* 164.

7. See Ezekiel 3:1–3; Revelation 10:9–11; Jerome, *Commentarium in ezechielem,* in *Patrologia Latina,* ed. J.P. Migne, 23: col. 17–704 (Paris: 1841–64).

8. Roland McHugh suggests "Moses Moses" in *Annotations to "Finnegans Wake"* (Baltimore: Johns Hopkins University Press, 1991), 3; Joseph Campbell and Henry Morton Robinson suggest "I am, I am" in *A Skeleton Key to "Finnegans Wake"* (New York: Penguin, 1986), 29; however, an annotation by Joyce himself interprets the Hebrew expression *misha mishinnah* as signifying, "a bad, violent and unprepared [unintelligible word] for death or end" (see *James Joyce Quarterly* 4, no. 3 [1966]: 194).

9. See McHugh, *Annotations to "Finnegans Wake,"* 3. The term "arclight" alludes to *arcobaleno,* Italian for "rainbow." The term "regginbrow" alludes to the German *Regenbogen.* The phrase "Rot a peck of pa's malt" contains "rot" for the process of fermentation, "malt" for a cereal used in beer brewing, and alludes to Robert Burns's song: "O, Willie brew'd a peck o' mant." The combination of names, "Jhem or Shen" evokes the phoneme *jameson,*

allusive of Jameson Whiskey, a favorite Dublin drink. I thank the Edwin Mellen Press for allowing me to reproduce the present paragraph and footnote from Balsamo, *Scriptural Poetics in Joyce's "Finnegans Wake,"* 100, 106–7.

10. See, respectively, William York Tindall, *A Reader's Guide to "Finnegans Wake"* (Syracuse: Syracuse University Press, 1996), 44; Danis Rose and John O'Hanlon, *Understanding "Finnegans Wake": A Guide to the Narrative of James Joyce's Masterpiece* (New York: Garland, 1982), 18.

11. A. Nicholas Fargnoli and Michael P. Gillespie, *James Joyce A to Z* (Oxford: Oxford University Press, 1995), 22.

12. See McHugh, *Annotations to "Finnegans Wake,"* 18. The modern Greek expression, *vivlion viou,* translates as "book of life."

13. Jean-Jacques Rousseau, *Essai sur l'origine des langues,* ed. Charles Porset, (Bordeaux: Ducros, 1970), 63–65 (my translation).

14. Rousseau, *Lettres à Burney,* éd. Houssiaux (Paris:, n.p., 1852), 3:557 (my translation).

15. See Paul de Man, *Allegories of Reading: Figural Language in Rousseau, Nietzsche, Rilke, and Proust* (New Haven: Yale University Press, 1979), 72–78.

16. Augustinus, *Confessiones,* Liber X, cap. 10, 29; Liber XI, cap. 6. See also Stock, *After Augustine,* 21–22.

BIBLIOGRAPHY

Adams, R. M. "Hades." In *James Joyce's "Ulysses": Critical Essays,* ed. Clive Hart and David Hayman, 91–114. Berkeley: University of California Press, 1974.

Adams Day, Robert. "How Stephen Wrote His Vampire Poem," *James Joyce Quarterly* 17, no. 2 (Winter 1980): 186.

Alighieri, Dante. *Cani Grandi de la Scala,* in *Tutte le opere di Dante,* ed. Fredi Chiappelli, 860–69, 890–98. Milan: Mursia, 1965.

———. *Convivio,* in *Tutte le opere,* 487–651.

———. *La divina commedia.* Ed. Carlo Grabher. 3 vols. Bari: Laterza, 1964.

———. *Inferno.* Ed. Carlo Grabher. Bari: Laterza, 1964.

———. *Paradiso.* Ed. Carlo Grabher. Bari: Laterza, 1964.

———. *Paradiso.* Translated by Charles S. Singleton. Princeton: Princeton University Press, 1991.

———. *Purgatorio.* Ed. Carlo Grabher. Bari: Laterza, 1964.

———. *Purgatorio.* Translated by Charles S. Singleton. Princeton: Princeton University Press, 1991.

———. *Vita nuova,* in *Tutte le opere,* 363–416.

Altizer, Thomas J. J. *Genesis and Apocalypse: A Theological Voyage toward Authentic Christianity.* Louisville: Westminster / John Knox Press, 1990.

———. *History as Apocalypse.* Albany: State University of New York Press, 1985.

———. "The Primordial Sacrifice," personal communication.

Aquinas, Thomas. *Quaestiones quodlibetales.* In *Opera Omnia,* Ed. Roberto Busa, 3:438–500. Stuttgart-Bad Cannstatt: Frommann-Holzboog, 1980.

———. *Summa Theologiae.* Cura et Studio Instituti Studiorum Medievalium Ottaviensis Commissio Piana. Ottawa: n.p., 1953.

———. *Summa Theologiae.* Vol. 1, *Christian Theology.* Translated by Thomas Gilby. London: Blackfriars, 1964.

———. *Summa Theologiae.* Vol. 58, *The Eucharistic Presence.* Translated by William Barden. London: Blackfriars, 1965.

———. *Summa Contra Gentiles.* Translated by R. Bernier and F. Kerouanton. Paris: Lethielleux, 1957.

Aschkenasy, Nehama. "Biblical Females in a Joycean Episode." *Modern Language Studies* 15, no. 4 (Fall 1985).

Auerbach, Erich. *Mimesis: The Representation of Reality in Western Literature.* Translated by Willard R. Trask. Princeton: Princeton University Press, 1991.

———. "Figura." Translated by Ralph Manheim, in *Scenes from the Drama of European Literature,* 9–76. New York: Meridian, 1959.

———. "Vico's and Aesthetic Historicism" in *Scenes from the Drama of European Literature,* 181–98.

Auerbach, Nina. *Woman and the Demon: The Life of a Victorian Myth*. Cambridge: Harvard University Press, 1982.

Augustine. *Confessions*. Translated by William Watts. Cambridge: Harvard University Press, 2000.

————. *Confessions*. Translated by R. S. Pine-Coffin. New York: Penguin, 1961.

————. *Confessions*. In *Nicene and Post-Nicene Fathers of the Christian Church*. Vol. 1. Ed. Philip Schaff. Edinburgh: T & T Clark, 1994.

————. *Confessions*. Translated by F. J. Sheed. Indianapolis: Hackett, 1993.

————. *Confessions*. Translated by John K. Ryan. Garden City, N.J.: Image Books, 1960.

————. *Confessions*. Translated by Rex Warner. New York: New American Library, 1963.

————. *De civitate dei*. Translated by David S. Wiesen. Cambridge: Harvard University Press, 1986.

————. *De catechizandis rudibus*. In *Corpus Christianorum, Series Latina* 46. Turnhout: Brepols, 1954– .

————. *De cura pro mortuis gerenda ad paulinum*. In *Corpus Scriptorum Ecclesiasticorum Latinorum* 41. Vindobonae: Hoelder-Pichler-Tempsky, 1866– .

————. *De immortalitate animae*. Vol. 32 *Patrologia Latina*. Ed. J. P. Migne. Paris: 1844–64.

————. *De libero arbitrio*. In *Earlier Writings*, Ed. J. H. S. Burleigh, 113–217. Philadelphia: Westminster, 1953.

————. *De libero arbitrio*. In *Corpus Christianorum, Series Latina* 29. Turnhout: Brepols, 1954.

————. *De magistro (Il maestro)*. Translated by Massimo Parodi and Cristina Trovò. Milan: Biblioteca Universale Rizzoli, 1996.

————. *De quantitate animae*. In *Corpus Scriptorum Ecclesiasticorum Latinorum* 89. Vindobonae: Hoelder-Pichler-Tempsky, 1866– .

————. *De Trinitate*. In *Corpus Christianorum, Series Latina*, 50. Turnhout: Brepols, 1954– .

————. *Enarrationes in psalmos*. In *Corpus Christianorum, Series Latina* , 38. Turnhout: Brepols, 1954– .

————. *Epistulae*. Vol. 33, *Patrologia Latina*. Ed. J.-P. Migne. Paris, 1844–64.

Augustinus. *Confessiones*. Ed. Martinus Skutella. Ed. corr. Curav. H. Juergens et W. Schaub. Bibliotheca Graecorum et Romanorum Teubneriana. Stutgardiae et Lipsiae: Teubner, 1996.

Austin, Lloyd James. *Essais sur Mallarmé*. Ed. Malcolm Bowie. Manchester: Manchester University Press, 1995.

Badaloni, Nicola. *Introduzione a Vico*. Bari: Laterza, 1988.

Baird, J. L. and Owens, Coilin. "Shem as Crucified Word: FW 185–86." *James Joyce Quarterly* 14, no. 3 (Spring 1977): 251–54.

Balsamo, Gian. *Pruning the Genealogical Tree: Procreation and Lineage in Literature, Law, and Religion*. Lewisburg, Pa.: Bucknell University Press, 1999.

————. *Rituals of Literature: Joyce, Dante, Aquinas, and the Tradition of Christian Epics* Lewisburg, Pa.: Bucknell University Press, 2004.

————. *Scriptural Poetics in Joyce's "Finnegans Wake."* Lewiston, N.Y.: Edwin Mellen Press, 2002.

Balzac, Honoré de. *La peau de chagrin*. In *La comédie humaine*. Ed. P. Citron. Paris: Gallimard, 1976.

Barbi, Michele. *La nuova filologia e l'edizione dei nostri scrittori da Dante al Manzoni* (Florence: n.p., 1938).

Barbier, Carl Paul and L. A. Joseph, eds. *Documents Mallarmé* VI. Paris: Nizet, 1977.

Basevorn, Robertus De. *Forma praedicandi*. In *Artes praedicandi: Contribution à l'histoire de la rhétorique au moyen âge*, Ed. Thomas Marie Charland O. P. Paris: J. Vrin; Ottawa: Institute d'études médiévales, 1936.

Bellet, Roger. *Stéphane Mallarmé: L'encre et le ciel*. Seyssel: Champ Vallon, 1987.

Bennett, John Z. "Unposted Letter: Joyce's Leopold Bloom." In *Critical Essays on James Joyce's "Ulysses,"* ed. Bernard Benstock, 89–98. Boston: G. K. Hall & Co., 1989.

Benstock, Bernard. *Joyce-Again's Wake*. Seattle: University of Washington Press, 1965.

———. "The Temptation of St. Stephen: A View of the Villanelle." *James Joyce Quarterly* 14, no. 1 (Fall 1976): 31–38.

———, ed. *Critical Essays on James Joyce's "Ulysses,"* Boston: G. K. Hall & Co., 1989.

Benvenuto da Imola, *Commentum super Dantis Aldigherii Comoediam*, ed. I. F. Lacaita, Florence, 1887, II.

Berengarius Turonensis. *De Sacra Coena adversus Lanfrancum*. Ed. W. H. Beekenkamp. The Hague: n.p., 1941.

Bishop, John. *Joyce's Book of the Dark: "Finnegans Wake."* Madison: University of Wisconsin Press, 1986.

Blake, William. *Complete Writings*. Ed. Geoffrey Keynes. London: Oxford University Press, 1967.

Blanchot, Maurice. *La part du feu*. Paris: Gallimard, 1949.

Boccaccio, Giovanni. *Il Decameron*. Ed. Attilio Momigliano and Edoardo Sanguineti. Turin: Petrini, 1965.

Boldrini, Lucia. "The Artist Pairing His Quotations: Aesthetic and Ethical Implications of the Dantean Intertext in *Dubliners*," In *ReJoycing: New Readings of "Dubliners,"* ed. Rosa M. Bollettieri and Harold F. Mosher Jr.,. Lexington: University Press of Kentucky, 1998.

———. *Joyce, Dante, and the Poetics of Literary Relations: Language and Meaning in "Finnegans Wake."* Cambridge: Cambridge University Press, 2001.

Boyle., Robert , S. J. "*Finnegans Wake*, Page 185: An Explication," *James Joyce Quarterly* 4 (Fall 1966): 3–16.

———. *James Joyce's Pauline Vision: A Catholic Exposition*. London: Feffer & Simons, 1978.

———. "Miracle in Black Ink: A Glance at Joyce's use of His Eucharistic Image," *James Joyce Quarterly* 10 (Fall 1972): 47–60.

Bremmer, Jan "Scapegoat Rituals in Ancient Greece." *HSCP* 87 (1983): 299–320.

Bresciani, E. *Letteratura e poesia dell'antico Egitto*. Turin: 1969.

Brugsch, Heinrich Karl, trans. *Le roman de Setnau (contenu dans un papyrus démotique du Musée égyptien à Boulaq)*. In *Revue archéologique*, no. 16. Paris: Leleux 1867), 161–79.

Bultmann, Rudolph. "Paul's Demythologizing and Ours." In *The Writings of St. Paul*, ed. Wayne A. Meeks, 409–22. New York: Norton, 1972.

Burkert, Walter. *Creation of the Sacred: Tracks of Biology in Early Religions*. Cambridge: Harvard University Press, 1996.

Campbell, Joseph and Henry Morton Robinson. *A Skeleton Key to "Finnegans Wake."* New York: Penguin, 1986.

Caputo, John D. "Apostles of the Impossible." In *God, the Gift, and Postmodernism*, ed. John D. Caputo and Micheal J. Scanlon, 185–222. Bloomington: Indiana University Press, 1999.

———. "Toward a Postmodern Theology of the Cross." In *Postmodern Philosophy and Christian Thought*, ed. Merold Westphal, 202–28. Bloomington: Indiana University Press, 1999.

Carlson, Thomas A. *Indiscretion: Finitude and the Naming of God*. Chicago: Chicago University Press, 1999.

Carruthers, Mary. *The Book of Memory: A Study of Memory in Medieval Culture*. Cambridge: Cambridge University Press, 2002.

Cary, Phillip. *Augustine's Inventions of the Inner Self: The Legacy of a Christian Soul*. Oxford: Oxford University Press, 2000.

Chambers, Ross. "Gabriel Conroy Sings for His Supper, or Love Refused," in *James Joyce's "Dubliners,"* ed. Harold Bloom, 97–119. New York: Chelsea House, 1988.

Cheng, Vincent J. "Stephen Dedalus and the Black Panther Vampire," *James Joyce Quarterly* 24, no. 2 (Winter 1987): 161–76.

Chomsky, Noam. *Aspects of the Theory of Syntax*. Cambridge: MIT Press, 1965.

———. *New Horizons in the Study of Language and Mind*. Cambridge: Cambridge University Press, 2000.

Citron, Pierre. Introduction to *La Comédie humaine,* by Honoré de Balzac. Paris: Gallimard, 1976.

Coleman, Janet. *Ancient and Medieval Memories: Studies in the Reconstruction of the Past*. New York: Cambridge University Press, 1992.

Coleridge, Samuel Taylor. "The Rime of the Ancient Mariner." In *The Norton Anthology of Poetry,* 4th ed, ed. M. Ferguson, Mary Jo Salter, and Jon Stallworthy, 744–59. New York: Norton, 1996.

Cullingford, Elizabeth B. "At the Feet of the Goddess: Yeats's Love Poetry and the Feminist Occult." In vol. 9 of *Yeats Annual,* ed. D. Toomey, . London: Macmillan, 1992.

Damrosch, David. *The Narrative Covenant: Transformations of Genre in the Growth of Biblical Literature*. Ithaca: Cornell University Press, 1991.

Danesi, Marcel, ed. *Giambattista Vico and Anglo-American Science*. Berlin: Mouton de Gruyter, 1995.

———. *Lingua, metafora, concetto: Vico e la linguistica conoscitiva*. Modugno: Edizioni del Sud, 2001.

Deane, Seamus. "Dead Ends: Joyce's Finest Moments," in *Semicolonial Joyce,* ed. Derek Attridge and Marjorie Howes, 21–36. Cambridge: Cambridge University Press, 2000.

de Man, Paul. *Allegories of Reading: Figural Language in Rousseau, Nietzsche, Rilke, and Proust*. New Haven: Yale University Press, 1979.

Derrida, Jacques. *The Gift of Death*. Translated by David Wills. Chicago: University of Chicago Press, 1995.

———. *Given Time: I. Counterfeit Money*. Translated by Peggy Kamuf. Chicago: University of Chicago Press, 1992.

———. *Glas*. Translated by John P. Leavey, Jr. and Richard Rand. Lincoln: University of Nebraska Press, 1990.

———. *Of Grammatology*. Translated by Gayatri Chakravorty Spivak. Baltimore: Johns Hopkins University Press, 1976.

Devlin, Kimberly J. "Visible Shades and Shades of Visibility: The En-Gendering of Death in 'Hades.'" In *"Ulysses"—En-Gendered Perspectives: Eighteen New Essays on the Episodes,* ed. Kimberly J. Devlin and Marilyn Reizbaum, 67–85. Columbia: University of South Carolina Press, 1999.

Doucet, Dominique. "L'*Ars memoriae* dans les *Confessions*." *REA* 33 (1987): 49–69.

Dragonetti, Roger. *Dante, pélerin de la sainte Face,* Romanica gaudensia, no. 11, Ghent.

Duffy, Enda. "Interesting States: Birthing and the Nation in 'Oxen of the Sun.'" In *"Ulysses"* *—En-Gendered Perspectives: Eighteen New Essays on the Episodes,* ed. Kimberly J. Devlin and Marilyn Reizbaum, 210–28. Columbia: University of South Carolina Press, 1999.

Durkheim, Émile. *Les Formes élémentaires de la pensée religieuse: Le système totémique en Australie.* Paris: Félix Alcan, 1937.

Durling, Robert M. and Martinez, Ronald L. *Time and the Crystal: Studies in Dante's Rime Petrose.* Berkeley: University of California Press, 1990.

Durling, Robert M., trans. and annotator, and Martinez, Ronald L., annotator, *Inferno.* Vol. 1, *The Divine Comedy of Dante Alighieri.* New York: Oxford University Press, 1996.

Eco, Umberto. *Il problema estetico in Tommaso d'Aquino.* Milan: Bompiani, 1970.

Ellmann, Richard. *James Joyce.* Oxford: Oxford University Press, 1983.

———. *Oscar Wilde.* New York: Vintage, 1988.

———. *Ulysses on the Liffey.* New York: Oxford University Press, 1972.

Ericsson, K. A. and W. Kintsch. "Long-Term Working Memory." *Psychological Review* 102, no. 2 (1995): 211–45.

Fargnoli, A. Nicholas and Michael P. Gillespie, *James Joyce A To Z.* Oxford: Oxford University Press, 1995.

Fraser, Jennifer Margaret. *Rite of Passage in the Narratives of Dante and Joyce.* Gainesville: University Press of Florida, 2002.

Frayne, John P., ed. *Uncollected Prose, by W. B Yeats.* New York: Columbia University Press, 1970.

Freccero, John. *Dante: The Poetics of Conversion,* Cambridge: Harvard University Press, 1986.

———. *Dante's Cosmos,* Bernardo Lecture Series 6. Binghamton: Center for Medieval and Renaissance Studies, SUNY, 1998.

———. "Moon Shadows: *Paradiso* III," in *Studies for Dante,* ed. Franco Fido, Rena A. Syska-Lamparska, and Pamela D. Stewart, 100. Fiesole: Cadmo, 1998.

Furnivall, F. J., ed. *The Burial of Christ.* In *The Digby Plays.* EETSes 70. London: Oxford University Press, 1967.

Gifford, Don. *"Ulysses" Annotated.* Berkeley: University of California Press, 1988.

Gilbert, Stuart. *James Joyce's "Ulysses."* New York: Vintage, 1958.

Glasheen, Adaline. *Third Census of "Finnegans Wake,"* Berkeley: University of California Press, 1977.

Gordon, John. *"Finnegans Wake": A Plot Summary* (Syracuse: Syracuse University Press, 1986).

———. "Notes in Response to Michael Seidel's '*Ulysses's* Black Panther Vampire.'" *James Joyce Quarterly* 15, no. 3 (Spring 1978): 229–35.

Grabher, Carlo, ed. *"La Divina Commedia" di Dante Alighieri: "Inferno,"* Bari: Laterza, 1964.

———, ed. *"La Divina Commedia" di Dante Alighieri: "Paradiso,"* Bari: Laterza, 1964.

———, ed. *"La Divina Commedia" di Dante Alighieri: "Purgatorio,"* Bari: Laterza, 1964.

Grassi, Ernesto. "Joyce and Vico: The Demythologization of the Real." In *Vico and Joyce,* ed. Donald Phillip Verene, 147–59. Albany: State University of New York Press, 1987.

Greene, Graham. *The End of the Affair.* New York: Penguin, 1975.

Gregorius Magnus, *Moralia in Job,* trans. Dom André de Gaudemaris, Paris: Éditions du cerf, 1975.

Hameury, Jean-Paul. *L'échec de Mallarmé.* Bédée: Folle Avoine, 1998.

Hart, Clive. *Structure and Motif in "Finnegans Wake."* Evanston, IL: Northwestern University Press, 1962.

Hart, Clive, C. George Sandulescu, Bonnie K. Scott, and Fritz Senn. *Images of Joyce.* 2 vols. Gerrards Cross: Colin Smythe, 1988.

Hawkins, Peter S. "Dante's *Paradiso* and the Dialectic of Ineffability." In *Ineffability: Naming the Unnameable from Dante to Beckett,* ed. Peter S. Hawkins and Anne Howland Schotter, 5–21. New York: AMS Press, 1984.

Hayman, David, *A First-Draft Version of "Finnegans Wake."* Austin: University of Texas Press, 1963.

———. *Joyce et Mallarmé.* 2 vols. Paris: Lettres Modernes, 1956.

Heidegger, Martin. *Being and Time.* Translated by John Macquarrie and Edward Robinson. San Francisco: Harper, 1962.

Herr, Cheryl. "Old Wives' Tales as Portals of Discovery in 'Proteus.'" In *"Ulysses"—En-Gendered Perspectives: Eighteen New Essays on the Episodes,* ed. Kimberly J. Devlin and Marilyn Reizbaum, 30–41. Columbia: University of South Carolina Press, 1999.

Hertz, Robert. *"Contribution à une étude sur la représentation collective de la mort,"* in *Année sociologique,* 1st series, tome X, 1907. Reprinted in Hertz, *Sociologie religieuse et folklore.* Paris: Presses Universitaires de France, 1970.

———. *Sociologie religieuse et folklore.* Paris: Presses Universitaires de France, 1970.

Higdon, David Leon. "Gendered Discourse and the Structure of Joyce's "The Dead," in *ReJoycing: New Readings of "Dubliners,"* ed. Rosa M. Bollettieri and Harold F. Mosher Jr. Lexington: University Press of Kentucky, 1998.

Homer, *The Iliad.* Translated by Robert Fitzgerald. New York: Anchor, 1975.

Hyde, Douglas, ed. and trans. *The Love Songs of Connacht.* Dublin: Irish University Press, 1971.

Isidorus of Seville, *De ecclesiasticis Officiis,* ed. Christopher M. Lawson, Turnholti: Brepols, 1989 (in *Corpus Christianorum, Series Latina* vol. 113).

Jaurretche, Colleen. *The Sensual Philosophy: Joyce and the Aesthetics of Mysticism.* Madison: University of Wisconsin Press, 1997.

Jeauneau, Edouard. "L'usage de la notion d'integumentum à travers le Gloses de Guillaume de Conches," in *Archives d'histoire doctrinale et littéraire du Moyen Age* 24 (1957); cited in Nicoló Mineo, *Profetismo e Apocalittica in Dante: Strutture e temi profetico-apocalittici in Dante dalla Vita Nuova alla Divina Commedia.* Catania: Facoltá di Lettere e Filosofia, 1968.

Jerome. *Commentarium in ezechielem.* In Patrologia cursus completus, Series latina. Ed. J. P. Migne. Paris: 1841–64, 221.

Joyce, James. "Drama and Life" and "Ibsen's New Drama." In *The Critical Writings of James Joyce,* ed. Mason Ellsworth and Richard Ellmann, 38–67. Ithaca: Cornell University Press, 1989.

———. *Dubliners.* Ed. Robert Scholes and A. Walton Litz. New York: Viking, 1976.

———. *Finnegans Wake.* New York: Penguin, 1976.

———. *Letters.* Ed. Richard Ellmann. 2 vols. New York: Viking Press, 1966.

———. *A Portrait of the Artist as a Young Man.* New York: Penguin, 1976.

———. *Stephen Hero.* New York: New Directions, 1963.

———. *Ulysses.* Ed. Hans W. Gabler with Wolfhard Steppe and Claus Melchior. New York: Vintage, 1986.

Keane, Patrick J. *Yeats, Joyce, Ireland, and the Myth of the Devouring Female.* Columbia: University of Missouri Press, 1988.

Kearney, R. "Myth and Motherland." In *Ireland's Field Day,* ed. Field Day Theatre Company. London: Hutchison, 1985.

Kenner, Hugh. *Dublin's Joyce.* Boston: Beacon Press, 1962.

———. *Joyce's Voices.* Berkeley: University of California Press, 1978.

Kinzie, Mary. *A Poet's Guide to Poetry.* Chicago: University of Chicago Press, 1999.

Kristeva, Julia. *Powers of Horror: An Essay on Abjection.* Translated by Leon S. Roudiez. New York: Columbia University Press, 1982.

———. "*Stabat Mater.*" In *The Kristeva Reader,* edited and introduced by Toril Moi, 160–86. New York: Columbia University Press, 1986.

Lanters, José. "Old Worlds, New Worlds, Alternative Worlds: "*Ulysses,*" *Metamorphoses* 13, and the Death of the Beloved Son." *JJ* Q 36, no. 3 (Spring 1999): 525–40.

Lawrence, Karen. "Legal Fiction or Pulp Fiction in 'Lestrygonians.'" In "*Ulysses*"—*Engendered Perspectives: Eighteen New Essays on the Episodes,* ed. Kimberly J. Devlin and Marilyn Reizbaum, 100–110. Columbia: University of South Carolina Press, 1999.

Lear, Edward. *A Book of Nonsense.* New York: Knopf, 1992.

Levinas, Emmanuel. *Le Temps et l'Autre.* Paris: Quadrige, 1979.

Lewis, Bernard, ed. and intro. *Land of Enchanters: Egyptian Short Stories from the Earliest Times to the Present Day.* London: Harvill Press, 1948.

Lewontin, Richard *The Triple Helix: Gene, Organism, and Environment.* Cambridge: Harvard University Press, 2000.

Lichtheim, Miriam. *Ancient Egyptian Literature: A Book of Reading.* Vol. 3, *The Late Period.* Berkeley: University of California Press, 1980.

Lobkowicz, Nicholas. *Theory and Practice: History of a Concept from Aristotle to Marx.* Lanham, Md.: University Press of America, 1967.

Maimonides, Moses. *The Guide of the Perplexed.* Translated by Shlomo Pines. Chicago: University of Chicago Press, 1963.

Mallarmé, Stéphane. *L'après-midi d'un faune.* Translated by Frederick Morgan. In *An Anthology of French Poets from Nerval to Valéry in English Translation,* ed. Angel Flores. New York: n.p., 1958.

———. *Collected Poems.* Translated by Henry Weinfield. Berkeley: University of California Press, 1994.

———. *Correspondance.* Vol. 1, *1862–1871.* Ed. Henri Mondor and J.-P. Richard. Paris: Gallimard, 1959.

———. *Oeuvres complètes.* Ed. Carl Paul Barbier and Charles Gordon Millan. Paris: Flammarion, 1983.

Malory, *Works.* Ed. Eugene Vinaver. Oxford: Oxford University Press, 1971.

Mandelbaum, Allen, trans. "*The Divine Comedy*" *of Dante Alighieri: "Paradiso,*" New York: Bantam, 1986.

Mariette, Auguste. *Les papyrus égyptiens du Musée de Boulaq.* Tome Premier, Papyrus nos. 1–9. Paris: Librairie A. Franck, 1871.

Marion, Jean-Luc. *Dieu sans l'être.* Paris: Fayard, 1982.

———. *Étant Donné: Essai d'une phénoménologie de la donation.* Paris: Presses Universitaires de France, 1997.

———. "Sketch of a Phenomenological Concept of Gift." Translated by John Conley, S.J. and Danielle Poe. In *Postmodern Philosophy and Christian Thought,* ed. Merold Westphal, 122–43. Bloomington: Indiana University Press, 1999.

Martella, Giuseppe. "*Ulisse*": *Parallelo biblico e modernità.* Bologna: CLUEB, 1997.

Mauss, Marcel. *"L'expression obligatoire des sentiments."* In *Journal de psychologie normal et pathologique,* vol. 18. Paris: Alcan 1921.

Mayes, Andrew R., Patricia A. Gooding, and Rob van Eijk. "A New Theoretical Framework for Explicit and Implicit Memory." *Psyche* 3, no. 2 (June 1997).

McGee, Patrick. "Gesture: The Letter of the Word." In *Critical Essays on James Joyce's "Ulysses,"* ed. Bernard Benstock, 304–26. Boston: G. K. Hall & Co., 1989.

McHugh, Roland. *Annotations to "Finnegans Wake."* Baltimore: Johns Hopkins University Press, 1991.

Mineo, Nicoló. *Profetismo e Apocalittica in Dante: Strutture e temi profetico-apocalittici in Dante dalla Vita Nuova alla Divina Commedia,* Catania: Facoltá di Lettere e Filosofia, 1968.

Moloney, Caitriona. "The Hags of *Ulysses*: The 'Poor Old Woman,' Cathleen Ni Houlihan, and the Phallic Mother." *James Joyce Quarterly* 34, nos. 1 and 2 (Fall 1996 and Winter 1997): 103–20.

Montanari, P. "Prefazione." In Sant'Agostino, *De libero arbitrio.* Trans. P. Montanari. Bag 21. Florence: n.p., 1939.

———. "Il problema della libertà in Agostino." *Rivista di filosofia neo-scolastica,* 29 (1937): 359–87.

Moseley, Virginia. "'Two Sights for Ever a Picture' in Joyce's 'The Dead,'" *College English* 26 (March 1965).

Nietzsche, Friedrich. *The Birth of Tragedy.* In *"The Birth of Tragedy" and "The Case of Wagner" by F. Nietzsche,* translated by Walter Kaufmann. New York: Vintage, 1967.

Norris, Margot. "Narration under a Blindfold: Reading Joyce's 'Clay,'" in *James Joyce's "Dubliners,"* ed. Harold Bloom, 143–60. New York: Chelsea House, 1988.

Nussbaum, Martha. *Upheavals of Thought.* Cambridge: Cambridge University Press, 2001.

———. *The Fragility of Goodness: Luck and Ethics in Greek Tragedy and Philosophy.* Cambridge: Cambridge University Press, 1986.

Nyberg, Lars and Endel Turving. "Classifying Human Long-Term Memory: Evidence from Converging Dossiciations." *European Journal of Cognitive Psychology* 8, no. 2 (1996): 163–83.

Nyberg, Lars, A. R. McIntosh, and Endel Tulving. "Functional Brain Imaging of Episodic and Semantic Memory with Positron Emission Tomography." *Journal of Molecular Medicine* 76 (1998): 48–53.

Ogden, Daniel. "Cleisthenes of Sycyon." *Classical Quarterly* 43, no. 2 (1993): 353–63.

O'Neill, John. "The Origins of Myth: Promethean or Orphic?" In *Giambattista Vico and Anglo-American Science,* ed. Marcel Danesi, 147–58. Berlin: Mouton de Gruyter, 1995.

Ovid. *Metamorphosen.* Dublin: Weidmann, 1969.

———. *Les Métamorphoses.* Edited and translated by Georges Lafaye. Paris: Les Belles Lettres, 1972.

Padoan, Giorgio. *Il pio Enea e l'empio Ulisse.* Ravenna: Longo, 1977.

Page Renouf, P. le, trans. *The Tale of Setnau.* In *Records of the Past,* vol. 4, *Egyptian Texts,* ed. the Society of Biblical Archeology, 129–48. London: Samuel, Bagster and Sons, 1875.

Pascasius Radbertus. *De corpore et sanguine Domini.* Cura et studio Bedae Paulus, O.S.B.. Turnholti: Typographi Brepols Editores Pontificii, 1969, 394m.

Pater, Walter. *The Renaissance: Studies in Art and Poetry.* London: Macmillan, 1877.

Pelikan, Jaroslav. *Mary through the Centuries: Her Place in the History of Culture.* New Haven: Yale University Press, 1996.

Piselli, Francesco. *Mallarmé e l'estetica.* Milan: Mursia, 1969.

Pius XI. Encyclical letter *Studiorum ducem* (1923). Washington, D.C.: National Catholic Welfare Conference, 1936.

Plato. *Symposium.* Translated by Alexander Nehamas and Paul Woodruff. Indianapolis: Hackett, 1989.

———. *Symposium.* Translated by Seth Benardete. Chicago: University of Chicago Press, 2001.

Proust, Marcel. Cahier I from *Fonds Proust de la Bibliothèque nationale,* Esquisse III, in Marcel Proust, *À la recherche du temps perdu.* Vol. 1. Ed. Jean-Yves Tadié. Paris: Gallimard, 1987.

———. *Contre Sainte-Beuve.* Ed. Pierre Clarac and Yves Sandre. Paris: Gallimard, 1971.

———. *Contre Sainte-Beuve.* Ed. Bernard de Fallois. Paris: Gallimard, 1954.

Rabaté, Jean-Michel. *James Joyce Authorized Reader.* Baltimore: Johns Hopkins University Press, 1991.

Restuccia, Frances E. *Joyce and the Law of the Father.* New Haven: Yale University Press, 1989.

Reynolds, Mary T. *Joyce and Dante: The Shaping Imagination.* Princeton: Princeton University Press, 1981.

Richardson, James. *Vanishing Lives: Style and Self in Tennyson, D. G. Rossetti, Swinburne, and Yeats.* Charlottesville: University Press of Virginia, 1988.

Rickard, John S. *Joyce's Book of Memory: The Mnemotechnic of "Ulysses."* Durham, N.C.: Duke University Press, 1999.

Ricoeur, Paul. *Time and Narrative.* Translated by Kathleen Blamey and David Pellauer. 3 vols. Chicago: University of Chicago Press, 1988.

Riquelme, John Paul. "Joyce's 'The Dead': The Dissolution of the Self and the Police," in *ReJoycing: New Readings of "Dubliners,"* ed. Rosa M. Bollettieri and Harold F. Mosher Jr. Lexington: University Press of Kentucky, 1998.

———. *Teller and Tale in Joyce's Fiction: Oscillating Perspectives.* Baltimore: Johns Hopkins University Press, 1983.

Robillard, Monic. *Le désir de la vierge: Hérodiade chez Mallarmé.* Geneva: Droz, 1993.

Rose, Danis and John O'Hanlon. *Understanding "Finnegans Wake": A Guide to the Narrative of James Joyce's Masterpiece.* New York: Garland, 1982.

Rossi, Paolo. *Clavis universalis: Arti della memoria e logica combinatoria da Lullo a Leibnitz.* Bologna: n.p., 1983.

Rousseau, Jean-Jacques. *Essai sur l'origine des langues.* Ed. Charles Porset. Bordeaux: Ducros, 1970.

Sallis, John. *Being and Logos: The Way of the Platonic Dialogue.* Atlantic Highlands, N.J.: Humanities Pres International, 1986.

Scanlon, Michael J. "A Deconstruction of Religion: On Derrida and Rahner." In *God, the Gift, and Postmodernism,* ed. John D. Caputo and Micheal J. Scanlon, 223–28. Bloomington: Indiana University Press, 1999.

Schieffelin, E. L. "Reciprocity and the Construction of Reality." *Man* 15 (1980): 502–17.

Scholem, Gershom. *The Messianic Idea in Judaism.* Translated by Micheal A. Meyer and Hillel Halkin. New York: Schocken Books, 1995.

Scholes, Robert. "Stephen Dedalus, Poet or Esthete?" In *A Portrait of the Artist as a Young Man: Text, Criticism, and Notes,* ed. Chester G. Anderson, 468–80. New York: Viking, 1968.

Segal, Alan F. *Paul the Convert: The Apostolate and Apostasy of Saul the Pharisee.* New Haven: Yale University Press, 1990.

Seidel, Micheal. "*Ulysses*'s Black Panther Vampire." *James Joyce Quarterly* 13, no. 4 (Summer 1976): 415–27.

Senn, Fritz. *A Conceptual Guide to "Finnegans Wake."* London: Pennsylvania State University Press, 1974.

Sicari, Stephen. *Joyce's Modernist Allegory: "Ulysses" and the History of the Novel.* Columbia, University of South Carolina Press, 2001.

Silvestris, Bernardus. *Commentum super sex libros Eneidos Virgilii.* Ed. Julian Ward Jones and Elizabeth Frances Jones. Lincoln and London: University of Nebraska Press, 1977.

Singleton, Charles S. *Dante Studies I: Elements of Structure.* Cambridge: Harvard University Press, 1957.

———, ed. and trans. *"The Divine Comedy" of Dante Alighieri: "Purgatorio."* Princeton: Princeton University Press, 1991.

———, ed. and trans. *"The Divine Comedy" of Dante Alighieri: "Paradiso."* Princeton: Princeton University Press, 1991.

———. *"The Divine Comedy" of Dante Alighieri: "Inferno": Commentary.* Princeton: Princeton University Press, 1989.

———. *"The Divine Comedy" of Dante Alighieri: "Paradiso": Commentary.* Princeton: Princeton University Press, 1991.

———. *"The Divine Comedy" of Dante Alighieri: "Purgatorio": Commentary.* Princeton: Princeton University Press, 1991.

Slote, Sam. *The Silence in Progress of Dante, Mallarmé, and Joyce.* New York: Peter Lang, 1999.

Stanford, W. B. *The Ulysses Theme: A Study in the Adaptability of a Traditional Hero.* Ann Arbor: University of Michigan Press, 1968.

Stock, Brian. *After Augustine: The Meditative Reader and the Text.* Philadelphia: University of Pennsylvania Press, 2001.

———. *Augustine the Reader: Meditation, Self-Knowledge, and the Ethics of Interpretation.* Cambridge: The Belknap Press of Harvard University Press, 1996.

Strand, Mark "2002." *New York Review of Books,* December 19, 2002, 59.

Stubbings, Diane. *Anglo-Irish Modernism and the Maternal: From Yeats to Joyce.* Houndmills: Palgrave, 2000.

Tindall, William York. *A Reader's Guide to "Finnegans Wake."* Syracuse: Syracuse University Press, 1996.

Thompson, David. *Dante's Epic Journey.* Baltimore: Johns Hopkins University Press, 1974.

Torchiana, Donald T. *Backgrounds for Joyce's "Dubliners."* Boston: Allen & Unwin, 1986.

Troup, Calvin L. *Temporality, Eternity, and Wisdom: The Rhetoric of Augustine's Confessions.* Columbia: University of South Carolina Press, 1999.

Verene, Donald Phillip. *Vico's Science of Imagination.* Ithaca: Cornell University Press, 1981.

Vico, Giambattista. *Principi di scienza nuova* (1744), in *Opere filosofiche,* ed. Paolo Cristofolini, Florence: Sansoni, 1971.

———. *Principi di una scienza nuova.* Ed. Giuseppe Ferrari. Milan: Società Tipografica dei Classici Italiani, 1843.

———. *La scienza nuova seconda.* Ed. Fausto Nicolini. 2 vols. Bari: Laterza, 1942.

Virgil. *Aeneis.* Turin: Einaudi, 1989.

Walzl, Florence L. "Gabriel and Michael: The Conclusion of 'The Dead,'" in Robert Scholes and A. Walton Litz, in *James Joyce's "Dubliners,"* ed. Robert Scholes and A. Walton Litz, 423–43. New York: Viking, 1976.

Watts, A. E., trans. *"The Metamorphoses" of Ovid*. Los Angeles: Los Angeles University Press, 1954.

Weir, David. "A Womb of His Own: Joyce's Sexual Aesthetics." *James Joyce Quarterly* 31, no. 3 (Spring 1994): 207–32.

Weir, Lorraine. "Imagination and Memory in Vico and Joyce." In *Giambattista Vico and Anglo-American Science,* ed. Marcel Danesi, 243–47. Berlin: Mouton de Gruyter, 1995.

Weldon, Thornton. *Allusions in "Ulysses."* Chapel Hill: University of North Carolina Press, 1987.

Westphal, Merold. *Postmodern Philosophy and Christian Thought*. Bloomington: Indiana University Press, 1999.

White, Hayden. *Figural Realism: Studies in the Mimesis Effect*. Baltimore: Johns Hopkins University Press, 1999.

———. *Metahistory: The Historical Imagination in Nineteenth-Century Europe*. Baltimore: Johns Hopkins University Press, 1973.

———. *Tropics of Discourse: Essays in Cultural Criticism*. Baltimore: Johns Hopkins University Press, 1985.

Willcock, M. M., ed., *"The Iliad" of Homer.* New York: St. Martin Press, 1984.

Wilson, John A. *The Culture of Ancient Egypt*. Chicago: University of Chicago Press, 1957.

Wlassics, Tibor. "Nota su Dante nell'*Ulisse,*" *Rivista di letterature moderne e comparate* 24, no. 2 (1971): 151–54.

Wood, Michael. "Experience's Ghosts." *New York Review of Books,* June 12, 2003, 71–73.

Yeats, William Butler. "The Autumn of the Body." In *Essays and Introductions*. New York: Collier, 1961.

———. "Easter 1916." In *Major British Writers*. Ed. G. B. Harrison. New York: Harcourt, Brace & World, 1967.

———. "Into the Twilight." In *The Variorum Edition of the Poems by W. B. Yeats*. Ed. P. Allt and R. K. Alspach. New York: Macmillan, 1957.

———. "To Ireland in the Coming Times" (*The Rose*). In *The Variorum Edition of the Poems by W. B. Yeats*. Ed. P. Allt and R. K. Alspach. New York: Macmillan, 1957.

———. *Mythologies*. London: Macmillan, 1959.

———. "Who Goes with Fergus?" In *Major British Writers*. Ed. G. B. Harrison. New York: Harcourt, Brace & World, 1967.

Ziarek, Ewa. "Working the Limit: (M)other, text, abject in *Ulysses.*" In *Images of Joyce,* ed. Clive Hart, C. George Sandulescu, Bonnie K. Scott, and Fritz Senn, 2:632–44. Gerrards Cross: Colin Smythe, 1988.

INDEX

abortion, 62, 84
Adams Day, Robert, 79, 83, 148n43
AE. *See* Russell, George William
Aeneid (Virgil), 37
"Aeolus" (*Ulysses*), 40, 63–64, 65, 82, 148n41
afterlife: Bloom, Leopold, on, 98, 102–3; bodily putrefaction in promise of, 98; Christ's descent into, 11–12, 30, 35, 39, 132n9, 138n8; Dante's/pilgrim's experience of, 9, 10, 11, 23, 31, 33, 34–36, 37–39, 46, 132n6, 138n9; Dedalus, Stephen, as poet of, 20, 61, 62, 76–92
allegory: Bible's spiritual meaning vs., 117, 154nn41–42; Dantean/Joycean use of, 57–58, 142n53; language and, 40; modernist, 57; Plato's cave, 30–31; of theologians, 21
Altizer, Thomas, 112–13
altruism, 5, 85, 89–90
anthropologists, French, 95–97
apophatic experience, 4, 22–23, 135n16; impossibility in, 9–11, 12, 15, 22, 62; linguistic dimension of, 20–28; ordinary experience and, 13, 31–32, 74; silence in, 39–40; stations of journey unto death in, 138n11
Aquinas, Saint Thomas, 145n46; on Bible's spiritual meaning, 117, 154nn41–42; hermeneutics of, 120–21; Psalm 44 cited by, 117, 154n42; topological interpretation doctrine of, 118, 121; on transubstantiation, 15, 109, 110, 111, 133n35, 153nn17–18; on vetero-Testamental types, 113
"Araby" (Joyce), 60
Aristophanes, 103

Aristotle: *Metaphysics* by, 66; on purgation/catharsis, 98; referenced by Dedalus, Stephen, 70
asceticism, Augustine's, 30, 137n6
Auerbach, Eric, 9, 10, 36, 142n34
Auerbach, Nina, 81
Augustine, Saint: asceticism of, 30, 137n6; Caputo on, 24; Dante linked to, 29, 35, 38; "The Dead" and, 46, 47, 53; Dedalus, Stephen, influenced by, 65–66, 68–71, 73, 74, 87, 144n22; existentialist revolution of, 12–13; Homer's *Odyssey* and, 38; identity paradigm of, 46–47; instantiation of negative existence by, 29, 32; journey unto death/necropolitan journey of, 29–33, 39, 138n11; Joyce expanding on, 40–41, 74, 115–16; on memory/God's Word, 4, 5, 12–13, 24, 72–73, 123, 127, 131n6; mental imprint notion of, 24, 136n32; messianic self and, 14, 20, 29–33, 138n11; mother of (Monica), 16, 29–32, 62, 64–65, 72, 144n22; *A Portrait of the Artist as a Young Man* influenced by, 71; *Paradiso* influenced by, 35; speech/silence and, 4, 20, 23, 31, 38, 39, 62, 72; touching experienced by, 30–31. See also *Confessions* (Augustine)

Baird, J. L., 131n13
Balsamo, Gian: *Pruning the Genealogical Tree* by, 78, 86, 146n1, 146n18, 150n80; *Rituals of Literature* by, 14, 17, 34; *Scriptural Poetics in Joyce's "Finnegans Wake"* by, 21, 29, 67
Balzac, Honoré de, 113–14, 115, 153n27
Bellet, Roger, 87

Benstock, Bernard, 138n12, 143n7, 148n46

Benvenuto da Imola, 139n32

Bernard de Clairvaux, Saint, 85

Bible: apostles in, 34; motherhood figures in, 90; of negative existence, *Finnegans Wake* as, 125–26; Old/New Testaments in, 29, 113, 120–21; spiritual vs. allegorical meaning in, 117, 154nn41–42; Thomist hermeneutics of, 33; typology in, 29. *See also* Scriptural poetics, in *Finnegans Wake*

bio-graphy, in *Finnegans Wake*, 120–21

birth control, 84, 120, 148n52

Bishop, John, 26

Blake, William: Dedalus, Stephen, influenced by, 16–17, 20, 40, 66, 67, 68, 69, 71, 80, 82, 112–13, 115, 144n31; in *Stephen Hero*, 77–78

Blanchot, Maurice, 40, 90

blood: drinking of, 94–95, 100, 101; menstrual/"Vampire Poem" and, 2–3, 5, 6, 16, 40, 52, 61–62, 76–78, 80, 83, 84, 86, 87, 88, 90, 91–92, 106, 108, 120, 148n43, 148n49, 149n61, 151n39, 152n1

Bloom, Leopold, 93–107; at Catholic Mass, 96; cocoa shared by, 106; daughter (Milly) of, 105; death/afterlife philosophy of, 98, 102–3; Dedalus, Simon, envied by, 101; dilemma of, 20; drinking of blood and, 94–95, 100, 101; eating by, 93–98, 99–107, 123; Eucharistic reenactment by, 108; existential predicament of, 3, 6, 104; homecoming of, 34; impossibility intrinsic to, 11; kiss between Molly and, 3, 6, 103–6, 111, 123, 151n39; limerick composed by, 94, 97, 98, 101; messianic self/negative character of, 123; son (Rudy) of, 98, 100–103, 105, 106, 107, 123; on women's role in burial, 100–101, 151n23. *See also Ulysses* (Joyce)

Bloom, Molly: adultery committed by, 102, 103; burial task given to, 100–101; Eucharistic reenactment by, 108; fecundity of, 107; kiss between Bloom,

Leopold, and, 3, 6, 103–6, 111, 123, 151n39. *See also Ulysses* (Joyce)

Boccaccio, *Decameron* by, 147n23

Boldrini, Lucia, 10, 21, 39, 54, 56, 71, 132n6

Bonaventura, Saint, 138n11

Book of Daniel, 91

Book of Dead, Egyptian, 124, 126

Book of Kells, 126

Boyle, Robert, 108–10, 113, 115, 116, 118–19

Brugsch, Heinrich Karl, 124, 155n1

burial: meal, 93–98, 99–107; as task of women, 100–101, 151n23. *See also* funeral, of Dignam, Patrick

Burial of Christ, The (Digby play), 131n13

Burkert, Walter, 99, 110

Calliope, Dante's invocation to, 146n18

cannibalism, 15, 93, 96–97, 101, 102

Caputo, John, 12, 24

Carlson, Thomas, 11, 14

Cary, Philip, 12

catharsis, 6, 14–15, 98, 99, 107, 110, 112

Catholicism: Bloom, Leopold, and, 96; on contraception, 84; Dante's devotion to, 81; Irish women and, 78, 84; maternal model of self-sacrifice in, 3; Requiem Mass, 93, 96, 97; virgin-mother in, 80, 81, 82

Cavalcanti, Guido, 147n23

cave, allegory of, 30–31

Cazalis, Henri, 87, 88

Chambers, Ross, 142n53

Cheng, Vincent, 61

childbirth, 151n23

Chomsky, Noam, 4–5, 24

Christ: *anima* of, 110–11; descent into hell by/necropolitan journey of, 11–12, 20, 29, 30, 33–34, 35, 39, 132n9, 138n8; *imitatio Christi* and, 11, 34; incarnation of, 85–86, 92; as Jesus-on-the-Cross, 121; Lucifer/Satan and, 112–13; Mary and, 85; in *Paradiso*, 85; Stephen, Dedalus, as Christic poet and, 62–64, 73, 74, 78; type, revision of, 113–15; vowel sequence and, 72. *See also* Crucifixion, Christ's; transubstantiation

Christianity: end of eschatology of, 116; epic tradition and, 34, 36, 39; sacrificial tradition in, 2–3, 14–15, 110, 111, 112, 123; salvation promised by, 11; on womanhood types, 92. *See also* Eucharist; Scriptural poetics, in *Finnegans Wake*

Christic poet, Dedalus, Stephen, as, 62–64, 73, 74, 78

Christological imagery, in "The Dead," 58–59

"Clay" (Joyce), 36–37, 45, 50

"claybook" (*Finnegans Wake*), 26–27, 126–27

coin imagery, 50–51, 141n26

Coleridge, Samuel Taylor, 67

Commedia (Dante): ending of, 38, 39, 139n36; individual consciousness/ historical contingency in, 52–53, 142n34; muse in, 80; on poetry, 145n46; praeterhistorical condition in, 53, 142n34; universal biographical model in, 35; Yeats and, 79. *See also* Dante Alighieri; *Inferno* (Dante); *Paradiso* (Dante); *Purgatorio* (Dante)

conception, maternal, 91–92, 100

Confessions (Augustine), 11, 12, 24–25, 132n9; in "Aeolus," 65; Christ's descent to hell in, 35; human speech in, 31; "I" used by Dedalus, Stephen, and, 68–70; intimacy with divine in, 30; mother and son in, 16, 29–32, 62, 64–65, 72, 144n22; will power in, 47. *See also* Augustine, Saint

Conroy, Gabriel: epiphany of negative self of, 54–59; as father figure, 45, 51; impossibility intrinsic to, 11; "incarnations" of, 45, 56; infernal/paradisiac transition of, 46, 48, 54–56, 142n43; in-numenation of, 55, 56; "journey westward of," 57–58; name of, 58, 143n58; necropolitan journey of, 20, 45–59; negative biography and, 52–53 sensory limitations of, 48. *See also* "Dead, The" (Joyce)

Convivio (Dante), 72, 73, 80, 145nn46–47

creation: to post-creation, 91–92; universal history of, 115

crucifixion: in *Finnegans Wake,* 42; maternal altruism of, 85

Crucifixion, Christ's, 6; *anamnesis* of, 110; Dante's/Joyce view of, 36; as death vs. cathartic experience, 14–15; incarnation of, 85–86, 92; Marion on, 13; "type of types" and, 113; victim as scapegoat, 99; Word and, 13–14

Danesi, Marcel, 24

Dante Alighieri, 10, 11, 132n6; biography of, 10, 11, 132n6; Catholic faith of, 81; Christian epic genre invented by, 34; *Convivio* by, 72, 73, 80, 145nn46–47; *cristallino* of, 115, 153n32, 154n33; Dedalus, Stephen, influenced by, 16–17, 18, 20, 40, 52, 60, 62, 71–73, 74–75, 145nn46–48; Homer's *Odyssey* and, 38; Ibsenian modernity of, 41; influence of, in *Finnegans Wake,* 40–41, 73, 115–16, 153n32, 154n34; in-numenation notion of, 34–35, 139n19; Joyce influenced by, 10, 11, 21, 38, 40–41, 52, 59, 73, 115–16, 153n32, 154n34, 154n48; linked to Augustine, 29, 35, 38; on miracle of Crucifixion, 36; muses of, 80; necropolitan journey of, 9, 10, 11, 23, 31, 33, 34–36, 37–39, 46, 132n6, 138n9; negative poetics of, 9–11, 32, 34–35, 36, 41, 46–50, 52–59, 80, 124, 140n7, 141n19, 142n34, 142n40, 142n43, 143n57, 143n59; nonreferentiality and, 9, 36, 124; planetary system of, 153n32, 154n33; silence and, 4, 38, 39, 40, 41, 42, 62; transmutation and, 31, 138n9, 154n48; *Vita Nuova* by, 39–40, 54–55, 71–72, 73, 74, 75, 80; Yeats influenced by, 79, 80, 82, 86. *See also Commedia* (Dante); *Inferno* (Dante); *Paradiso* (Dante); *Purgatorio* (Dante)

"Dead, The" (Joyce): Augustinian self and, 46, 47, 53; Christological imagery in, 58–59; Conroy, Gretta in, 45, 49,

"Dead, The" (Joyce) (*continued*)
50, 51–52, 140n5; Dante's poetics and, 46–50, 52–59, 140n7, 141n19, 142n34, 142n40, 142n43, 143n57, 143n59; *Inferno* and, 58, 143n59; naturalistic style in, 45, 46, 49–50, 51, 54, 59, 140n6, 140n9; *Paradiso* and, 48–49, 53, 54, 56, 58, 141n19, 143n57; self-validation in, 46, 50; symbolism in, 46–48, 50–51, 52, 54, 56–58. See also Conroy, Gabriel; *Dubliners* (Joyce)

Deane, Seamus, 58

death, 1–2, 131n3: Bloom, Leopold, on, 98, 102–3; of Dedalus, Stephen, 1–2, 17, 102, 123; of God, 42, 111, 153nn17–18; incorporation by, 93–99; maiden and, 82–86; metaphor of Paul's, 139n40; of mother of Dedalus, Stephen, 1–3, 5, 15, 16, 17, 18, 19, 32–33, 61–62, 64–68, 73, 76–79, 84–85, 102, 122–23, 134n44, 146n1; nutrition in psychology of, 95–98, 99–100; purgation by, 99–107; of son of Bloom, Leopold, 98, 100–103, 105, 106, 107, 123; of Word, 42, 111, 153nn17–18. *See also* Christ; crucifixion; Crucifixion, Christ's

death, journey unto: Augustine's, 29–33, 39, 138n11; catalog of typal expressions in, 41; existential stance of, 38; intimacy with divine in, 39, 40; language and, 40–41; stations of, 138n11; surrender / messianic instantiation in, 36. *See also* necropolitan journey

Dedalus, Mary Goulding, 16; children born to, 84; death of, 1–3, 5, 15, 16, 17, 18, 19, 32–33, 61–62, 64–68, 73, 76–79, 84–85, 102, 122–23, 134n44, 146n1

Dedalus, Simon, 18, 101

Dedalus, Stephen: as abortive poet, 1, 4, 16, 62, 73–75, 146n53; Aristotle's influence on, 70; Augustine's influence on, 20, 65–66, 68–71, 73, 74, 78–79, 87, 144n22; Blake's influence on, 16–17, 20, 40, 66, 67, 68, 69, 71, 77–78, 80, 82, 112–13, 115, 144n31;

Bloom, Leopold, with, 101, 106; as Christic poet, 62–64, 73, 74, 78; conversion experienced by, 32–33; Dante's influence on, 18, 60, 62, 71–73, 74–75, 79–80, 82, 85–86, 91, 145nn46–48, 146n18, 150n88; death of mother of, 1–3, 5, 15, 16, 17, 18, 19, 32–33, 61–62, 64–68, 73, 76–79, 84–85, 102, 122–23, 134n44, 146n1; death/mortality of, 1–2, 17, 102, 123; from esthete to poet, 32–33, 138n12; Eucharistic reenactment by, 108, 118; exile of, 18, 60–61, 77; existential condition of, 2, 3, 4, 5, 6, 18; extirpation of poetry and, 90–92; father of, 18; homecoming of, 34, 77; on "house of decay," 147n23; "I" used by, 68–70; impossibility intrinsic to, 11, 15, 17; infernal/paradisiac vision of, 55–56, 142n40; as laconic writer, 40, 89; Mallarmé's influence on, 16–17, 19, 20, 40, 52, 74, 77–78, 79–80, 82, 86–90, 146nn3–4, 149n64; messianic self of, 19, 123; Mulligan, Buck, and, 1, 4, 15, 16, 62, 64, 73–75, 84, 146n53; muse of, 81–82, 86–90; negative existence of, 3, 123; nocturnal emission of, 60, 143n7; obligations of, 2, 18; ordinary experience language of, 32, 122–23; as poet of afterlife, 61, 62, 76–92; as poet of maternal absence, 64–68; poetic vocation of, 5, 10, 18, 66–67, 73, 74; poets emulated by, 16–17, 19, 20, 40; self-enamorment and, 1, 3; silence of, 4, 5, 62, 65, 144n14; in *Ulysses*, 32–33, 69; "Vampire Poem" / kiss of menses by, 2–3, 5, 6, 16, 40, 52, 61–62, 76–78, 80, 83, 84, 86, 87, 88, 91–92, 106, 120, 148n43, 148n49, 149n61, 151n39; "Villanelle of the Temptress" by, 17, 32, 33, 40, 60, 83, 138n12, 143n7, 148n46; Yeats's influence on, 16–17, 20, 40, 67–68, 79–82, 83, 84–85, 86, 144n25, 144n35, 147n28, 154n48. See also *Portrait of the Artist as a Young Man, A* (Joyce); *Ulysses* (Joyce)

Derrida, Jacques: on apophatic discourse, 22; on existential experience vs. factual life, 12, 13, 133n29; on "Gift of the Poem," 89; *Glas* by, 18–19; on God's name, 5; on Idumaea, 149n75; on impossibility, 10; on poetics of self-forgetfulness, 74; on transcendental signifier, 136n39

Devlin, Kimberly, 102, 134n44, 151n23

dictionary, mental (Vico's), 4, 24, 131n8, 135n26

Digby Plays, 131n13

Dignam, Patrick, funeral of, 93–94, 96, 97, 101–2

divine: dictation, 110; intimacy with, 30, 39, 40, 62; light, 11; *Verbum*, 73, 74, 75, 116. *See also* God

dogs, copulating, 105

Dracula (Stoker), 83, 84, 86, 88

"Drama and Life" (Joyce lecture), 59

Dubliners (Joyce): Kenner on, 45; naturalistic style in, 45, 46, 49–50, 51, 54, 59, 140n6, 140n9; "spectacle of redemption" in, 20; "Uncle Charles principle" in, 45, 46, 49–50, 56, 57. *See also* "Araby" (Joyce); "Clay" (Joyce); Conroy, Gabriel; "Dead, The" (Joyce); "Two Gallants" (Joyce)

Durkheim, Émile, 5, 28, 95

Ellmann, Richard, 56, 58, 113–14, 152n1, 153n26

epic tradition, 33, 37–38; Christian, 34, 36, 39

epiphany, of negative self, 54–59

erotic lover, 92

Eucharist, 96, 101; Bloom, Leopold, in reenactment of, 108; Bloom, Molly, in reenactment of, 108; Dedalus, Stephen, in reenactment of, 108, 118; in *Finnegans Wake*, 108–11, 112, 115, 118; Joyce's reenacting of, 108, 112; in *A Portrait of the Artist as a Young Man*, 17

Eve, 82, 83, 85, 89, 91

existential condition/experience: Augustine's, 12–13; of Bloom, Leopold, 3, 6, 104; Dante's, 9; of Dedalus, Stephen, 2, 3, 4, 5, 6, 18; Derrida on, 12, 13, 133n29; factual life vs., 10–11, 13, 20; in *Finnegans Wake*, 4, 6; of journey unto death, 38; of negative historicity / nonreferentiality, 9; in *Ulysses*, 3; wake/vigil as, 2, 4

existential hermeneutics, Heidegger's, 12

Ezekiel, 125

Fall: Edenic, 83, 85, 91; fortunate, 113

feces, Shem's, 42, 111, 112

fertility, female, 107, 119

figurative interpretation, 20–21

Finnegans Wake (Joyce): apocalyptic notion in, 92; Augustine's influence on, 40–41, 74, 115–16; "bellicose figurines" in, 127; bio-graphy in, 120–21; Christ type in, 113–15; "claybook" in, 26–27, 126–27; completion of, 42; crucifixion in, 42; "crystalline world" in, 115, 153n32, 154n33; Dante's influence on, 40–41, 73, 115–16, 153n32, 154n34; Earwicker in, 26; Eucharist in, 108–11, 112, 115, 118; existential revolution/catharsis in, 4, 6; Holy Writ in, 41, 42; messianic poetics of, 5–6, 20, 39, 40, 41, 42, 114, 115, 116, 117, 118, 119; negative existence and, 26–27, 125–26; Proust's influence on, 104; punning-stylemes in, 101; reading of, 118–19, 127; Scriptural poetics in, 115–18; "spectacle of redemption" in, 20; transubstantiation and, 109, 110, 111; "true to type" in, 113, 153n24; twins in, 125–26, 155n8, 156n9; vestigial theory of language and, 4, 23–28, 40–42, 56, 73, 74–75, 123, 127; Word/flesh in, 42, 116, 118–21. *See also* Shem the Penman

Flaubert, Gustave, 45, 49

folklore, 99–100; Lucifer in, 112; medicine, 94–95

food/eating, 93–107, 123

Fraser, Jennifer Margaret, 80, 81

Freccero, John, 9, 10, 11, 35, 46, 142n34

free will, 35, 37, 47
freedom of choice, 120
Freeman's Journal, 63, 79
Freud, Sigmund, 74, 97, 98
funeral, of Dignam, Patrick, 93–94, 96, 97, 101–2. *See also* burial

Gaelic revivalism, 49, 51, 65
gaze. *See* sensory experience
Gide, André, 32
"Gift of the Poem" (*Don du poème*) (Mallarmé), 33, 77, 86–90, 149n64
Gilbert, Stuart, 77
glass imagery, 46–48, 54
God: arm of, 154n42; charity of, 14; death of, 42, 111, 153nn17–18; meal with, 95–96; name of, 5; soul fleeing from, 12; women's blood linked to, 152n1. *See also* divine; Word of God
Greek tragedy, 98–99, 110
Greene, Graham: *The End of the Affair* by, 131n3

"Hades" (*Ulysses*), 97, 98, 100–101, 102–3, 105
Hamlet (Shakespeare), 62, 144n14, 148n49, 154n48
Harrison, Robert, 139n36
Hayman, David, 77, 146n3, 152n4
Heidegger, Martin, 12, 13, 22, 25
hermeneutics: of Aquinas, 120–21; existential, 12; literal/metaphoric, 123; negative, 116
hero. *See* negative hero
Herr, Cheryl, 100
Hertz, Robert, 95, 96–97
Higdon, David, 141n26
history: escaping Irish, 61; memory/past and, 104; negative historicity and, 9; ordinary experience and, 75; personal, 62; poetic vocation vs., 5, 18, 19, 66–67, 73, 74; praeterhistorical condition and, 53, 142n34; silence at end of, 92; universal, of creation, 115; universal, of Shem, 108, 152n4
Holy Spirit, 110, 117, 152n11
Holy Writ, 39, 41, 42, 115–16

Homer: *Odyssey* by, 33, 38, 94–95, 101, 139n32
Hyde, Douglas, 40, 82, 148nn42–43

"I," used by Dedalus, Stephen, 68–70
Idumaea, 88–89, 149n75
imitatio Christi, 11, 34
impossibility: in apophatic experience, 9–11, 12, 15, 22, 62; Derrida on, 10; human discourse vs., 23; intrinsic to Joyce's protagonists, 11; Marion on, 10; poetics of, 9–11, 132n6
incarnations: of Christ, 85–86, 92; of Conroy, Gabriel, 45, 56; of Word in womb, 90–91, 92
infernal/paradisiac transition, 46, 48, 54–56, 142n43
Inferno (Dante): Christ's descent into hell in, 138n8; "The Dead" and, 58, 143n59; Dedalus, Stephen, as Ulysses and, 18; existential poetics in, 9; Francesca's speech in, 79; pilgrim's necropolitan journey and, 9, 10, 11, 23, 31, 33, 34–36, 37–39, 46, 132n6, 138n9. See also *Commedia* (Dante); Dante Alighieri
in-numeration: of Conroy, Gabriel, 55, 56; Dante's notion of, 34–35, 139n19
instantiation, 21; of messianic self, 28, 29, 36; of negative biography/existence, 28, 29, 32, 36, 37, 40, 41; self, into feces, 42; self, linguistic, 23; self, of Word, 13–14
intimacy with divine. *See* divine
Ireland: escaping history in, 61; Gaelic revivalism in, 49, 51, 65; Mother, 81; population growth in, 84, 148n52; women in, 78, 84
irony: crisis of, 36–38; ironic reduction and, 123

Jesus Christ. *See* Christ
John the Divine, 125
journey unto death. *See* death, journey unto; necropolitan journey
Joyce, James: allegory used by, 57–58, 142n53; anthropologists' influence on,

95, 96–97; Augustine expanded on by, 40–41, 74, 115–16; case studies/typal expressions in, 41–42; Christological influence on, 21; Crucifixion duplicated by, 36; Dante's influence on, 10, 11, 21, 38, 40–41, 41, 52, 59, 73, 115–16, 153n32, 154n34, 154n48; "Drama and Life" by, 59; Eucharist reenacted by, 108, 112; influences obscured by, 154n48; Mallarmé read by, 146n3; on miracle of Crucifixion, 36; negative hero of, 15–19; negative poetics of, 20, 37, 41–42; Nora's elopement with, 17, 61; philosophy of life of, 98; protagonists of, 11, 20, 23, 29; reading of, 118–19, 127; reductionist language vs., 32; "scrupulous meanness" style of, 50, 141n22; silence and, 38–39, 62; thunder feared by, 25; "underbred" writing of, 17, 133n40; on Vico/Freud, 74. *See also specific works*

Joyce, Nora, 17, 61

Kenner, Hugh, on *Dubliners,* 45, 49, 51, 56, 58
Kinzie, Mary, 80
kiss: Bloom, Leopold & Molly, 3, 6, 103–6, 111, 123, 151n39; of menses / "Vampire Poem," 2–3, 5, 6, 16, 40, 52, 61–62, 76–78, 80, 83, 84, 86, 87, 88, 91–92, 106, 120, 148n43, 148n49, 149n61, 151n39
Kristeva, Julie, 81, 102

language: allegory and, 40; Augustine and, 4, 20, 23, 31, 38, 39, 62, 72; journey unto death and, 40–41; Joyce vs. reductionist view of, 32; of ordinary experience, 32, 122–23; silence and, 20, 23, 31, 38, 39, 40–41, 42, 62, 72; vestigial theory of (Vico's), 4, 23–28, 40–42, 56, 73, 74–75, 123, 127; wordless communication vs., 31–32. *See also* speech, human
Lawrence, Karen, 98, 101, 105–6, 151n39
Leonard, Garry, 49, 50, 52, 57

"Lestrygonians" (*Ulysses*), 101–2, 104
limerick, Bloom's, 94, 97, 98, 101
"liquid letters of speech" (*A Portrait of the Artist as a Young Man*), 32, 40, 60, 62, 73, 75
literalism, 20–21, 40
literary discourse, four tropes of, 36
liturgical repetition, 104
"Lotus Eaters" (*Ulysses*), 96
Love Songs of Connacht, The (Hyde), 82, 148nn42–43
Lucifer/Satan, 112–13

Madonna, 82, 85
Magnus, Gregorius, 109–10
maiden/maidenhood: death and, 82–86; maternity and, 81, 147n28
Mallarmé, Stéphane, 155n52: *Aûmone* ("Alms") by, 18–19; Dedalus, Stephen, influenced by, 16–17, 19, 20, 40, 52, 74, 77–78, 79–80, 82, 86–90, 146nn3–4, 149n64; "Gift of the Poem" (*Don du poème*) by, 33, 77, 86–90, 149n64; "Immaculate Creation" poetics of, 17; maternal muse of, 134n46; on maternal power, 87–88; silence and, 4, 62; trilogy of *faune* by, 32
Mandelbaum, Allen, 141n19
Marian legend/cult, 3–4, 85
Marion, Jean-Luc, 10, 12, 118
Martella, Giuseppe, 120
maternal model: of altruism, 89; *maternante* in, 18, 134n46; of nurturing, 87; of self-sacrifice, 3. *See also* mother
maternity. *See* pregnancy
Mauss, Marcel, 95, 100
McGee, Patrick, 102
memory: Augustine on God's Word and, 4, 5, 12–13, 24, 72–73, 123, 127, 131n6; "daughters of," 66, 67, 69, 71; episodic vs. semantic, 21–22, 135n7; fermentation linked with, 106; "hidden crevices" of, 74; imagination and, 144n31; past and, 104; perpetuated by men, 101; poetry and, 1–2; silence and, 12–13; time/intentionality in, 70, 72;

memory (*continued*)
  vestigial theory of language in, 4,
    23–28, 40–42, 56, 73, 74–75, 123, 127;
    words in, 72–73
men: burial role of, 100–101, 151n23;
    memory perpetuated by, 101
menstruation, 90, 108, 119; "Vampire
    Poem" and, 2–3, 5, 6, 16, 40, 52,
    61–62, 76–78, 80, 83, 84, 86, 87, 88,
    91–92, 106, 120, 148n43, 148n49,
    149n61, 151n39
messianic self: as alternative identity, 123;
    Augustine's, 14, 20, 29–33, 138n11; of
    Bloom, Leopold, 123; of Dedalus,
    Stephen, 19, 123; in *Finnegans Wake*,
    5–6, 20, 39, 40, 41, 42, 114, 115, 116,
    117, 118, 119; inexpressible, 28; instan-
    tiation of, 28, 29, 36; irony in, 36–38;
    life-giving altruism in, 89–90; logor-
    rhea of, 38–42; negative biography /
    existence in, 14, 15, 28, 33–36; self-
    expression of, 39; stations, 12
midwives, 100
milkwoman, 84, 148n53
Milton, John, 115, 153n32
mirror imagery, 46–48, 54
mnemonic mediation, 104
moon-tomb-womb amalgam, 82, 83, 86
Moseley, Virginia, 48
mother: Augustine's (Monica), 16,
    29–32, 62, 64–65, 72, 144n22; biblical
    figures of, 90; carnal, 92; of Dedalus,
    Stephen, 1–3, 5, 15, 16, 17, 18, 19,
    32–33, 61–62, 64–68, 73, 76–79, 84–
    85, 102, 122–23, 134n44, 146n1; vir-
    gin, 80, 81, 82. *See also* maternal model
Mulligan, Buck: Dedalus, Stephen, as
    server to, 64, 73–74; Dedalus, Stephen,
    in conflict with, 15; extemporary
    verses of, 62; milkwoman and, 84; as
    poet, 1, 4, 16, 62, 73–75, 146n53. See
    also *Ulysses* (Joyce)
muse: from crypt, 86–90; of Dante, 80;
    of Dedalus, Stephen, 81–82, 86–90;
    Herodiade as, 88; immaculate/nurtural,
    79; sepulcher, 76–78
"My Grief on the Sea" (Gaelic song), 40

Narcissus, 46–47
naturalistic tradition, 37; in "The Dead,"
    45, 46, 49–50, 51, 54, 59, 140n6,
    140n9; mimesis, 36l; in *Ulysses,* 69
nature, nurture and, 5
necks, metaphor of two, 91
necropolitan journey, 122–27: Augustine's,
    29–33, 138n11; Christ's, 11–12, 20, 29,
    30, 33–34, 35, 39, 132n9, 138n8; of
    Conroy, Gabriel, 45–59; Dante's/pil-
    grim's, 9, 10, 11, 23, 31, 33, 34–36,
    37–39, 46, 132n6, 138n9; end of indi-
    viduality in, 35–36; instantiation of, 40,
    41; matrix, 47, 54–55; in messianic self,
    33–36; negative biography, 33–36; as
    negative hermeneutics / poetics, 116
negative existence, 20–28: Augustine's
    instantiation of, 29, 32; Dante's instan-
    tiation of, 32; Dedalus, Stephen, and, 3,
    123; *Finnegans Wake* and, 26–27,
    125–26; instantiation of, 36, 37, 39; of
    messianic self, 14, 15, 28, 29, 36; nega-
    tive interpretation and, 20–23; radical
    choice of, 74; recognizing, 13; Shem's
    instantiation of, 32; vestigial theory of
    language and, 23–26
negative hero, 15–19
negative historicity / nonreferentiality, 9
negative poetics, 20–23: Dante's, 9–11, 32,
    34–35, 36, 41, 46–50, 52–59, 80, 124,
    140n7, 141n19, 142n34, 142n40,
    142n43, 143n57, 143n59; Joyce's, 20,
    37, 41–42; negative hermeneutics as,
    116; of nonreferentiality, 9, 36, 124; in
    Paradiso, 9, 80, 147n26
negative representation, logic of, 11–15,
    19, 25
negative self, 9–19, 25, 34–35, 47, 54–59,
    123
"Nestor" (*Ulysses*), 66
Nicodemus, apocryphal gospel of, 35,
    138n8
Nietzsche, Friedrich, 47, 98, 141n10
nonreferentiality. *See* negative poetics
Norris, Margot, 36–37, 45, 50
Nussbaum, Martha, 98, 137nn6–7
nutrition, linked to burial, 93–107, 123

Odyssey (Homer), 33, 38, 139n32; Augustine/Dante and, 38; drinking of blood in, 94–95, 101; preternatural travelers and, 38
Oedipus, King, 99
Ogden, Daniel, 99
Old Testament, 29, 113, 120–21
ordinary experience: apophatic experience and, 13, 31–32, 74; history and, 75; Joyce's characters outside of, 29; language of, 32, 122–23; Shem in world of, 42; transubstantiation of, 32
Ovid, 146n18
Owens, Coilin, 131n13
"Oxen of the Sun" (*Ulysses*), 80, 91–92, 101, 144n22, 148n51

Page Renouf, P. Le, 124, 155n1
papyrus (*Tale of Setnau, The*), 123–24, 155n1, 155n3
"Parable of the Plums" (*Ulysses*), 63–64, 73
Paradiso (Dante): Augustian self in, 35; conflicting selfhood in, 34; "The Dead" and, 48–49, 53, 54, 56, 58, 141n19, 143n57; influence on Dedalus, Stephen, of, 80; logic of in-numenation in, 34–35, 139n19; menstrual discharge metaphor in, 90; negative poetics in, 9, 80, 147n26; pilgrim's necropolitan journey in, 31, 138n9; Saint Thomas in, 80, 147n26; shadows in, 9, 10; universal daughter and, 150n88; Virgin Mary / Christ in, 85. See also *Commedia* (Dante); Dante Alighieri
past. See history
Pater, Walter, 52, 116, 149n61
patriarch, 3; Conroy, Gabriel, as, 45, 51; Earwicker as, 26
Paul, Saint, 14–15, 37, 139n40
Pelikan, Jaroslav, 85
phenomenal identity, Augustinian paradigm of, 46–47
phenotype, 25, 136n42
Picture of Dorian Gray, The (Wilde), 32, 113–14, 115, 141n10

pièce de résistance, 4, 21
planetary system, Dante's, 153n32, 154n33
Plato: cave allegory of, 30–31; *Symposium* by, 103; transcendence and, 30, 137n7; use of sight by, 30, 137n4
poet/poets: abortive, 1, 4, 16, 62, 73–75, 146n53; of afterlife, 20, 61, 62, 76–92; Christic, 62–64, 73, 74, 78; "disempowered," 89; emulation of great, 16–17, 19, 20, 40; from esthete to, 32–33, 138n12; history vs. vocation of, 5, 10, 18, 66–67, 73, 74; of maternal absence, 64–68; Mulligan, Buck, as, 1, 4, 16, 62, 73–75, 146n53
poetry: *Commedia* on, 145n46; extirpation of, 90–92; memory and, 1–2; self-enamorment in, 1, 131n2
population growth, 84, 148n52
Portrait of the Artist as a Young Man, A (Joyce); Augustian artistic identity in, 71; "eucharistic hymn" in, 17; influences obscured in, 154n48; "liquid letters of speech" in, 32, 40, 60, 62, 73, 75; "Tower of Ivory" in, 56; "Villanelle of the Temptress" in, 17, 32, 33, 40, 60, 83, 138n12, 143n7, 148n46. See also Dedalus, Stephen; *Stephen Hero* (Joyce)
pregnancy, 81, 92, 100, 147n28
Primum Mobile, 115, 153n32
"Proteus" (*Ulysses*), 40, 65, 67, 68, 83, 88, 90–91, 144n25
Proust, Marcel, 66, 104, 105, 144n27
Pruning the Genealogical Tree (Balsamo), 78, 86, 146n1, 146n18, 150n80
Psalm: 44 of Vulgate Version, 109, 116–17, 152n9; 64:2, 90
purgation, by death, 99–107
Purgatorio (Dante), 91. See also *Commedia* (Dante); Dante Alighieri

Rabaté, Jean-Michel, 71
Raphael, Balzac's, 114
reading: allegory of, 127; of Joyce, 118–19, 127
recognition, 21
Requiem Mass, 93, 96, 97
Reynolds, Mary, 56, 73

Riquelme, John Paul, 49, 50, 58, 140n6

Rituals of Literature (Balsamo), 14, 17, 34

Robillard, Monic, 134n46

Rosetti, Dante Gabriel, 52

Rousseau, Jean-Jacques, 126

Russell, George William (AE), 66, 68, 69, 144n35

Ryan, John, 30

Sacrificial tradition, 2–3, 14–15, 110, 111, 112, 123

Sainte-Beuve, Charles-Augustin, 65–66, 144n27

Sandymount Strand, 76, 79, 80, 83, 85

Satan. *See* Lucifer/Satan

scapegoating, 99, 110, 121, 129

Schaff, Philip, 30

Scholes, Robert, 138n12

Scriptural poetics, in *Finnegans Wake,* 109–10, 113, 115–18, 120–21, 125–26, 152n11. *See also* Bible

Scriptural Poetics in Joyce's "Finnegans Wake" (Balsamo), 21, 29, 67

"Scylla and Charybdis" (*Ulysses*), 62–64, 65, 71–72, 73, 89, 91, 144n14

self: consciousness of modern, 41; end of individuality in, 35–36; instantiation, 13–14, 23, 28, 29, 36, 42; negative, 9–19, 25, 34–35, 47, 54–59, 123; self-forgetfulness of, 74; self-validation of, 46, 50; transcendental *elsewhere* and, 41. *See also* messianic self

sensory experience, 30–31, 38–39, 48, 137n4; of sight, 30, 48, 65, 85, 137n4, 138n9, 144n25; of touch, 30–31

shadows, in *Paradiso,* 9, 10

Shakespeare, William: *Hamlet* by, 62, 144n14, 148n49, 154n48; *Winter's Tale, The,* by, 148n49

Sheed, F. J., 30

Shem (Noah's son), 64

Shem the Penman: feces of, 42, 111, 112; impossibility intrinsic to, 11; Isobel as sister of, 119; messianic self of, 5–6, 20, 39, 40, 41, 42, 114, 115, 116, 117, 118, 119; Scripture and, 109–10, 113, 115–18, 120–21, 125–26, 152n11; text on body of, 5–6, 10, 39, 42, 108, 110, 113, 114–16, 118, 121, 131n13, 152n4; transaccidentation of, 106, 109, 113, 115, 116, 117, 118–19, 120, 121; universal history of, 108, 152n4; Veronica of, 117, 118; wake for, 26; in world of ordinary experience, 42. *See also* *Finnegans Wake* (Joyce)

Sicari, Stephen, 16, 21, 39, 66, 68, 139n40

sight. *See* sensory experience

silence: in apophatic experience, 39–40; Augustine and, 4, 20, 23, 31, 38, 39, 62, 72; Dante and, 4, 38, 39, 40, 41, 42, 62; of Dedalus, Stephen, 4, 5, 62, 65, 144n14; at end of history, 92; Joyce and, 38–39, 62; language and, 23, 38, 39, 40–41, 42; Mallarmé and, 4, 62; memory and, 12–13; "whiteness" of, 89, 150n80; Word as, 92

Singleton, Charles, 37

Slote, Sam, 23, 40, 62, 89

Socrates, 65, 137n7

Sophocles, 99

"spectacle of redemption," 20

speech, human: in *Confessions,* 31; in *A Portrait of the Artist as a Young Man,* 32; in *Ulysses,* 40. *See also* language

Stephen Hero (Joyce): Blakean influence in, 77–78; Clery, Emma, in, 148n46; influence of, 154n48; mother's death in, 16; Yeats and, 147n28. *See also* *Portrait of the Artist as a Young Man, A* (Joyce)

Stock, Brian, 24

Stoker, Bram, *Dracula* by, 83, 84, 86, 88

Strand, Mark, 1, 131n2

Stubbings, Diane, 81, 82, 85, 90

symbolism: in "The Dead," 46–48, 50–51, 52, 54, 56–58; French, 52

Tale of Setnau, The, 122, 123–25, 155n1, 155n3

Taylor, John, 63, 65

"Telemachus" (*Ulysses*), 64, 79, 80, 146n1

Tertium datur, 4
thaumaturgical tradition, 2
Thomas, Brook, 39
Thomas, Saint (*Paradiso*), 80, 147n26
thunder, 25, 97
Torchiana, Donald, 49, 57
touching, experience of, 30–31
"Tower of Ivory," 56
transaccidentation, 106, 109, 113, 115, 116, 117, 118–19, 120, 121
transcendental signifier, 25, 136n39
transcorporealization, 106
trans-figuration, liturgical, 116
transmutation, 31, 138n9, 154n48
transubstantiation, 15, 109, 110, 111, 133n35
trinitarian reflexivity, 35
Troup, Calvin, 25
"Two Gallants" (Joyce), 51
typal expressions, catalog of, 41
"type of types," 113, 115, 120

Ulysses (Joyce): "Aeolus" in, 40, 63–64, 65, 82, 148n41; anthropologists' influence on, 95, 96–97; body vs. self in, 116, 120; Dante's rebellious Ulysses in, 18; "daughters of memory" in, 66, 67, 69, 71; dogs copulating in, 105; "Hades" in, 97, 98, 100–101, 102–3, 105; Homer's Odysseus and, 33, 34; human speech in, 40; "Lestrygonians" in, 101–2, 104; "Lotus Eaters" in, 96; modernist allegory in, 57; muse in, 81–82, 86–90; naturalistic style in, 69; negative hero in, 15–19; "Nestor" in, 66; "Oxen of the Sun" in, 80, 91–92, 101, 144n22, 148n51; "Parable of the Plums" in, 63–64, 73; "Proteus" in, 40, 65, 67, 68, 83, 88, 90–91, 144n25; Proustian influence in, 104, 105; "Scylla and Charybdis" in, 62–64, 65, 71–72, 73, 89, 91, 144n14; silence in, 4, 5, 62, 65, 144n14; "spectacle of redemption" in, 20; *Telemachiad* in, 112; "Telemachus" in, 64, 79, 80, 146n1; "Vampire Poem" / kiss of menses in, 2–3, 5, 6, 16, 40, 52, 61–62, 76–78, 80, 83, 84, 86, 87, 88, 91–92, 106, 120, 148n43, 148n49, 149n61, 151n39; vowel sequence in, 71–72, 145nn47–48; "Wandering Rocks" in, 68, 144n30; westward journey in, 77; Yeats and, 16–17, 20, 40, 67–68, 79–82, 83, 86, 144n25, 144n35
"Uncle Charles principle," 45, 46, 49–50, 56, 57

Valéry, Paul, 32
"Vampire Poem." See *Ulysses* (Joyce)
vera icona, 117, 118–19
Veronica, of Shem, 117, 118
vestigial theory of language: vestigial traces and, 56; Vico's, 4, 23–28, 40–42, 73, 74–75, 123, 127
Vico, Giambattista: Freud anticipated by, 74; on literary discourse, 36; mental dictionary of, 4, 24, 131n8, 135n26; vestigial theory of language of, 4, 23–28, 40–42, 56, 73, 74–75, 123, 127. *See also* vestigial theory of language
victim: holy/sacrificial, 2–3, 14–15, 110, 111, 112, 123; as scapegoat, 99, 110, 121, 129
vigil. *See* wake
"Villanelle of the Temptress" (*A Portrait of the Artist as a Young Man*), 17, 32, 33, 40, 60, 83, 138n12, 143n7, 148n46
Virgil, 37, 89
virgin: fertile, 92; mother, 80, 81, 82
Virgin Mary, 60, 80–82, 85, 89, 90, 91, 111
Vita Nuova (Dante), 39–40, 54–55, 71–72, 73, 74, 75, 80
vowels: in Book of Clay, 126; sequence of, 71–72, 145nn47–48

wake: burial meal as, 97; as existential condition, 2, 4; male privilege in, 101
Walzl, Florence, 46, 49, 51–52, 58, 140n7
"Wandering Rocks" (*Ulysses*), 68, 144n30
Warner, Rex, 30
waste. *See* feces, Shem's
Weir, Lorraine, 24

westward journey: of Conroy, Gabriel, 57–58; in *Ulysses,* 77

"wet sign," 83, 148n49

White, Hayden, 25, 136n44

"whiteness," 89, 150n80

Wilde, Oscar, 153n26; *The Picture of Dorian Gray* by, 32, 113–14, 115, 141n10

Winter's Tale, The (Shakespeare), 148n49

Wolf, Virginia, 133n40

womb: amalgam, 82, 83, 86; of Bloom, Molly, 103–4

women: burial role of, 100–101, 151n23; Catholic Irish, 78, 84; Christian types of, 92; contraception and, 84; fertility of, 107, 119; as midwives, 100; milk, 84, 148n53; pregnancy in, 81, 92, 100, 147n28

Word of God: Augustine on, 4, 5, 12–13, 24, 72–73, 123, 127, 131n6; death of, 42, 111, 153nn17–18; as divine *Verbum,* 73, 74, 75, 116; in *Finnegans Wake,* 42; incarnated in womb, 90–91, 92; made flesh, 116, 118–21; self-instantiation of, 13–14; as silence, 92

words: language tied to, 72; power of, 3

Wordsworth, William, 144n31

Yeats, William Butler, 18, 52, 58: *Commedia* and, 79; Dante's influence on, 79, 80, 82, 86; Dedalus, Stephen, influenced by, 16–17, 20, 40, 67–68, 79–82, 83, 84–85, 86, 144n25, 144n35, 147n28, 154n48; *Stephen Hero* influenced by, 147n28